SUCCESSFUL MERGERS
Planning, Strategy and Execution

Michael Simmons
and contributors

WATERLOW PUBLISHERS

First edition 1988
© Waterlow Publishers 1988

Waterlow Publishers
Oyez House, PO Box 55
27 Crimscott Street
London SE1 5TS
A division of Pergamon Financial and Professional Services PLC

All rights reserved. No part of this publication may be reproduced, stored in a retrieval system, or transmitted, in any form or by any means, electronic, mechanical, photocopying, recording or otherwise, without the prior permission of Waterlow Publishers.

ISBN 0 08 036902 2

Simmons, Michael
   Successful mergers: planning, strategy and
   execution.
   1. Companies. Mergers and take-overs.
   Management aspects
   I. Title
658.1'6

Printed in Great Britain by
Dramrite Printers Ltd, Southwark, London SE1

Contents

Introduction		*Michael Simmons*	v

Part 1 – Planning the merger

1	Reasons for and against merger	*William C Cobb*	1
2	Alternatives to merger	*Michael Simmons*	10
3	Search techniques and initial evaluation	*Michael Simmons*	13
4	Choosing the right partner	*Michael Simmons*	17
5	Whether or not to merge	*Michael Simmons*	23

Part 2 – Practicalities of merger

6	Managing change	*William C Cobb*	31
7	Accounts and taxation	*Nigel Davey*	48
8	Drafting the merger documents	*Michael Simmons*	66
9	Administration	*Gilda Buckwell*	70
10a	Personnel and remuneration	*Lynda King Taylor*	74
10b	Personnel and remuneration – the practitioner's viewpoint	*Michael Simmons*	83
11	Integrating the systems	*Michael Simmons*	89

Part 3 – Experiences of merger

12	Large firms (Clifford Chance)	*Sir Max Williams*	95
13a	Mid-sized firms (Withers Crossman Block)	*Tony Thompson*	102
13b	Mid-sized firms (Fladgate Fielder)	*Anthony Baker*	106
13c	Mid-sized regional firms (Taylor Vinters)	*Philip Swift*	111
14a	Regional groupings (M.5 Group a critical view)	*Michael Simmons*	117
14b	Regional groupings (Eversheds)	*Peter Bromage*	120
15	Mid-sized firm taking over smaller firms (Malkin Cullis & Sumption)	*Michael Simmons*	125
16	Small firms (Townsend Livingston)	*Alan Dunn*	132

Part 4 – Post merger

17	Post-merger accounts	*Nigel Davey*	141
18	Marketing the merged practice	*Aubrey Wilson*	147

19 De-merger – a strategy for growth
   (Egerton Sandler) *Tony Sacker* 153
20 Putting assunder *Michael Simmons* 156

Epilogue *Michael Simmons* 160

Appendices

1a Merger procedure checklist 163
1b Holborn Law Society's amalgamation service 169
2 An amalgamation case study 173
3 Partnership bust-up case study 197
4 Anatomy of a law firm merger 200
5a To merge or not to merge 207
5b Law firm merger evaluation information 212
6 Draft heads of agreement 215
7 Dealing with the library 221
8 Law Society Rules relevant to merger 222
9 'I married a myth' 225
10 Inland Revenue press release 18/6/79 239
11 Inland Revenue Statement of Practice SP 9/86 241
12 Selected major mergers and amalgamations since 1.1.87 243
13 Bibliography 245

Index 251

Introduction

Nearly every professional firm is likely within the next twelve months to consider in abstract the possibility of merger, receive a merger approach, or actually merge. The present climate, both economic and professional, is such that we feel vulnerable on the one hand, while we worry about coping with the ever increasing workload on the other.

While merger consultants are beginning to appear, who will offer their services in advising on the practicalities of merger, our library shelves to date have totally lacked a work on this particular subject. This book is designed to fill that gap. It is designed essentially to be a practical work of reference and is in no way intended by the authors to be a legal text book in the accepted sense of the word, with the exception perhaps of Chapters 7 and 17 in those parts where Nigel Davey deals with the taxation aspects.

Solicitors and the members of the other professions are having to learn the hard way, but management is not an exact science. There are no hard and fast rules, but merely guidelines. Managers, unlike those perfect professionals, will make mistakes. This book is about guidelines and indications for those engaged, or likely to be engaged in the merger process. It is designed to be a helpful book based in part on the actual experience of its authors. We have endeavoured to balance the practical illustrations with the views and concepts of some of the more eminent consultants available to the professions on both sides of the Atlantic.

Having had the role of managing partner thrust upon me at an early age, the problems of growth forced me to seek solutions to the management difficulties, which my firm was then facing. Having had an academic background before becoming a practising lawyer I looked for academic solutions on the management side, but I found that the United Kingdom had little or nothing to offer me of use in the professional services sector. I was pointed in the direction of the Economics of Law Practice Section of the American Bar Association, and I have been making my annual pilgrimage to the United States ever since to sit at the feet of the great and learn from them. A lot of the success which my firm now enjoys, such as it is, is a result – on the management side – of what I learned in America. This applies to the science, if it should be called that, of mergers. The concepts of management taught by the Harvard Business School, among others, have been applied to law office management and the subject of merger has come under full scrutiny.

I commend readers particularly to chapter 1 by William C Cobb, the doyen of American legal consultants, the breadth of whose perception and original thinking is matched only by the vividness of his Texas ranching metaphors.

We have been singularly fortunate in the quality of those on this side of the Atlantic who have been persuaded, by fair means or foul, to contribute to the book. I have to mention specially Aubrey Wilson, who is recognised at the Harvard Business School as well as in the U.K., as the foremost consultant on marketing for the professional services sector.

Messrs Spicer & Oppenheim have achieved a particular reputation in the quality of the advice that they give professional partnerships, which is a subject which they seem to have made their own. We are extremely fortunate in having Nigel Davey as a contributor in chapters 7 and 17. Among a long list of solicitors contributing, I hope that he does not feel lonely as the only accountant.

Lynda King Taylor has made a special study of the treatment, good or otherwise, of personnel in professional firms, and she was an obvious choice to write chapter 10a on that particular topic. We have not been disappointed and the chapter in question offers a great deal of food for thought.

When Part 3 of the book was conceived, it was my private opinion that those solicitors approached for their personal views of their own mergers would adopt the traditional lawyer's attitude of silence and secrecy. I think that it is fairer to say that I was overwhelmed rather than merely pleasantly surprised by the total openness and co-operation, which I received from all those whom I approached. I am particularly indebted to Sir Max Williams for the Clifford Chance story, bearing in mind that he must be one of the busiest men in the legal profession. Not only did he deliver the goods, as it were, but produced it in absolutely record-breaking time.

Over the years, one makes many friends in one's own profession, and I feel that the total co-operation which I received in that section owes a lot to that friendship. Thank you, gentlemen.

Part 4 is designed once again as a practical section and is designed to show readers that the actual consummation of the merger is by no means the end of the road. A great deal of work still has to be done on a continuing basis to realise a 'Successful Merger'.

I make no apology for the fact that chapter 20 on the subject of de-merger effectively ends the book. In due course, I expect to see a number of books written on this particular subject alone. As the rush to merge accelerates, so the converse physical situation will arise, and there will be an increasing number of hive-offs, de-mergers, defections, split-offs, or what you will. For the moment, the subject has been restricted to one chapter only, but future experiences will, no doubt, impel an expansion.

I have tried to stress that this is intended as a practical book. The rights and wrongs of a merger appear after the event. The book is intended to guide readers through the process, but new situations and different experiences will occur all the time and will, I hope, form the subject of the second edition. I encourage you all to write to me with those experiences, even if they are at variance with what appears in this book.

Michael Simmons was educated at St. Paul's School and Emmanuel College, Cambridge. He qualified as a solicitor in 1958 being placed equal first in the Honours' List and was joint winner of the Clements Inn Prize.

After National Service in the Royal Air Force, he joined his present firm, Malkin Cullis & Sumption as the junior of two partners. He is now senior of twenty partners and concentrates on company and Commercial Law generally.

In recent years he has written, broadcasted and lectured on a number of legal topics particularly with reference to professional practice problems.

He is now specialising in advising the legal and other professions in relation to their problems of practice and is the author of "Anatomy of Professional Practice".

Part I

PLANNING THE MERGER

1 Reasons For and Against Mergers

Over the past few years, many firms have contemplated mergers or acquisitions as a tactic to achieve their perceived goals. Unfortunately, merger, as an answer, does not usually fix the problem. In fact, many firms have difficulty defining the problems they are trying to solve. Such firms are using the "herd" method of planning. After all, if all the other firms are doing it, why shouldn't we? Cobb Consulting Group's experience indicates that, of the mergers and acquisitions Cobb is introduced to after a merger has been accomplished, eighty percent do not measure up to the expectations of the partners. Mergers and acquisitions, therefore, are not the answer for most of the problems firms perceive to be solvable through such a tactic.

Throughout this overview chapter the terms merger and acquisition mean the combination of a large percentage of two firms. Merger and acquisition are used interchangeably in that the approach is the same but the relative size of the two firms is different. Merger implies the combination of two fairly equal entities, and acquisition implies the combination of entities of unequal size. Another set of definitions would be:

Merger: $A + B = C$
Acquisition: $A + B = A$

Experience shows that most combinations are acquisitions even though the assets and resources of the two firms are pooled.

Why Merge?

Arguments for merger are many. Successful mergers and acquisitions are the result of firms doing their homework, defining a unique strategy and using the merger or acquisition tactic as the most viable alternative available to them. The most obvious reasons for using merger or acquisition strategies are outlined below.

Joint client strategies

The first major reason to merge or acquire is to take advantage of client development and maintenance opportunities. The merger or acquisition activity is a result of a well-developed strategy, not a knee-jerk reaction to the first apparent opportunity. There are three client service areas to consider: service to existing clients, development of new clients and geographic presence.

Service to Clients

The first goal of the merger tactic is to increase services to the firm's current client base. The firm's strategy should be to focus on the development of its current client base and to maintain a high level of client service. When this strategy is fully developed, the criteria for targeting and integrating another firm are established. The initiating firm then understands the tough questions that it must ask when proceeding through the pre-merger, merger, and post-merger phases.

Development of new clients

Developing new clients is a key reason for merging. This strategy uses the existing expertise and accumulated knowledge of the firms. Where the firms have found their current expertise could be more efficiently used with a higher volume of work, a merger or acquisition may be an appropriate tactic to acquire the clients that need the expertise of the joined firm.

Geographic presence

Another strategy is the expansion of a firm to gain access to clients through a broad geographic presence. This is a volatile and potentially risky strategy. Distant office locations may highlight inherent problems such as lack of synergy; cultural differences; significant differences between legal markets and the way a firm gains access to those markets; differences in the level of expertise required to practice in one region versus another and similar problems. The firm using the merger or acquisition tactic to expand geographically must have deep pockets and a real commitment to spending the hundreds of hours and actual capital required for integration of the two firms.

Utilisation of expertise

A second major strategy that drives a merger or acquisition tactic is the need for additional expertise to service the firm's existing client base. It is assumed that the acquiring firm has a realistic assessment of its practices and the services it delivers and has identified the needed expertise most critical to the viability of the firm. Having accomplished that assessment, the firm has identified those areas of expertise it requires and under what circumstances that expertise is to be acquired.

Capitalisation on the expertise of others

The primary purpose of going through the merger or acquisition negotiation is to communicate the expertise needed and to determine whether the target firm has that expertise. The group being brought in will perform best against the expectations of the acquiring partners if the expectations are clearly defined and discussed. It is better to communicate expectations before attempting to integrate than to find out later that the groups involved do not understand the expectations.

Increasing the representation of current clients

The merger or acquisition may be a strategy for expanding services to current clients of the firm. The merger or acquisition tactic should identify, assign and develop new areas of support through the added firm.

Two plus two must equal five

Merger or acquisition is a tactic employed as part of a firm strategy. Most firms will find, if they go through the planning process and develop a viable strategy, that a merger is not an appropriate tactic to solve their perceived problems or to move them towards critical opportunities. To be successful, the firm must be independently viable and have solved their internal problems. To make a merger work, two plus two must equal five. All the effort involved in making a merger work should, over time, lead to a better firm in terms of client service and partnership profitability. The following discussion focuses on the adverse consequences of 'not doing it right'. In order to 'do it right', the firm must adopt the operating philosophy of using the planning process to lay the foundation for the firm's future. Tactics such as mergers or acquisitions must be implemented in the context of the

Successful Mergers

firm's overall goals, objectives and specific strategies that flow from the objectives.

Risks

The risks to firms involved in a merger or acquisiton are numerous and complex. Without a well thought out strategy that will legitimatise a merger effort, it is highly probable that one of the following adverse consequences will materialise.

Risk to the acquiring firm

The risks to the acquiring firm include the initial investment of time and money, playing the role of venture capitalist without control of the return on investment, and the increased complexity and pressure of managing a merger process.

Investment.

The firm must invest a great deal of time and money in the effort. This diverts resources away from clients and the firm's capability to generate revenues. Typically, the most valuable partners are involved in the effort, and, therefore are diverted from the practice of law and firm clients.

Venture capital with no 'Golden handcuff'.

The acquiring firm will be committing critical resources to the combination effort. The effort, however, may provide the target firm with clients and capital to establish itself in a market. If the firm acquired is in another city, the acquiring firm may be financing the other firm. When the acquired firm becomes self-sustaining, the practice is portable, and there is no need for the acquirer.

Seeds of spin off.

Every time a branch office is established, the firm sows the seeds of a new spin off. Even if the firm acquires a firm in its own city, individuals in the acquired firm may decide that the new effort is not to their liking and position themselves to leave. If these partners are key to the acquired firm's viability, their departure can have a disastrous effect.

Number and complexity of decisions.

The number and complexity of decisions will go up exponentially with the acquisition of each new partner. The combining firms must deal with complex problems of management, communication, coordination, effectiveness and cost of delivery of services. The key partners of the acquiring firm must begin to focus on the management of people who have not been inculcated with the traditions and culture of the acquiring firm. The operating philosophies and unique values of the acquiring firm must be continually communicated and reinforced by the mangement group with constructive discussions of how the two firms' cultures can be accommodated. Communication needs will increase dramatically as a function of the number of new partners. Not only must management position itself to listen to the partners, but it must also set up a more formal decision-making hierarchy to ensure that communications and resulting decisions are effectively actuated.

The combination of management and communication will drive the merger firms towards a more accountable structure. Accountability means that every partner must have a solid sense of his or her responsibility for functions such as client management; practice management; project management; section management; supervision; committee chairmanship and management. Accountability also assumes that the partners know their performance in assigned functions will be consistently evaluated and reflected in their share of partnership profits.

Suffice it to say that very few firms have reached a point where their management functions are effective enough to meet the above criteria. Therefore, they are not in a position to take on the complexities involved in a merger or acquisition.

Every firm that merges with a firm outside its own city is a little more realistic about coordination problems than are firms that are within the same city. If one of the combining firms has problems with coordination between practice groups and lacks efficiency in cross selling and cross support, the problems are going to be magnified by a merger. In reality, those firms that have a strong sense of direction; effective strategies operating within the firm before the merger and a sophisticated set of guidelines for using the merger or acquisition tactic are the ones that will succeed in integrating new personnel and practices quickly and effectively. Managing professionals must treat their combined firms with the same respect they give their most significant clients.

Given the coordination problems in the delivery of professional services, efficiency goes down, not up, when a new group of people comes on board. The combined firm must deal with integrating the new partners into the operating procedures of the acquiring firm, with delivery services and with passing work among the practice groups of both firms. More importantly, the new firm may not be able to use efficiently the informal networks of the acquiring firm for example in the referral between lawyers.

Owing to the inefficiencies discussed above, the economies of scale that firms think will be part of the delivery system in the merged firm will not mature for at least twelve to eighteen months. When expectations are too high, the partners become disenchanted with the merger and a 'we' versus 'they' attitude may begin to prevail.

Risk to the acquired firm

The risks to the firm being acquired are even more pronounced. Typically, the firm to be acquired is not blessed with the depth of resources of the larger firm and therefore must allocate already stretched talent to the effort. Key individuals will be distracted from vital client relationships and practice responsibilities. The firm may suffer a loss of identity in the market as the merger discussions continue and news of the potential merger leaks to the public. Discussions with the acquiring firm may cause some partners to envision a new firm they do not wish to be part of and precipitate an exodus. Also, the acquiring firm may not want all of the partners of the target firm. Finally, the integration of the partners into the new firm may upset some old partner synergies and referral networks developed over the years, thus magnifying some of the acquired partners' insecurities.

Distraction.

When negotiating a merger, the partners who are part of the acquired firm's management group will be time pressured. These partners are usually key to current important client relationships, lead the practice groups and participate in the mangement of the firm. During the merger discussions, critical daily mangement functions may fall through the cracks endangering the firm's viability. If the negotiations fail, the ability of the minor firm to hold key clients may be endangered. The competition will certainly use the failure of the negotiations to their advantage in establishing footholds with key and significant clients.

Reasons For and Against Mergers

Loss of identity.

As the firm begins to negotiate with the potential acquiring firm, the internal identity of the firm may suffer. If the acquired firm does not have a strong consensus on its direction, its market niche, culture, shared values and negotiations will constantly be coloured by the perception of the acquiring firm. All the values of the old firm become suspect, and the firm may begin to flounder even before the merger negotiations become serious. Should the discussions break off, the firm could be subject to some very tough times. Discussions held in the merger-failure environment may drive the firm members apart. With a strong sense of direction and consensus prior to merger discussions, negative consequences are less likely to occur.

The firm may run the risk of irreparable damage being done to its client market share. As competition and clients get wind of the merger, questions will begin to surface about the underlying changes in the firm. Clients start asking if the new firm will be less responsive and more costly. The competition may comment that the firm is in trouble and needs to be bailed out. The firm's significant clients will become opportunity targets for aggressive competitors. Should the merger fail, the firm may be stuck with the image that it could not be bailed out or that it was not good enough for the acquiring firm. A failed merger is thus almost a no-win situation for the non-acquired firm.

Break off.

As the culture and operating philosophy of the acquiring firm becomes clearer, some key partners may decide they do not want to practise law in the perceived new environment. These partners may either stonewall the merger, adopt an attitude of quiet resistance or start to place themselves with other firms.

Break up to old synergies.

Assuming the merger goes through, the new partners will have to be integrated into the acquiring firm. As the new partners are integrated, old ways of allocating work, methods of practice and office procedures will change. This will be uncomfortable for some patners and may amplify their sense of insecurity. The new partners must learn to operate in a large firm environment where accountability for client management, allocation of work, management of projects and firm management will be more structured and place greater burdens on partners. The pressure of the new environment and the performance standards may constructively isolate and eventually force out some of the acquired firm partners.

Messes

Law firms seeking to merge or be acquired not only run the risks discussed above but compound their problems by taking a casual attitude towards the merger by assuming that once agreement is reached in principle everything will work out and they can go back to practising in their traditional manner. This is not the case, as decisions made 'up front' must be implemented. The most difficult part of a merger is its implementation. The better the preparation and process for negotiating the merger, the more effective and efficient the implementation will be. There are many opportunities in mergers for wishful thinking. There are also many pressures for taking short cuts in the process. Many examples of disasters can be cited when wishful thinking and short cuts were involved in the negotiations.

Summary

The combination of two firms is a difficult process but one that can be accomplished if the firms have properly prepared themselves before finding one another and if both firms have taken a concerted and objective approach toward pulling the two firms together. It is crucial that all preparatory time involved on behalf of both firms is aimed at ensuring the integration of the two firms by the end of the first twelve to eighteen months of operation. Once a merger agreement is signed, it is not a contract that will enact itself automatically. It requires a tremendous amount of work and commitment from every partner within both firms. Given the nature of professional practice and the pressures on professionals today from clients and competitors, it is the exception when two firms will take the time and effort to prepare themselves adequately and conduct themselves in proper sequence for negotiations and implementation.

Mergers or acquisitions are not appropriate for most firms and there will always be niches for small and medium sized firms. A firm cannot represent all clients and cannot be all things to all people in the current competitive environment. Firms must have a strategy and take actions based upon that strategy. A merger or acquisition may not be an appropriate tactic for your firm, but, if it is, do it right.

William C. Cobb is the managing partner of the WCCI, Inc. in Houston. Mr. Cobb has been a consultant to professional firms since January 1, 1978. Prior to starting his consulting practice 1978, he was Executive Director of Bracewell and Patterson, a large law firm in Houston, Texas, and immediately prior to that, Management Consultant with the CPA firm Touche, Ross & Company.

Mr. Cobb is a frequent speaker on strategic planning, value billing, organisational structure, partner compensation marketing and other management issues to professional service organizations.

In 1978, the American Bar Association published Mr. Cobb's book, *"A Planning Workbook for Law Firm Management"*. He has contributed many articles to periodicals for the legal profession and is often quoted in the national press on management issues involving law firm policy formulation.

Mr. Cobb received his Bachelor of Science degree in Engineering from the University of Texas in Austin in 1966 and his Masters degree in Business Administration from Ohio State University in 1970. He is a Certified Public Accountant in the State of Texas and a member of the AICPA. He has worked with the ABA Section of Economics of Law Practice and its Council since 1974. Mr. Cobb is a member of the Texas Society of Certified Public Accountants Coordinating Committee for Managing the Accounting Practice, since 1971.

2 Alternatives to Mergers

The obvious alternative to merger is the exact converse of merger; not to merge. Those who succeed are sometimes those who do nothing. The illustration is that of the busy professional person, who always answers letters by return of post. Correspondence is in perpetual motion. Suddenly, he or she is away from the office for a couple of weeks, and it is amazing the number of problems which solve themselves without the need to do anything. The very problems, which Bill Cobb has highlighted as being capable of solution by merger, will often solve themselves by effluxion of time:

The firm is not growing quickly enough. A sudden burst of organic growth created by changing economic conditions provides the boost to turnover and profits for which you have long been looking.

We have no specialists in company and commercial Law. An equally sudden downturn in the economy means that there is now a shortage of such work, and the lack of personnel to deal with it becomes a little or no importance.

The firm is top heavy in that we have too many older partners and not enough younger ones to ensure the succession. Suddenly, you realise that some of the young assistant solicitors, whom you have bred from articled clerks are of far greater calibre than you anticipated. They are of the quality to take over the mantle of the senior partners and will attract others of similar capability around them.

However, inertia is not going to be the solution for all a partnership's problems. In fact, successes, when there are structural weaknesses, arising out of doing nothing, are likely to be the exceptions rather than the rule. It will sometimes be easy, with the benefit of hindsight, to see that failing to make a decision has produced the right results, but it goes against the planning culture, and one of the main hypotheses of this book is that professional firms must start and continue to plan, merging or otherwise. On balance, unplanned inaction is not the recipe for any type of success.

Merger has been suggested as one of the main methods of achieving one's goals as part of the strategic planning process. To reach that goal requires a full appraisal of the market position of the firm including an analysis of strengths, weaknesses, opportunities and threats. The result of that appraisal and analysis may well be that the firm should not expand, but should contract. There may well be areas of work which are currently unremunerative, or which are likely to die out because of legislation or economic changes. The answer may be, therefore, to close down departments and re-train staff.

Alternatives to Mergers

Another potential solution will be the hiving-off of certain branches or parts of the practice into separate firms. I particularly refer readers to chapter 19, where Tony Sacker gives his own account of his particular reorganisation and shake-out, and the thought processes which led up to them.

Another possibility may be that merger is the ultimate scheme to secure the firm's main goal; however, as the firm stands at the moment, it would be unattractive to a potential suitor. A typical example could be a law firm which wishes to expand its corporate and commercial side by merger. It may be a firm with a very large debt collecting department, which by its nature would be unattractive to a commercial firm. The average bill of a debt collection department is likely to be extremely small and will contrast with the much higher average billings of a good company and commercial department. Before the firm making the merger decision can sensibly look for suitable merger prospects, it may need to divest itself of the department with the low paying work.

The management buy-out has become fashionable throughout commerce and industry. The strategic planning process which leads a company to agree a management buy-out of its divisions or subsidiaries will be on much the same lines as the professional firm which decides to divest itself of part of its operation. In most instances such an operation will not find a ready buyer in the outside market, but it may well be that those working within its ambit will wish to acquire it, in order to secure continuity of employment, as well as the chance to show faith in the buyers' own efforts.

The debate over the next few years in professional firms is likely to be whether to be a general service firm, being all things to all clients, or whether it is better to become a boutique firm, concentrating on a few or more specialities which those in the firm know are done well. Those who make the decision to operate as a boutique may well wish to dispose of those activities being offered which do not fit within the particular framework of the boutique services.

Thus, alternatives to merger, inertia apart, may include the shutting down of unproductive branches or departments, or the disposal of them to those running them or outsiders, not necessarily because their functioning is uneconomic, but merely because their continued presence within the firm does not fit within the strategic plan.

An unplanned result of this might be a partner, other fee earner, or department voting with its feet and moving away. However, this chapter is concentrating on the planned aspect of hiving-off and reorganisation, and such a situation is likely to lead to the search for a merger partner, as, if what has gone was valuable, there is likely to be a vacuum created, which only a merger can fill in the short-term.

The conscientious reader who has followed the arguments so far is likely to feel that the professions are changing rapidly, and not necessarily for the better. The old days of stability, continuity and partnership for life seem to be gone, perhaps forever. The growth of mergers means that firm names are changing with bewildering rapidity. We must never forget how confusing this must be for clients, and this needs to be considered in the marketing context: chapter 18 deals particularly with this aspect. A de-merger is also likely to unsettle clients and, once again, chapter 18 needs careful study as to the best way of marketing in the situation, both from the point of view of the firm disposing and those acquiring.

Bigger is not always better, and while merger ought to be considered as part of the strategic planning process, nevertheless an alternative will often be the more logical solution to the problems of the day, not only in economic, but also in human terms.

Michael Simmons

3 Search Techniques And Initial Evaluation

Finding the appropriate merger partner may or may not be easy. Rather like the girl next door, the firm to approach may be the obvious one, and may be the one which you have known all your professional life. However, even the obvious has sometimes to be pointed out to you. The right merger partner may be staring you in the face but it may still require a third party to point it out to you.

In the absence of the obvious candidate, it is necessary to look a little further. Does one's professional body maintain a registry of likely candidates or offer a merger service? For example, the Law Society maintains an employment registry which has a mergers section. Details are contained weekly in the Law Society's Gazette. The section is divided somewhat haphazardly into three headings: –

Practices, partnerships and amalgamations.
Practices for sale.
Legal practice disposal, merger and acquisition.

The choice of sections seems to be that of the advertiser and advertisements are normally anonymous with a box number quoted, although there are some from merger agencies, of which more later. The advantage of anonymity is with the advertiser, who can reject out of hand applications from firms which are not considered suitable. The response to such advertisements is usually bewilderingly varied. It is normally best to compile a short list of suitable applicants. In case there is any doubt of suitability, outside help may be required in the form of a consultant who knows the particular profession.

Turning now from the central professional body, a number of local professional associations maintain merger registers or have an official designated to deal with appropriate enquiries. This is often a more fruitful source than the centralised system, as local knowledge is likely to be more prevalant and, once the introduction is made, there are often the advantages of having worked together in the past. In fact, once you know who is looking for a merger locally, the reaction is often surprise that you had not thought of that particular partner before and made a direct approach.

In the absence of suitable professional registries, the obvious next port of call is one's accountant. Most auditors of professional firms have more than one client within that profession. They may already have been approached with a view to finding a suitable partner, if one comes along. A word in the accountant's ear may often produce some profitable results, particularly as almost everyone within the professions is thinking of merger, if only as something at the back of the mind.

Having exhausted the sources already mentioned, where the likely expense or fee payable to the introductory source will be small, it is necessary to consider the merger agencies, or those who hold themselves out as capable of providing that facility. We are now in the realms of the commercial entity, who will want to be paid substantially for services rendered. As is to be expected, some of these are better than others.

An initial approach via recommendation is obviously best. If this is not available, then answer the various advertisements. A preliminary discussion will probably help sort out the sheep from the goats and then at the earliest possible moment, ascertain their charging basis. Some will work on a consultancy basis, while others charge only for success. The fee is usually a percentage of the gross fees of the target firm.

However, John Hamilton Associates for example offer a different fee structure for solicitors. This consists of an initial tranche, payable on receipt of instructions. This amount is not refundable, if the enquiries on the client's behalf are unsuccessful or if instructions are cancelled. An additional fee is payable for each equity partner and any other fee earner, who joins or who is employed by the client firm as a result of his enquiries on their behalf. This amount is payable on the date upon which a legally binding agreement is entered into between any of the parties concerned to merge with the client firm. There is a longstop provided in that the aggregate fee payable under both headings will not exceed a previously agreed amount.

Yet another alternative is where a charge is made on a consultancy basis on a hourly rate, and the consultancy fees are taken into account against the percentage fee on a successful merger. Any agency seeking to charge a consultancy fee and a substantial percentage fee on top will have some important questions to answer as to the excellence of its service!

A typical agency with a reasonable reputation within the professions is one which will have started a number of years ago specialising in accountancy mergers, acquisitions and disposals. The next move will have been into the legal field and then into other professions, where a market exists for the sale, purchase and merger of practices.

An agency will require fairly full particulars of your firm so that they can try and match them with those already registered with them as

Search Techniques and Initial Evaluation

seeking merger. If there is none available, they will go out into the market on your behalf, preserving your anonymity until you are ready to disclose your identity, and seek suitable candidates within your profession.

The approach of John Hamilton is to target several selected practices (a list of which would have been agreed beforehand) in the appropriate area in order to establish interest. This is done by means of a letter from him, or a telephone call to someone within that particular firm with whom he is already acquainted. Once interest has been established, he arranges, if appropriate to visit the firm concerned to discuss further details so that he can make a recommendation about further action. He needs to be able to disclose to interested parties certain details about his client firm, which would be listed in advance in following consultation with the client. He then keeps his client informed of progress and further action is decided in the light of the response received.

The details which he would need to have about his client's practice so that interested firms can form a preliminary view about their continued interest are basically as follows:

1. Size of firm – fee earners and non-fee earners as well as age and brief details of professional experience of each partners.
2. Types of work undertaken.
3. Client base.
4. General indication of turnover and profitability.
5. Brief details of firm's premises and equipment.
6. Reason for desire to merge.
7. Any other relevant factors.

In the current climate, it is not surprising that most firms approached in this way show an interest.

Strangely enough, as far as lawyers are concerned, the response to an enquiry on behalf of an unnamed principal by an agency not within the particular profession seems to produce better results than a direct approach made by you to such firms. This is probably based on the reluctance, which still exists, to reveal our inner workings, even including our possible desire to merge, to what we still consider to be the competition, even though the competition is very much more powerful outside the legal profession these days than within it.

After the agency has made their initial introduction, it is up to you to decide how much you require of their services. They will certainly offer consultancy services and assistance with the details of the merger. The merger procedure and checklist recommended by one particular agency in fact comprises appendix 1 of this book.

However, once the initial introduction has been made, you may decide that you have sufficient expertise inhouse to deal with the details from thereon youself. Alternatively, or additionally, you may require the help of your firm's accountants, but the agency's experience of similar situations will always be useful when difficulties arise.

As the pace of mergers increases within the professions, there is going to be a greater place for the competent agency outside the particular profession to help negotiate the terms. These agencies are not cheap, but their services seem increasingly necessary in our complex society.

Michael Simmons

4 Choosing A Partner

The parallel with courtship and marriage is almost irresistible. Some of us marry the girl next door and never give it another thought. Others of us assiduously haunt the disco floor in the hope that our ideal will eventually appear. What we fail to realise is that, even if he or she did, by the time that we actually met them, we would be so jaded that we would not even recognise them. Others lack the confidence to go it alone and seek the help of a dating agency or marriage bureau.

A similar situation exists on the merger front. Some firms seem effortlessly to proceed from successful merger to successful merger. How do they do it, when others of us are agonising lengthily over the choice?

There is the apocryphal story of two well-known London firms where the partners met weekly over a period of eighteen months. The consumption of sherry was phenomenal but the merger never took place, nor did either side ever seriously grapple with the problems involved. One of those firms met its eventual merger partner on the rebound and the deal was consummated four weeks after the first meeting. In other words, there is no pattern to be found in all this.

Reverting to the marriage analogy for the moment; although we all have our ideal partner in our mind's eye and reality often differs greatly from the image: we have to start somewhere. In choosing a partner for a merger, the partners of the seeking firm ought, as part of their planning process, to work out and reduce to writing the profile of their ideal merger partner. Just as, when recruiting staff, the job specification should be available in advance, against which the calibre of the various candidates should be tested, so the merger specification will immediately eliminate those potential candidates who are manifestly unsuitable. As a result, a great deal of valuable time and effort will be saved in pursuing undesirable prospects. Time, after all, is money to the professional firm, and it is not fair to waste the time of those who have no chance of fitting your pre-agreed specification.

The ideal candidate will have complementary strengths to match your weaknesses and, other things being equal, complementary weaknesses to match your strengths. For example, if you have a remarkably fine administration, which is under-used, a desirable merger partner might be a firm which has grown speedily, where the administration has fallen behind and needs a boost. If you have a strong and profitable private client department, your ideal will be a firm with a thriving commercial side which is otherwise weak on the personal client front.

If you have five partners over sixty and none under thirty five, you will want a firm where the accent in the partnership is on youth, although do not be surprised if they look somewhat askance at what you are bringing to the negotiating table, particularly if the firm is heavily burdened with potential retirement obligations to those elderly partners.

A number of firms have good workers, but no producers of new clients. The ideal merger partner will be a firm with extrovert partners who produce more business than they can handle, where there is a shortage of suitably qualified partners to do the work.

The examples are endless, but the principle is clear. In the present market, to merge two firms with strong private client departments, but little else, makes no logic. To group together two firms with five partners each over sixty, but none under the age of thirty five, may create a superb nursing home, but will not produce a very effective firm. These propositions ought to be self-evident, but it is not difficult to look around and see a number of current mergers which defy commercial logic. In other words, the parties have not done their homework in advance and prepared their ideal merger candidate specifications.

It is also vital to consider whether what is happening is a merger; a takeover or a reverse takeover.

The hardest of all is the so-called merger of equals. The truth is that it very rarely exists. To find oneself with joint senior partners and joint managing patners, one of each taken from the two constituent firms, is not normally a recipe for long-term success. One side needs to be in charge and perceived as such. Of course, in an ideal world, you might find yourselves with a situation where one firm provides the senior partner and the other the managing partner, and everything slots neatly into place. However, reality is usually far more untidy.

For this reason, the takeover is often so much more effective than the merger of so-called equals, as one firm, normally the larger, more powerful, will be imposing its culture, organisation and systems on the other smaller. However, having said that, size is not necessarily the only criterion.

The reverse takeover is a well known phenomenon, where the seemingly smaller firm provides the actual dynamic. A typical situation will be a town where the larger firm has become somewhat sleepy, as the founders retire or lose interest. Such a firm lacks marketing thrust, and tends to drift. If it has perceptive partners, they may well appreciate what is wrong as part of their strategic planning progress and may seek to merge with a younger, more dynamic firm, which has the marketing appetite the larger entity lacks. The only problem is that the larger and better established firm will have to subordinate its partners' egos and pride. It is a very adult quality to be able to admit to one's inadequacies in this respect and go out and seek the remedy by merging with an ostensible inferior.

I have hinted at the cultural problems which surround mergers, and these now need to be explored in greater detail. No two professional firms are exactly alike, and most are remarkably dissimilar. Talk to a few perennial assistant solicitors who have done the rounds. They will tell you how firms in the same street differ totally in culture and philosophy.

It is these differences which make the merger exercise such a difficult one and at the same time so fascinating to accomplish. The problem is felt in industry too, but often is overcome by the brute force of the buying power and dynamic of the predator where the companies are publicly quoted. The differences in philosophy will be expressed in the management styles and hence in the personalities of the directors. However, the company intent on a takeover will ignore the objections of the directors and will appeal on economic grounds alone to the shareholders, a separate body. Shareholders are normally motivated by financial considerations only and will sell out for the best offer.

Solicitors and certain other professionals are still bound by the partnership format where directors and shareholders are effectively the same. It is, therefore, not possible to by-pass management and appeal to the proprietors. The proprietors are the management.

Not only are firms culturally diverse, but they also experience cultural changes. The firm which is initially successful will rely on the entrepreneurial skill of its founder or founders. Their success will often be based on marketing abilities rather than pure legal skills. Such people normally surround themselves with good legal technicians who can process the work brought in by the founders. Very often the younger partners in these types of firms are drawn from the ranks of their articled clerks so that they know no other types of working environment. Sooner or later, either the hunger of the founders becomes satisfied so that they lose their appetite as hunters and providers of work, they retire, or they die.

Such firms then move into the second phase, where the remaining partners find that their work providers have left them. It is very rare for second generation partners to have the same hunger or ferocity which produced clients in a similar way. Firms at this stage have much more of an institutional nature. They rely on their own dynamic to produce work. A great deal will depend on the past effectiveness of the founding fathers on the one hand and of the working skills of the second generation on the other.

Firms can successfully exist through this phase without substantial "rain-makers" as hitherto in the shape of the founding partners. If the situation has been anticipated and planned for effectively, the transition from entrepreneurial to institutional firm can be effected more or less painlessly. If not, there is often a crisis of confidence and the younger partners, left on their own at last, feel lost and leaderless. They need to seek the comfort and reassurance of another parental bosom. Firms at this stage often seek a merger with another firm still in the entrepreneurial first phase because they lack the confidence to go it alone.

If they do have the confidence, the chances are that a third generation will arise of younger and more aggressive partners who, while marketing their talents in a different way from the entrepreneurs, nevertheless will produce similar results. This third generation should be allowed to flourish in the marketing sense, freed from the shadow and example of their entrepreneurial founding fathers. By comparison with the second generation institutional partners, the third generation's marketing talents will shine and should be extremely effective.

On the basis of action and reaction, firms will presumably move into a fourth phase of renewed institutionalism. As yet it is probably not possible to chart that development as most professional firms have not been sufficiently long established.

Two institutional firms may well have the cultural ability to merge successfully if they have sufficient of the "rolling stone" dynamic. However, they may well lack leadership, drive and marketing ability so that such a merger is not a success.

If two firms in the entrepreneurial stage merge there may well be cultural and personality clashes. Such a merger may be doomed to failure in that entrepreneurs often suffer from particularly large egos.

In terms of philosophy, the best merger, once again, is an attraction of opposites. The joining of an entrepreneurial firm with an institutional one, if the cultures are not too far apart, may well produce the best results in the long term. Obviously it depends on the individual personalities of the partners in each case.

The truth of the matter is that generalisation is not really possible; each situation has to be looked at on its merits. However, this particular analysis may help those engaged in the choosing of an appropriate and potential merger partner. Extreme entrepreneurs are unlikely to mingle well with extreme institutionalists, although moderate entrepreneurs may well combine nicely with a firm whose move towards an institutional culture is as yet in the early stages.

Some commentators take the view that the financial elements in a merger are of the greatest importance and that, if these elements are right, then the philosophies and cultures will automatically mesh. I do not adopt that view at all and feel that it is fallacious, particularly where the legal profession is concerned. We are notoriously innumerate and tend to consider financial rewards as of far lesser importance than professional and job satisfaction generally. Thus we like to work with colleagues whose professional qualities we respect and who share the same outlook and standards. It is for this reson that I have stressed the aspects of philosophy and culture as of paramount importance. Having said that however financial harmony, or the possibility of it in the merged firm, must exist, otherwise the merger will not take place.

In this chapter I am not dealing with financial matters in detail; those far more qualified than I do so in other chapters. My comments go far more to philosophy, which will be reflected in the financial dealings of the firms contemplating merger.

For example, one partnership may have an extremely conservative policy with regard to capital accounts, bank borrowings and partners' drawings. Such a firm is likely to frown on the concept of an office account overdraft. The one which it approaches may be financed almost totally by its bankers. Every penny earned, or even future earnings, may be drawn by the partners and the bank manager may be prepared to allow this situation to continue because of historical reasons, inertia, or his knowledge that the firm's growth and management is such that it will all come right in the end.

In another situation, one firm may allow its partners to take part in other businesses, perhaps including those of clients. The other may expressly prohibit such activities or provide for the proceeds to be paid into the firm's account.

One set of partners in each such case is likely to find itself very uncomfortable with the financial policy of the other. I have deliberately painted a picture of two extremes and I even doubt if either side can so modify its policy as to reach an accommodation in the middle, as it were. Such a merger is almost destined to fail.

A divergence in financial philosophy will also be reflected in the partners' life-styles. It sounds petty, but very often the key is in the cars that the partners drive. One firm may specialise in new white Porsches while the partners in the other may be content to drive around in ten year old Fords. This is fine until merger is contemplated, when comparative life-styles will be scrutinised most carefully. Cars may be the start but it goes on to housing, children's schools, holidays and all the rest of it.

On the subject of holidays and overseas trips, one firm may have a policy of a strict two weeks annually, while the other firm may believe that the quality of life demands at least six weeks holiday annually to recharge the batteries. One set of partners will look askance at the others' way of life and a compromise will probably satisfy nobody. Attendance at overseas conferences may be required for the partners in one firm while the partners in the other may consider that such attendance is merely an excuse for yet further holidays, this time at the firm's expense. It is difficult to dispel such suspicions as the marketing results of overseas conferences are often difficult to chart in quantitative terms.

The above are merely examples of philosophical divergencies expressed in financial terms. I will leave Nigel Davey in chapter 7 to talk about the financial differences which, from the accounting point of view, are likely to inhibit merger.

It is impossible in a mere chapter, or probably even in a book, to categorise all the potential philosophical differences, (or financial ones for that matter, which after all only reflect a firm's philosophy) which have to be overcome if a merger is to proceed. As more mergers take place further examples will occur and the next edition of this book may well contain an appendix of additional examples. These of course will be without attribution, to spare the blushes of those involved.

Michael Simmons

5 Whether or Not to Merge

There are decisions and decisions where mergers are concerned. There is the decision to proceed in principle and the final binding contractual decision which creates the contract for merger. Experience shows that there is many a slip twixt cup and lip. There is obviously no such thing as an ideal partner in the merger situation. Reverting for a moment to the last chapter, no firm will totally fit your merger specification. Series of meetings are required at a number of levels to decide whether the parties are compatible.

Possibly the initial approach will have been made at senior partner level, or perhaps one partner in one firm is well acquainted with one in the other, so that the approach has been made other than at the very top of the firm.

At the very earliest possible moment, as many partners in one firm should be exposed to the partners in the other firm. In some of the vast mega-enterprises of today this is impractical and a counsel of perfection. However, the more exposure at the outset the more chance there is of eliminating the possibilities of an unsuccessful merger later.

The principle behind these meetings is for the partners of one firm to explore philosophy and culture with their counterparts in the other; each will be probing to examine each other's work methods. Our American counterparts place great emphasis on professional ethics at this level. We either tend to take the subject for granted or cloak it in some other apparel. It is, of course, a matter of greatest importance, although British professionals tend to assume that other firms have the highest standards unless and until they are found lacking.

If the firms are departmentalised then it is probably best to conduct these meetings on a departmental basis. The heads of the respective departments will be comparing notes with each other on the management and organisation of their departments, while the departmental partners will be talking on a more professional and personal level. Meanwhile, parallel discussions will be going ahead between the managing partners on the subject of leadership; management; administration; accounting; finance and tax (which subjects must not be treated as an exhaustive list).

Where disclosure is concerned we find ourselves in something of a 'chicken and egg' situation. Obviously both parties must agree total confidentiality as to what is disclosed, particularly in the event of the merger not proceeding to completion. However, if agreement to proceed is going to be reached it is necessary to bare one's financial soul. In fact, as little as possible, if anything at all, should be held back. Thus, the setbacks and failures must be revealed along with the successes and strengths. The opportunity must be given to both sides to make a totally realistic assessment of each other, based on facts, good or bad. Impressions will obviously count for a great deal as well, but these are more subjective.

The making of the initial decision to proceed will vary in form, depending on the cultures of the firms in question. One firm, by size and structure, may require written reports to be exchanged among its leading partners, and a written proposal may be put at that stage to the partners on a democratic basis. The other firm may deal with matters by informal soundings and discussions in corridors. I repeat that the initial decision to proceed can only be made on full disclosure, followed by even fuller disclosure subsequently. The question of conflict will have to be explored and it should be dealt with at the earliest possible moment, before the first decision.

Few firms will not have important clients who represent a substantial part of the firm's practice. The partners may have sleepless nights worrying about their best clients being taken over, but the facts have to be recognised. Those vital clients should be informed in confidence at an early date of the merger talks. If they state that the merger does not have their approval and that, if it goes ahead, they will remove their work, then this is a very strong reason for not proceeding with negotiations. Forewarned is forearmed in this context and it is better to know earlier rather than later that the merger will become uneconomic if one of the largest clients will not remain with the new merged firm. Of course, a decision may be made to proceed regardless but it will at least be an informed decision.

What should be avoided as far as possible is the unpleasant surprise. This, once again, is a counsel of perfection, but such surprises will be reduced to a minimum by the maximum disclosure, discussion and questioning at these early stages of negotiation. This is all time consuming and the doomed merger is often considered by the participants as a disaster. This need not be the case in certain respects. As well as learning about the other firm, you also learn about yourselves in these discussions. This information need not be wasted and may form the basis for an important strategic planning process subsequently.

Let us take the situation where all has gone well and the decision to proceed is reached in principle. I stress that this is a decision in principle and it should be stated that both sides have the ability to withdraw without disclosing reasons up to the date of final consummation. This should be expressed rather than implied because it is a situation that happens.

There have been a number of instances, some more public than others, where mergers have been announced early, but have not actually taken place. There are arguments for not making such announcements, or hedging them about in some way, which will offend the public relations consultants but may save blushes later. The parallel is the court martial sentence, which is always reported as subject to confirmation. 'A merger is announced subject to confirmation...' may not sound too effective from the marketing point of view, but the point has been made and probably some sort of cosmetic wording can be found. 'Merger talks are in process...' perhaps gives the true flavour and the fact that agreement has been reached in principle, subject to the right to withdraw, can be left as implied rather than actually expressed.

Once agreement to proceed has been reached in principle some sort of announcement needs to be made to the senior staff, and possibly junior as well, to dispel the worst kind of rumours. Everybody knows that an office is a place where rumours abound and become exaggerated and few mergers take place where staff economies are not affected. The appropriate announcements need to be made and reassurances given to key staff at the earliest possible moment.

Those staff who are not to be required in the merged firm should be told as soon as possible and their terms of compensation negotiated. By contrast, those staff who are required must similarly be told of this fact as well as of details of any changes in their compensation. Such changes are invariably upwards as the salary scales of the firm which pays less will have to be harmonised with those of the firm which pays more. Once this stage has been reached the hard work really starts. Departmental partners will be seeking to merge the respective departments of the two firms and resolve the conflicts which will undoubtedly arise. Senior partners will be dealing with questions of leadership and managing partners will be deciding how the firm is to be managed. Administrators will be working together to harmonise the administration; accounts; and personnel whilst they consider the timetable and details of the necessary moves which will follow the actual merger.

All of this is a considerable distraction from the business of client development and fee earning. The clients must not be neglected in the general merger activities, otherwise the reasons for the merger may be eliminated.

The period from the agreement to merge to final consummation is one of intense and exhausting activity for all concerned. It is obviously one which is very unsettling. The stress factors in life have now been charted and changing jobs and moving house are high on the list. A merger very often is a combination of the two plus an added element.

On the financial front, without pre-empting Nigel Davey in chapter 7, both firms' financial advisors will be busy. They will be advising on the effects of termination; preparing budgets, forecasts and pro-forma merged accounts to take into consideration any economies of staff or premises to be achieved, as well as the expense of the probable move or moves; and considering the enhanced expenses of running a larger practice.

The draftsmen in both firms will also be extremely busy. The terms of merger need to be reduced to writing, if only for the avoidance of doubt. This is not to say that the parties do not trust each other, but matters will come up in the negotiation; often small points will be agreed and then forgotten if they are not included in the heads of agreement.

At the same time, the partnership agreement for the new merged firm must be discussed; its detailed terms put into full written form. The draft will probably have to be circulated among those who will ultimately be signing it for their approval and reaction.

The detailed timetable for the merger will have to be prepared. This document will give responsibility for the various actions to be taken by relevant partners and those in the administration. As little should be left to chance as possible and reduction to writing does aid this process, if only that looking at the written word often brings into focus matters which would otherwise have been overlooked.

Meanwhile, the decision-making process continues. The larger the firm and the greater the numbers of partners, the more difficult it is to achieve consensus for the final decision to merge. There have been classic cases of management committees in firms who have agreed on a merger only to have the final decision subverted by the vote of the partnership at large. This is a situation which cannot be avoided as firms increase in size; more's the pity.

As the days pass, the date of the final decision will have to be reached. In fact, it is best if this date is laid down in advance as part of the overall timetable. To leave the date open is to pile on the agony of uncertainty.

The final, ultimate and irrevocable decision to merge is a contractual event. This is the date which can be given the maximum publicity by your public relations people. Announcements will be made in all the appropriate journals, to bodies such as the Law Society, and local law societies, directories, and all the myriads of others who need to know. If the job has been done properly, all those concerned will have been listed in advance, the appropriate notices prepared and the whole operation will go through smoothly.

In an imperfect world, which it normally is, too much will have been left to chance, as most of our firms do not have the excess management and administrative capacity which the nuts and bolts of merger require. The preliminary decision, to merge subject to contract, may have been made some considerable time ago. The final decision is only reached after a great deal of exploration and hard work.

Michael Simmons

Part 2

PRACTICALITIES OF MERGER

6 Managing Change

Editor's note

This is probably the most important chapter of the book. However, for those who are not accustomed to the language of the consultant, it may be a difficult one. Nevertheless, it is a chapter which should be read by everyone interested in the principle of merger or a specific merger case. It is written by my friend, Bill Cobb, who is the foremost American law firm consultant. He has written this chapter for the merger of two large firms.

However, even a merger of two sole principals can cull from this chapter enough material to make their merger a success. Obviously, a lot of what Bill includes will not affect the smaller firm, but, as the firms involved in the merger become larger, so more of the contents of this chapter will be relevant. Even that which is not specifically relevant will be interesting and will strike responsive chords in the mind of the reader.

In fact, if you read no other chapter, read this one and it will give you the essence of the theme of this book, Successful Merger.

The firm entering into merger discussions has many questions:

1 How does the firm deal with the anomalies and the actions of partners and employees that are not in conformance with agreements made during the merger discussions?

2 How should the discussions cope with egos and the firm name?

3 How should the new firm be structured for managing the joint practice and for running the administrative systems that will support the practice?

4 How and when should communications be initiated internally and externally?

5 How does the joint firm identify and integrate the facilities, equipment and technology of supporting the practice?

We always use an office design analogy in dealing with these issues. A partnership should not begin to choose the colour of the carpets and the size of a partners's office until preliminary steps of design can be accomplished. These include programming the relationship among professionals, schematically designing the placement of critical functions in the firm and then proceeding to detailed layouts of the space. Dealing with the colour of the carpet would be out of context with setting the objectives for the space. Without the primary objectives in place, discussions on the size of an office degrade to personal and emotional issues that have little to do with the overall success of the space design. The firms in a merger discussion must deal with the above issues in the context of a process that ensures the primary objectives of the combination are met and personal issues do not distract the firms from the ultimate success of the merger.

Primary objectives of a merger discussion

The discussions are to create long term compatibility between the two firms. Integration and assimilation of the practices and clients are the key to a successful merger. The process for developing this compatibility and integration should start before the consummation of the merger and not be left to chance after the merger has been consummated!

Each phase of effort discussed in this chapter builds upon the previous phase. With each phase of effort, the firms should be:

1 Increasing the base of understanding of the other firm's culture, clients, method of practice, governance and partner accountability system.
2 Building a mutual understanding of expectations essential to the success of the combined firms after the merger.
3 Opening lines of communication between partners.

All discussions in each phase of effort are designed to approach issues objectively, without threat to egos. Each phase is designed to get personal agendas on the table and objectively discussed in the context of what is best for both firms.

Each phase ends with a milestone. That milestone is one of summary of agreements and understandings on joint operations and allows each firm to make a 'go' versus 'no go' decision before proceeding to the more detailed, and time consuming, next step.

Caveats

First, this is a tremendously dynamic process. It is impossible to draw out the entire decision tree for the process in one chapter, or even in one book, because so many variables are possible. Only experience and familiarity with all the implications of a particular choice can help. A recap of the decision tree would be helpful as an overview:

1. Preliminaries.
   a. Strategy of the firm and the appropriateness of using the merger or acquisition as a tactic in implementing the strategy.
   b. Search for an appropriate partner in the context of criteria established in the development of strategy.
2. Phase I, The chemistry test.
3. Phase II, Developing a joint strategy for the combined firms.
4. Phase III, Logistics and due diligence.
5. Phase IV, Documentation.
6. Phase V, Implementation.

At the end of each step there should be a 'go' or 'no go' decision.

Second, it is never too late to cut off discussions and not proceed. The expenditure of a lot of time and money does not constitute a reason to plunge blindly ahead.

Management consultant versus recruiting consultants (brokers)

Simply put, the management consultant gets paid on a per diem and for services rendered with the long term benefit of the client in mind. The recruiting consultant, headhunter or broker gets paid for making a match. For a consultant to say they do both creates a conflict.

Management consultants bill on a per diem or by the hour and are useful in keeping the parties up the learning curve and efficient in making decisions and moving ahead in the process. Timing must be exquisite if a merger or acquisition is going to come out successfully.

A management consultant will be more objective in asking questions. The consultant will be able to ask questions that are better asked by a consultant than by partners who may be living together in the combined firm. A management consultant should be the one who constantly challenges the reality of the strategy, the potential partner and the feasibility of moving to the next step.

A broker is one whose compensation will be tied to making the

Successful Mergers

match. Brokers are excellent for finding a potential partner among a large population. To proceed through the phases outlined below with only a broker whose financial pay off will come if the combination is made, is to risk having a combination forced together only to fall apart after the fees are paid.

The Preliminaries

Although the following two items have been covered in previous chapters, their importance cannot be over emphasised.

Strategic Thinking. The firms must satisfy themselves that their client service and growth strategies are best served by a merger or acquisition tactic. Some typical strategies that have led to merger include:

Client Strategies. The firm has clients which would be better served by a more diversified practice or a practice with more depth in a specific area of expertise.

Practice Strategies. The firm has developed a great deal of depth in a specific line of services and needs more clients that can use those services.

Joint Clients. The best mergers are when the criteria above are promoted by the fact that the two firms share some significant clients. Such a condition guarantees that the key partners of the two firms will be coordinating their efforts immediately.

Search. The search for a partner must be based upon a sound strategy that allows the firm to be very specific in its selection criteria.

Assuming the strategy is sound and the search turns up a qualified candidate to merge with, go to the next phase of the efforts.

Phase I; The chemistry test

This phase is the first series of meetings between the management groups of the two firms. Each of the groups should have the list of questions before them with supporting exhibits. Each group should have read through the entire process outlined in this chapter so they know when certain issues will be dealt with and so the first discussion does not degenerate into minutiae. As the name implies, this is a series of overview meetings to see if there is a possible fit and the chemistry of the two firms is compatible.

Organisation. Each firm should appoint the following to serve in this first phase. A liaison partner should be appointed by each firm. The liaison partner is the primary representative from each firm in all deliberations. The liaison partner is the partner charged with all the coordination and efforts. A second and larger group should be formed from the executive group of each firm to deal with the initial discussions. This merger committee has usually two or three members from the executive committees of each firm.

Exhibits. Each firm should circulate to the other group a copy of any brochures, capability statements, recruiting brochures, and any other knowledge the firm makes available to its clients or the general public. It should also bring supporting documentation for the following questions that might be exchanged if the first series of meetings go well.

Questions. The following questions should be dealt with in the first set of meetings in the chemistry phase.

1. Identify the liaison partner from each firm for all consolidation of agreements and key negotiating points.

2. What is the core group of:

    (a) Clients. Who are the most significant clients to the firm owing to volume of work; prestige; access to other clients and work; training and similar criteria for significance?

    (b) Areas of service or expertise. What are the areas of strength of the firm in areas of expertise? What areas would be enhanced by additional expertise or depth?

    (c) People. Who are the key business getters; key managers of work and clients; key producers or key trainers of others?

3. Are there any significant conflicts that appear formidable to the combination of the two firms?

4. How does the governance and decision making process in each of the two firms operate? For policy issues of the firm, where does the style of decision making lie between utter democracy and benevolent despotism? Start with the question of:

Successful Mergers

"How would you make a decision in your firm regarding the move to new office space; the acceptance of a new client; the admission of a lateral partner; the admission of a senior lateral, qualified professional not coming in as a partner, etc.

5. What is the culture and strategy of the firm and reflected by:
   (a) The identification and acquisition of clients. The types of matters and engagements accepted. What does this tell you about the way they select work? Do they have standards or criteria that fit your firm's.
   (b) The work ethic of the other firm and their responsiveness in the delivery of services. What is the difference in the pace for generating billable hours? Are they much harder workers? Are they only focused on the generation of billable hours not efficiency?
   (c) The strategy of the other firm in competitively positioning themselves in the market. Is their statement more or less specific and focused than your own? Does their statement make you challenge your own strategies or feel more comfortable with your own strategies?
   (d) The range of partner participation in profits. In general, will their approach fit your own? What is the ratio of compensation for the highest to the lowest partner? Does it tend to fit your range and ratio given the their partners' ages and contributions?
   (e) The approach used to determine compensation. What do they value in partner performance? How do they conduct their annual review and evaluation of partner performance?

Firm name. This will depend upon the tradition of the two firms and the relative value and impact of each firm on the combined firms. Two scenarios will help in approaching the issue:

The Acquisition, A + B = A

1. Firm A is a traditional firm with an institutional, brand name that does not change when new partners are admitted.
2. Firm B has a key partner whose name is an essential part of the brand name image of the practice.
3. Firm B has not developed an institutional, brand name in the market in which the combined firms plan to compete.
4. If 1 is true then the name will probably remain as Firm A.
5. If 1 and 2 are true then the name may be altered to include the brand name from Firm B.

6. If 1 is not true and 2 is true, then the firm name will probably be changed to include the brand names from Firms A and B.

Merger, A + B = C

1. In this scenario, the two firms are joining together as basic equals even though one may be larger than another.
2. The names will probably be combined into one institutional name based upon the brand name identification of the two firms.
3. It would be best to take the traditional names of the two firms that are associated with dead partners.

From this information, the liaison partners should have a good feel for the relative cultures of the two firms and where the fits and misfits might be. The liaison partners should summarise all the conversations in the meetings and prepare a presentation to their respective merger committees.

Should the executive committee and merger committee of each firm feel comfortable with the combination, the firms can proceed to the next and more rigorous phase.

Phase II; Developing joint strategies

The primary objective of this segment of effort is to set up a forum for determining how the various areas of each firm will work together. This effort expands the effort to include more partners.

Organisation. In addition to the liaison partners and the respective merger committees for each firms, other entities must be set up for the conduct of Phase II. Those groups include:

1. PAM; Practice Area Management group from each firm to supervise and guide the discussions of each of the practice groups placed together for discussions.
2. CAM; Client Assessment and Management group to supervise the discussions of the significant client teams that will be joined between the two firms.
3. PSA; Practice Support Area group to deal with the initial stages of the combination of the administration of the two firms.

These three liaison groups should include one to three partners from each firm and are responsible for dealing with the questions below.

Exhibits. Each of the firms should provide the following information to the other firm in this phase. They include:

1. Financial statements for the last three years. Also include any comparison information on the firm to other firms, e.g. ratios of staff to lawyers, expenses and revenue per lawyer, or other comparisons from national and city studies.
2. Staffing and organisational structure of the two firms. What are the levels of experience in each of the practice groups of the two firms. Show the demographic mix of expertise of each segment of the practice.
3. More detailed lists of significant clients and the work being performed for the clients.

Questions. The following questions are broken up into the PAM, CAM and PSA segments for better delegation.

PAM: Each of the major practice areas of each firm should have three members who work with their counterparts in the other firm to answer the following questions:

1. Identify the major cases or transactions in the area and the clients tied to those cases or transactions.
2. Identify the major conflicts and the way in which those conflicts will be resolved.
3. How will the expertise and talents of each of the two firms in the homogeneous areas be combined to strengthen the practice of the combined firm in the competitive market?
4. What are the areas of weakness in the combined groups that will have to be addressed through lateral entries; additional recruiting of newly qualified lawyers; pruning the groups to produce a leaner and more profitable combination?
5. Identify the issues that should be addressed in the next phase of effort.
6. Document the understandings and results in a joint memorandum.
7. The liaison partners should have a cover memorandum on the joint memorandum expressing the perceptions of the risks and benefits of the combination.

CAM: Each of the significant clients of the firm probably has one or two partners who are informally or formally charged with the relationship with the clients. Where there are many clients in any one industry or the significant clients are large enough to command a combined firm approach, clients teams should answer the following questions:

1. What is the current marketing and positioning strategy for developing the relationship with the significant clients?
2. What are the possibilities for using current, significant client relationships as access to new work of the combined firm? What elements of the combined firm will enhance the combined firm's ability to get that access and acquire the client work?
3. How will the combined capabilities be marketed to current and prospective clients?
4. What would the presentation of capabilities look like and in what format would it be delivered (e.g. conference with the key client personnel; presentation; letter; press release; etc.) What would be the content in the presentation? Who would give the presentation? How would each of the following be treated?
   (a) The very few critical clients of the combined firm.
   (b) Very significant clients of the combined firm?
   (c) Significant referral sources of work for the combined firm?
   (d) Most of the other clients of the combined firm?
   (e) The Bar?
   (f) Other clients of other law firms?
   (g) The general public?

(In all of the cases above the CAM group would have put together the marketing and PR strategy for the merged firms. The group would also have to come up with whatever strategy and media would be used to inform persons outside the firm of the merger and the benefits of same.)

5. What are the issues that should be dealt with in Phase III, the logistics and due diligence phase.
6. Document the understandings and results in a joint memoranda.
7. The liaison partners should create a cover memoranda on the joint memoranda expressing the perceptions of the risks and benefits of the combination.

PSA: With the information from the above discussions, develop a summary profit plan for the combined firm showing the impact on the profitability of the combined firm over the next three years. This should provide a summary picture of the 'bridge' costs in hard and soft costs to getting the combined firm up and running in twelve to eighteen months. The profit plan should show:

1. The impact on earnings.
2. The cost in hard pounds of bringing the combined firm up to full operation.

3. The soft cost in lost management time taken away from revenue production.
4. The obligations of the combined firms.

Liaison Partners. Using all of the previously developed information, develop a memorandum and supporting exhibits for use by the merger committee in preparing for a presentation to the partnership. That presentation should include:

1. The combination plan for pulling homogeneous practices together and filling in the holes in expertise and support.
2. A marketing support plan on how the combined firms will market the combination.
3. A rough estimate of how the compensation systems of each of the firms will be merged.

If the sub-groups work well together, the liaison partners and the merger committee will have created another group of partners who will have bought into the combination. A presentation can now be made to the partners. If a 'go' decision is made a presentation should be made to the other employees of the firms. Press releases on the fact that the two firms are talking can now be sent out.

Phase III; Logistics and due diligence

The primary objective of this phase of effort is to test the trends and the statistics generated in the previous phases. The items in this phase are usually not large enough to kill the combination, but represent details that must be addressed. It is not likely that any revelations will be discovered in this phase but should one arise, the due diligence will pay off.

Many law firms think this is the Phase II effort; that if the chemistry test works they go to this detailed phase. That may work for corporations but it does not work for a professional service affiliation. Professional service organisations do not have hierarchical systems of organisation and their assets go up and down in the lift every day.

Some consultants would have firms move directly to this phase because this is where most of the detail staff work can be done with the leverage most accounting firms need to make a profit. This is the *third* phase. It is now appropriate to create a larger team of partners, accountants and technical people, to work out the details of the merger.

Organisation. PSA begins to play a major role in this phase. Under the

Managing Change

direction of the liaison partners and based upon the items raised for this effort by the PAM and CAM groups in Phase II, the questions below become the focal point. Also the DOC, documentation group begins to form up the articles of partnership and operating agreements based upon the previous work. The documentation group will be charged with assembling the merger book detailing the implementation of the merger.

Exhibits. All of the documentation and memoranda of understanding from previous meetings should be part of the information base. In addition, the following is a sampling of the other information required for this phase.

1. All information on the financial performance of the firms over the last three years and any budgets on operations for future years.
2. All information on the benefits, insurance and taxes of the two firms.
3. A description of all the furniture, fixtures and equipment of the two firms to insure a proper accounting of all the hard assets of the two firms.
4. Any information on the leases and leasehold improvements of the two firms and any future obligations associated with those leases and leasehold improvements.
5. Obligations and liabilities; on and off balance sheet items.
6. Any other information that can be tied back to the financial conditions of the two firms and that can be used in developing a joint proforma and combined statement of operations.
7. All operating policies and procedures. Include the current ones and the revisions made by agreement in Phase II.
8. A complete list of clients and matters for the last five years. This list should be detailed enough to allow the firm to identify any minor but important conflict.
9. A complete list of personnel, including employment histories, compensation packages and other pertinent information needed to combine the firm's personnel and compensation systems.

Questions. Much more detailed questioning is used to deal with the following:

1. Minor conflicts.
2. Clarification of the assumptions and the resulting financial proforma.
3. Combination discussions on the practice support areas of the two firms:
   (a) Time and accounting systems (people, procedures, equipment, software, etc.).
   (b) Office equipment and facilities.

(c) Administration support structure.
(d) Taxes, insurance and benefits.
(e) Implementation plan and milestones.

Documentation. From the above information and agreements a merger book will be developed to summarise all agreements and action plans. The merger book developed by DOC should include the following sections:

1. Section I. The executive summary of the remaining sections.
2. Section II. The primary objectives of the combination and the benefits to be accrued to the clients and the partnerships as a result of the combination.
3. Section III. A description of the practices, areas of expertise, bundles of services offered, clients and relative competitive position of the combined firm. There should be a subsection on each firm.
4. Section IV. A description of the combined firm outlining the interim management structure; the focus of the marketing and competitive positioning efforts; organisation of the areas of practices and operating agreements for the combined firm.
    There should be a subsection on each practice group within the combined firm describing the competitive positioning strategy of the practice group; the implications on the structure of the group in delivering services and the staffing of the group with the appropriate mix of seniors and juniors; clerks; paraprofessionals and administrative staff.
5. Section V. The implementation plan outlining how the firm will combine its practices. An action plan will be included showing the milestones for the completion of each task, product, event or similar action item.
6. Section VI. The financial proforma for the next three years and the assumptions that went into the proforma's generation.
7. Section VII. A draft of the articles of partnership and the operating policies of the combined firm.

All but Section VI and VII can be distributed to all employees of the combined firm as part of the communications on the merger. The document can also be used as a basis for any press releases and presentations to clients and the referral base. The communication steps which follow should use the merger book as a guide.

Communication. Liaison partners should review the documentation and discuss it with each working group (e.g. PAM, CAM, PSA) to test the clarity of thinking and the reality of the milestones discussed in the

Managing Change

summary memoranda of agreements produced in Phase II. Can this document and its implications be explained to the partners of each firm? Can the liaison partners convince their partners that the document satisfies the due diligence ?

The liaison partners will then submit the documents to the merger committee one week in advance of a meeting. The first meeting after this submittal is used to 'lawyer' the document; i.e. are there any holes, misrepresentations of intent, misdirections, unclear and/or non-measurable objectives and similar items?

The second meeting will review the changes to the documentation. The merger committee will develop the agenda for explaining the key provisions and the implications to the other partners of each firm, then to the non partners and then to the rest of the firm.

Group meetings tend to work best so that everyone hears the approach and questions at the same time. Distribute the appropriate portions of the merger book to each group about three to five working days before each meeting. Each of the presentations must be very professional, well rehearsed, and clear in describing the merger and its implications. The presentation must also be clear in spelling out the implications of the firm's approach to client development and delivery of service.

Group meetings will be held to deal with individual questions. Those group meetings will be organised by area of practice and by significant client group.

Based upon the discussions in the lawyer meetings and the information developed during the due diligence, Phase III, deals with each of following groups for the 'go' versus 'no go' decisions:

1. Start with the executive committee and the key leadership of the two firms.
2. Then include the other leaders of the firm and the heads of departments that will be bound by the action plans. Determine the measurable objectives that will be used to measure the success of the combination at close intervals.
3. Deal with the partnership and describe the approach that will be used.
4. Communicate the merger agreement and the action plan to all the employees with full discussion so they understand the action plan and the measurement criteria for success.

If the consultants, executive committees and liaison partners have been doing their jobs throughout Phases I through III, almost all of the problems of communication, understanding of implications of the merger and the development of a consensus will have been created on:

1. The purpose and benefits of the merger.
2. The implications of the merger on how the two firms will practise together and build a strong combined firm.
3. The expectations of one another within realistic parameters.

Phase IV; Documentation

The primary objective of this phase is to consolidate all the documentation and finalise any of the information required for the merger book and the articles of partnership.

Given the discussions toward the last part of Phase III and the decision to go forward, make any adjustments to the merger book and its contents.

Make any final presentations to the various decision making levels of the firm, starting at the top.

Finally, communicate the contents of the merger book to the employees of the two firms. The liaison partners will be accountable but may delegate such briefings to others in the two firms.

Obtain signatures on the articles of partnership and the merger parties for the employees.

Phase V; Implementation

The primary objective of this phase is to make the merger agreements come to life and to ensure the combined firm is constantly evaluating its progress against its plan. *This does not mean that the plan outlined in the merger book is in concrete.* The firms will find that adjustments must be made based upon reality and new information that comes to light during the implementation.

This is *the* most important phase of effort. Everyone *will not* cooperate according to the policies and procedure formulated in Phases II and III. Successful implementation will require constant attention, meetings, jawboning and decision making through accountable partners.

The firms will have to commit the management time to making the merger work over the first 18 months. Here is a sampling of the time it will take:

1. Top management review of progress and problems at the end of months 3, 6, 9, 12 and 18. Resolve any problems immediately after they are identified.
2. Management time in assimilation will require 4 to 6 hours per week.
3. Departmental management time will be from 2 to 4 hours per week.

4. Joint client development and client acquisition time will require 2 to 4 hours per week per client team for significant clients identified in Phase II.

Summary

A firm deals with the anomalies and the actions of partners and employees who are not in conformance with the intentions of the merger through:

1. Dealing with the relationships of the partners and their expectations before the merger is consummated. This occurs through increasing commitment to the purposes of the merger as each Phase is accomplished.
2. Building a consensus on the purposes of the merger so the firm has clear criteria against which to compare the performance of partners and employees after the merger. Only then will management be in a position to deal with the hard people-decisions required when anomalies occur.

Egos within a partnership are an appropriate character trait of very talented, aggressive and successful professionals. The phased approach to the merger allows key partners to see the benefits to their practice of the merger and support it. It also lets those key partners talk through and overcome their perception of the risks.

Although name is critical, too many professionals have an unrealistic view of their reputation and the image of their firm. Only by going through the process and seeing where another firm brings a significant reputation and client base to their firm can a partner see his own competitive position objectively.

The structure of a new firm will follow:

1. The joint strategies of the combined firm and the expectations of the combined firm in accountability of partners,
2. Organisation for delivery of services,
3. The firm management that creates an unincumbered environment for the accomplishment of strategies, and
4. The practice support structure to support the combined firm management.

Communication is carried out internally throughout the process. An increasing number of people are informed of and brought into the process as each phase progresses. It is common for the firms to try to keep the

Successful Mergers

combination quite confidential until the end of Phase II.

During Phase II, the liaison partners should hire a public relations consultant. That consultant has three functions:

1. Helping the firm plan for the releases of information at the end of Phase II should there be a 'go' decision.
2. Helping the practice groups and clients groups shape the capability statements that will be used for communication to the significant clients and referral networks of the two firms.
3. Helping the firm cope with the press and others should leaks of information occur before the firm has made a 'go' or 'no go' decision at the end of Phase II.

Use of consultants is a consideration that any firm dealing with a merger should consider. As stated in the opening paragraphs there are two specific consultants who are needed besides technical, accounting and public relations consultants. The management consultant and the broker have two different functions. The management consultant should be used for dealing with long term considerations and implications. The consultant must bring objectivity to deal with the following:

1. Helping the firm establish strategies that will set the context for firm growth and expansion. The tactic of mergers or acquisitions is one of many strategies that might be apporpriate. Too many firms choose merger or acquisitions as a panacea to solve their perceived problems without having any underlying strategy that supports such a tactic.
2. Involvement in all phases to keep the discussions on track and to ask questions that the two firms may be too polite to ask or may fail to ask. The management consultant brings a discipline to the process that will ensure attention is paid to the right issues at the right time.
3. Objectively assessing the potential success of the merger and recommending the 'no go' decision when experience shows trends in discussion are pointing toward an ineffective combination. The consultant should look beyond some of the personality issues to the opportunities and problems that may come from the merger that partners may not or may not want to recognise.
4. Providing the technical and management support in assessing the information from the other firm. Examples include:
   (a) In Phase I; chemistry test; providing the initial assessment of the hard and soft bridge cost of combining the two firms.
   (b) Helping the liaison partners prepare presentations to the executive merger committees, leadership and others in the two firms.
   (c) Conducting an unbiased assessment of the structures – delivery

of services and practice support – of the firm and recommend alterations.
  (d) Conducting an unbiased assessment of the combination of the equipment, systems, management information and facilities.
5. Instilling the discipline to follow up on the performance measurement and management of the combination after the merger is consummated.

There are hard and soft costs of making a merger effective. The hard costs include the assumptions of obligations; building up the work in progress and accounts receivable of the combined firm; the start up costs in combining the systems of the two firms and similar issues already discussed in Phases I, II and III.

The soft costs include time (lost revenue), leadership for the assimilation of the two entities, joint efforts of the partners and the other personnel of the two firms in planning and consummating and implementing the merger.

Finally two key points of this process must be re-emphasised:

1. Compatibility and integration are functions of how well expectations are identified and then satisfied.
2. Do not go to the next phase of efforts until every member of the core group of each firm has reached a consensus on proceeding. Do not go to second base until the core group has reached the first and understands the implications of going on. THERE ARE NO SHORTCUTS!

It does not cost nearly as much to call off the merger and deal with the implications of that decision as it costs to correct a bad merger. Examples abound in the United States, and in UK as well, where firms joined into a bad merger have blown apart, like a grenade – not as the groups they were before the merger.

Mergers can be a tremendous tool to build a firm in conformance with a solid strategy. Do it right and the benefits will be reflected by the popular synergistic relationship; $1 + 1 = 3$.

William C Cobb

7 Accounts and Taxation

Introduction

One of the great advantages of practising within a partnership rather than a company is the privacy that this affords. Company accounts are on public record at the Companies Registry, but it is only the partners, the Inland Revenue and, possibly, the bank manager who have to see partnership accounts. Having been brought up in a tradition of secrecy regarding financial information, therefore, partners may be somewhat reluctant to disclose sensitive financial information to potential merger partners. However, a great deal of time can be saved if there is fairly open disclosure of critical financial data at the early stages of negotiation so that, if this demonstrates that the potential stumbling blocks to a merger represent insuperable obstacles, that decision can be reached sooner rather than later.

There are perhaps three matters in the financial arena which are potential deal breakers. These are:

1. differences in absolute profit shares
2. different accounting bases
3. divergent obligations for retired partners – both currently and potentially retired.

Differing absolute profit shares

While the question of the relative profit shares of partners in the merged firm is discussed in greater detail in chapter 9, a chapter on the financial aspects cannot ignore the potential difficulties of widely divergent absolute profit shares in the two firms contemplating merger.

While the philosophy of merger will normally embrace the concept of 'two plus two equals five' so that there is a hope and expectation that as a result of the merger, all partners will be better off in terms of profit share, it is very difficult within a single partnership for profit shares to be very different for partners of roughly the same seniority and experience.

Such a divergence may be acceptable where the two existing firms are operating in geographically separate areas, but where it is expected that the merged firm will occupy the same premises or be operating within close proximity of each other, it will be difficult for partners to accept significant profit differentials.

Thus if the average earnings of one firm are one and a half or twice those of the other, there would be a significant problem in attempting to integrate the two firms. With the best will in the world, it would be difficult to sell to the partners of the more profitable firm that there are significant benefits in the longer term to outweigh the reduction in current earnings which the merger would be likely to necessitate.

Incompatible accounting bases

A fairly superficial examination of the balance sheets of the two firms will indicate whether there is likely to be a problem in reconciling the accounting bases of the two firms. Professional partnerships, not being governed by the Companies Act's requirement for their accounts to show a 'true and fair view' can adopt one of three basic variations in the manner in which the accounts are drawn up. In broad terms these are:

1. an earnings basis
2. a bills issued basis
3. a cash basis

A firm which accounts on an earnings basis will, broadly, account for income as it is earned. This will involve taking credit each year for the work which is undertaken, even though this work may not have been billed to clients or paid for by clients. In the financial statements of a firm which accounts on an earnings basis, one will find figures for work in progress and fee debtors. However, even amongst firms which would regard themselves as adopting an earnings basis of accounting, there will be wide variations in the value attributed in each year's accounts to work in progress, and a close examination of that basis of valuation will need to be undertaken on each side.

A firm which accounts on a bills issued basis takes no credit for work which has been done at each accounting date but is unbilled, but takes credit merely for the bills issued to clients during the accounting period, whether or not those bills have been paid by the accounting date. In the balance sheet of such firms there will be no figure for work in progress, although client debtors will feature.

The third basis of accounting is the cash basis whereby income is only brought into account for the purposes of the financial statements (and for tax purposes) when the firm's bills are paid. Such firms' accounts will therefore show no balances in respect of work in progress or client debtors.

Successful Mergers

It may be regarded as surprising that the Inland Revenue accepts accounts for tax purposes drawn up on such potentially widely divergent bases. Undoubtedly the Inland Revenue would prefer accounts to be drawn up on an earnings basis because, with inflation and the natural growth of firms, this basis will report higher profits year by year than either of the other two, but the principal concern of the Inland Revenue is for consistency from one year to the next. Thus while newly established firms (including those that are deemed to be new firms for tax purposes following a change in the composition of the partnership for which no continuation election for tax purposes is made) are required to produce accounts on an earnings basis for at least their first three years, established firms are permitted to change to or continue with one of the other two main bases of accounting referred to as 'conventional bases'.

For the merged firm to be a fully integrated firm from the accounts point of view, it is obviously essential for a single, consistent accounting basis to be adopted after the merger. If, therefore, the two predecessor firms have hitherto adopted different accounting bases, one or other or both of them will need to make a change in order to enable consistency to be achieved. This can be an expensive and painful process, and may not be achievable. It is for this reason that an early discussion of each firm's basis of accounting is essential so that if it transpires that this particular hurdle is an insuperable one, much time is not spent in the fruitless debate and negotiation and other, less critical areas.

Where negotiations are between two fairly substantial firms, and one accounts on a cash basis and the other on a full earnings basis, it is quite probable that a fully integrated merger from the accounting point of view cannot be achieved. The possibility of continuing the two firms in parallel should be considered; this is discussed in greater detail in the paragraphs below.

The impact of a change in basis

For the purpose of illustrating the potential problems, let us consider the adjustments that might be required to reconcile the accounting basis of a firm which accounts on a cash basis with one adopting the full earnings basis of accounting. The abbreviated balance sheets of the two firms at a common accounting date might be as follows:

Accounts and Taxation

	Cash basis firm £000's	Earnings basis firm £000's
Partners' capital and current accounts	20	220
Cash	100	–
Debtors	–	250
Work in progress	–	200
	100	450
Current liabilities	(80)	(230)
Net assets	20	220

The Inland Revenue will allow firms to change their basis of accounting as long as the change is to be a permanent one. Thus it would be open to either the cash basis firm to introduce debtors and work in progress into its accounts, or for the earnings basis firm to write off its debtors and work in progress and thereafter to account on a cash basis. From an accounting point of view either of those changes can easily be achieved although the taxation implications and the effects on partners' balances can be pretty devastating.

However, before considering the impact of any changes, there perhaps ought to be a brief discussion of the advantages and disadvantages of each of the 'extreme' bases of accounting: the earnings and the cash bases. The bills issued basis is a mid-way point between these two extremes.

The earnings basis comes closest to the accountant's accruals concept, and perhaps therefore should be favoured. Under this basis, partners are given credit for the work done in any year whether or not that has been billed by the accounting date. The reported profit each year is therefore not dependent either upon the decision of a client to pay a bill on one day – perhaps the last day of an accounting period – or the next. Similarly, it is not entirely dependent upon the efficiency of the fee earner in issuing his bills.

However, it will be seen from the abbreviated balance sheets above, that the amount of capital required of partners in a firm which accounts on a full earnings basis is significantly more than that required of partners in a cash basis firm, notwithstanding that, in the above example, there is also much greater recourse to outside finance.

By bringing into account as income amounts that have not yet been received in cash, the reported profits are higher, the amounts therefore credited to partners' current accounts are higher and the tax liability of the firm is higher than it would be for the cash basis firm. If a retiring partner is able to withdraw from the firm all his undrawn profits – including those that are unrealised in cash terms – then inevitably the cash required of the continuing partners to finance the business will be higher.

By contrast, if credit is only taken for income when cash is received, reported profits and tax liabilities are lower and the amount of capital required from partners is correspondingly less. It is perhaps a matter of opinion as to which accounting basis is better. The writer's general philosophy is that the amount of capital which a partner has in the business should be kept to a minimum, and for this reason the cash basis of accounting gives the greatest advantage. Tax liabilities year by year are kept down, but the basis does mean that a retiring partner leaves behind that element of the profit which has been earned during his period as a partner but which has not been realised in cash.

What then is the impact of a change from an earnings basis on to a cash basis of accounting? This means that after the change the firm does not need to bring into account at the end of its accounting period the debtors and work in progress which exist at that date.

However, for the Inland Revenue to accept that the annual accounts ending on that day give a fair measure of the profit earned during that year, they will not allow any deduction at the beginning of the year for the opening work in progress and debtors. Those balances therefore have to be eliminated from the accounts, and ultimately the only balances against which they can be written off are the balances on the partners' capital and current accounts.

In the situation illustrated above there would be a need to write off debtors and work in progress amounting to £450,000 while the credit balances on partners' capital and current accounts amounted to only £220,000. Those balances would therefore be eliminated and replaced with a debit balance on partners' accounts of £230,000.

It is unlikely that such a course of action would meet with the approval of a partner who was nearing retirement. Previously he would have expected to be able to withdraw his capital and current accounts from the firm but, as a result of this decision, he finds himself in a position of owing money to the firm. What is more, while the build up of the figures for debtors and work in progress will have been subject to income tax year by year, the writing off of debtors and work in progress on making the change in the basis of accounting does not attract any tax relief.

As and when a cash basis firm comes to an end (either through actual dissolution, through incorporation or as a result of a partnership change

Accounts and Taxation

treated as a discontinuance for tax purposes), the previously unrecorded value of debtors and work in progress will have to come into account for tax purposes. There is thus the possibility that the £450,000 in the simple example above will not only have been taxed as it accumulated, but having been written off without tax relief, will also be taxed a second time when the business ultimately ceases.

It is likely, therefore, that partners will be prepared to write off debtors and work in progress only if they are relatively modest in absolute amount, or the partners can be reasonably sure that there will be no discontinuance of the business, thereby causing the then unrecorded debtors and work in progress to be taxed a second time, within the foreseeable future.

The Inland Revenue have a press release dated 18 June 1979 which describes the view they take with regard to the cash basis of accounting. This is reproduced in Appendix I.

The press release also describes the conditions that the Revenue may apply when a firm chooses to change its basis of accounting on to a cash basis. It states that the change 'must be a complete one', and this merely reinforces the fact that cash received in an accounting period after the change will form part of that period's taxable income even though the cash is realised from a debt which was effectively taxed in the previous accounting period.

The press release does indicate an area where perhaps advantage may be obtained from the change. Tax relief will be granted, after the change, for expenditure incurred in cash, even where relief was given in an earlier period when the accruals basis was being used, for the same accrued expense.

The change on to an earnings basis

Is the reverse change any easier to effect? Certainly the impact on partners' balances is favourable rather than unfavourable. If, to use the same figures as used above, the cash basis firm were to introduce debtors and work in progress into its accounts at a figure of £450,000 the debit to those accounts will be matched by a credit to partners' capital or current accounts. However, the drawback of this move is that it is not possible to introduce debtors and work in progress into the accounts without their being taxed.

Thus tax at, let us assume, 40% on the £450,000 will soon be required to be paid over to the Inland Revenue, and will therefore be debited against the credit to partners' capital or current accounts. More significantly, however, tax of £180,000 will need to be found to be paid over to the Inland Revenue, even though the mere introduction of debtors and work in progress into the accounts does not give rise to any realisation of cash. There is thus a permanent additional financial burden on the business which has to be financed, at a cost.

It can be argued, of course, that the payment of income tax on the introduction of debtors and work in progress is only an advance payment of tax which will be due at some stage in the future. This is obviously correct since, as explained above, ultimately tax will be paid on all the partnership's income. However, if there was otherwise little likelihood of the business ceasing for tax purposes (which would thereby trigger a tax charge on the unrecorded debtors and work in progress) the advance payment of this income tax represents a significant financial burden for the ongoing firm. It is impossible to say, in the abstract, whether the burden would be worse than the double taxation of certain profits which occurs when an earnings basis firm moves on to the cash basis.

Who should bear the cost?

In relation to the writing off of debtors and work in progress on a move on to a cash basis, there was a simple presumption that the amounts would be written off against the capital and current accounts of the firm concerned. However, since the write off in one firm was made in order to facilitate the merger of the two firms, there is a case for saying that the cost of the write off should be borne by the partners of the merged firm as a cost of the merger rather than a cost of one of the predecessor firms.

Furthermore, the amounts could be carried forward in the accounts to be written off, over a number of years after the merger, against the profits of the early years of the merged firm rather in the same way as purchased goodwill might, in the past, have been treated.

The cost of financing the tax burden that would arise on the firm moving from a cash to a full earnings basis is something which would, in any event, be borne by the merged firm if the cash were to be raised by way of a firm's overdraft. However, it would probably not be appropriate for the credit arising from the recognition of debtors and work in progress to be given to all the partners of the merged firm; the credit would merely put the capital accounts of the partners of the former cash basis firm on a level footing with those of the earnings basis firm.

It will be appreciated from the foregoing analysis that the merger of two firms which account on these two extreme bases of accounting may prove to be difficult. If the firms are unwilling to bear the costs involved the incompatibility of the accounting bases may cause the negotiations to break down entirely. It is for this reason that it is important to exchange information on each firm's accounting basis at an early stage in the negotiations.

In some cases it may be possible for the impact of the adjustments to be reduced by each firm moving to the middle ground. Thus the cash basis firm might introduce debtors into the accounts (and bear the appropriate tax charge) thereby moving on to a bills issued basis. The earnings basis firm might write off work in progress so as to enable it, too, to account thereafter on a bills issued basis. It will be appreciated, however, that both the difficulties described will be encountered, though on a reduced scale.

Parallel partnerships

As was suggested above, one way of enabling a merger to take place while retaining, within the ongoing business, two different bases of accounting is for the two firms to continue with their separate identities, albeit with an identical composition of partners. Thus all the partners of Firm A would be admitted to Firm B and all the Firm B partners would be admitted to Firm A, and the profit sharing arrangements which applied in each would be identical. Since the measure of profit reported in the accounts of each firm will be comparable with that of earlier years, no mischief will be done in relation to the sharing of profits between the two firms.

However, before giving their approval to the parallel approach, the Inland Revenue will need to be satisfied that the profit streams of each firm can be readily identified, and the parallel structure is not being used to achieve some kind of tax advantage for the partners.

It is for this reason that parallel arrangements are probably only appropriate where the merging firms operate in separate geographical areas or distinct areas of professional business. Thus within the same town or city, a specialist litigation practice may be able to operate in parallel with a predominantly conveyancing firm of solicitors without the Inland Revenue raising any objections. However, mergers of this kind are perhaps unusual, and more frequently there is, following the merger, an interchange of business and personnel, making it extremely difficult to identify whether new instructions are properly attributable to one firm or the other.

In these more frequently encountered mergers, a parallel partnership arrangement may not be feasible, thereby ruling out this possible solution to the problem of incompatible accounting bases.

Retirement obligations

A third potential deal breaker relates to the actual and contingent obligations of each firm to reward partners in retirement. Many larger practices are now attempting (with difficulty in some cases) to abandon any payments to partners in retirement on the grounds that a partner now has a good opportunity to make adequate provision for his retirement by way of personal pension contributions during his active years as a partner.

However, there remain in many firms long-standing commitments to partners to reward them in retirement by way of a sinecure consultancy or a partnership annuity. If the rights of current and future retired partners in the two firms are widely different, this can give rise to serious difficulties, and the position needs to be openly discussed at an early stage.

If the split of the profits of the merged firm is arrived at through a comparison of the profits of the predecessor firms in the year or two prior to the merger, and those adjusted profits take into account annuity payments or consultancy arrangements with one firm's retired partners, then there is no reason why that particular item of expense should be singled out for special treatment. It would probably not be unreasonable for the obligations to be assumed by the merged firm before the profits are appropriated to the partners.

There may be difficulties, however, if there are annuity arrangements in one firm linked to the profitability of that firm. Obviously a partner entitled to an annuity of, say, 5% of the profits of the firm cannot be entitled to 5% of the enlarged profits following the merger. It will therefore be necessary to renegotiate with any such annuitants to ensure that the annuity is calculated by reference to a measure of profit or other variables that are likely to give a sensible answer.

The principal difficulty, however, is likely to relate to the annuity entitlements of existing partners rather than the obligations to already retired partners. It is probably unacceptable for partners of one firm to have retirement entitlements while their contemporaries in the other do not. There can be no simple solution to this dilemma.

It is probable that the partners with retirement entitlements will have to relinquish these; to award equivalent rights to the partners of the other firm would be a retrograde step. The debate will centre around whether the relinquishing of retirement rights should be made with or without compensation.

Inevitably, there may need to be a tapering of entitlements, with those partners near to retirement perhaps receiving from the merged firm retirement entitlements not much reduced from their original expectations.

It will not be surprising if partners who have accumulated substantial retirement rights are reluctant to relinquish these even if they represent an entitlement unlikely to be realised for some years. It is therefore an area which needs to be explored sooner rather than later in case a resolution of the problem cannot be found.

The basis of taxation of the merged firm

Any change in the basis of accounting in one or other or both firms should ideally take place within the final accounts of the predecessor firms. It is important for the opening position of the merged firm to be on a consistent basis as between the two firms. Ideally, too, the accounting date of each firm immediately prior to the merger date (if it does not take place at an accounting date) should be the same.

Thus, for example, if one firm previously accounted to December in each year and the other one to June, it would be easier for the merger to take place with effect from 1 July. If that is not possible but it is nevertheless decided that the merged firm should make up accounts to 30 June each year, the December firm should change its accounting date to the 30 June immediately prior to the merger unless the change can be made more advantageously to the previous 30 June.

If, for example, the merger is to take place with effect from 1 January 1989, the accounts for both firms should be made up to 30 June 1988 so that the accounts of the merged firm can be made up to 30 June 1989, and thereafter to 30 June.

Each firm will need to make up accounts to 31 December 1988, but these will not be used for tax purposes but only to enable the relevant assessments to be properly allocated between the partners of the predecessor firms and those of the merged firm.

This book is not the appropriate place to debate the merits of different accounting dates, but it can be stated with confidence that an accounting date ending early in the fiscal year gives a tax advantage to firms compared with an accounting date ending late in the year. If profits are to rise year by year – which undoubtedly will be the expectation following the merger – then an accounting date of, say, 30 April gives not only a cash flow advantage to the firm but also the real likelihood of enabling them to make absolute savings of tax year by year.

The Inland Revenue produced a Statement of Practice in December 1986 (reproduced as Appendix 11) in which it went on record as formally acknowledging three ways in which a partnership merger might be treated from the tax point of view. Thus:

1. the event could give rise to a discontinuance for tax purposes of

both the predecessor firms, and the commencement of a new business;
2. one firm might be treated as discontinuing and recommencing while the other continued to be assessed on the preceding year basis; or
3. both firms could elect for continuation treatment.

Prior to the issue of this Statement of Practice, the Inland Revenue's official position was that a merger would normally give rise to the first of the options described above, namely, the discontinuance of both firms and commencement of a new one. In practice, however, the third option for the continuation of both firms could frequently be negotiated. The formal statement is to be welcomed inasmuch as it now recognises as possible all three options.

In the vast majority of cases, it will be in the interests of all the parties to opt for continuation treatment for both firms. Thus although the possibility is recognised of the discontinuance of one firm and the continuation of the other, the practical outworking of that would give rise to serious accounting problems for four years following the date of the merger through the application of sections 62 of the Taxes Act 1988.

This section provides that where a firm could make a continuation election under s 113(2) of the Taxes Act 1988 but decides against doing so, the profits of the first four years of the new business will be taxed on a current year basis. Thus if there is a merger of two streams of income, one of which is to be assessed on the preceding year basis and one on a current year basis, it will be necessary to keep separate records within the merged firm of the profits derived from each of the former businesses.

Although this might have been possible under the old rules for a twelve month period, it would become increasingly difficult as time passes for any accurate split to be made of the profits derived from each of the former businesses. Certainly three or four years after the merger, one would hope that new clients would be identified with the new firm rather than either of the predecessor firms. It is fairly unlikely in practice that this basis of dealing with the tax implications of merger will commend itself.

Indeed, a discontinuance of either firm is rarely going to be in the partners' interests. When profits are rising year by year a discontinuance will crystallise higher tax liabilities for the two or three years immediately prior to the merger, and it will normally be better for both firms to make the election required for the assessment to continue on the preceding year basis.

Each firm will admit to their partnership the partners in the other

Accounts and Taxation

firm and make the appropriate continuation elections. In theory this will result in two firms with an identical composition of partners, such that the Inland Revenue will treat them as a single firm and the merger will have been effected from the tax point of view.

The assessment for the first year or two of the merged firm will then be based on the aggregate of the profits of each of the predecessor firms for the appropriate basis period. This is best illustrated with a numerical example on the basis of a merger of two firms with effect from 1 July 1988, as follows:

	Tax adjusted profits		
	Firm A	Firm B	Merged firm AB
Year ended 30 June:			
1987	400	600	–
1988	500	800	–
1989	–	–	1,500
Assessments:			
1988/89			
6/4/88 to 30/6/88	25% x 400	25% x 600	–
1/7/88 to 5/4/89	–	–	75% x 1,000
1989/90			1,300

Thus for the part of the 1988/89 fiscal year prior to the merger, there would be an assessment on each firm based on the appropriate proportion of the profits that would normally be assessed on the preceding year basis for 1988/89 – ie the profits for the year to 30 June 1987. After the merger, the assessment is raised on the merged firm for the appropriate proportion (ie based on the period from 1 July 1988 to 5 April 1989) of an assessment based on the aggregate of the profits of the two predecessor firms for their years ended 30 June 1987. In 1989/90 the assessment of AB is again based on the profits of the predecessor firms for the year ended immediately prior to the merger.

In practice, partners of the merged firm will each pay tax by reference to profits which were actually earned by the partners of the other firm, but as long as the earnings of the merged firm exceed the assessment of that firm based on the previous year's profits, all the partners will benefit.

While there is sometimes a temptation to think that if the constituent elements of the assessment on the merged firm arising from the predecessor firms' profits are in different proportions from the way in which the profits of the merged firm are shared as between the partners of the two original firms, some tax equity adjustment may be needed. In the writer's opinion, such adjustment should be resisted unless the pattern of profits of one or other firm immediately prior to the merger was particularly erratic. As long as all the partners in the merged firm are earning more than the amounts on which they are being asked to pay tax, everyone should be satisfied and there should be no attempt to strive for an ultimate degree of fairness as between the partners.

The operation of the preceding year basis is always going to give rise to some minor degree of inequity, and this should be accepted as one of the normal features of partnership life on the swings and roundabouts principle.

Other accounting differences

The main part of this chapter has been concerned with the different treatment in accounts of debtors and work in progress arising out of the adoption of different accounting policies. Differences may also arise, however, even where both firms purport to account on an earnings basis. This is because of the widely different values that are attributable to work in progress in different firms' accounts.

Some firms will allocate a value to the element of work in progress attributable to the partners' time. While it could be argued that this is only fair to each year's partners since it credits them with the value attributable to partners' work carried out in any year, it does not accord with best accounting practice. Work in progress is the mechanism by which costs incurred in one accounting period are carried forward to be matched against the revenues generated from that work in a succeeding accounting period. In that accounting sense, partners' time has no value since there is no 'cost' attributable to partners' time; their remuneration is an appropriation of profit rather than an expense.

Other firms, conscious of the arguments against carrying in the accounts high values for work in progress, will carry forward in work in progress the minimum that can be justified.

When it come to the merger of two firms, there may be a need to look at the unrecorded profit inherent in the valuation of work in progress. Thus if two firms have work in progress which could be billed at £100,000 and this is valued in one firm at £60,000 and the other at £20,000 the second firm will be introducing into the merged firm an asset which contains a significantly larger unrecorded profit element than the corresponding asset brought to the party by the other firm.

It may be appropriate, therefore, for some adjustment to be made between the partners of the two firms to recognise this difference.

If such an adjustment is to be made, it is most easily effected by means of a prior share of the profits out of the first year (or possibly two years if the adjustment is too large to make out of one year's accounts) of the merged firm. If such an adjustment is to be made, care needs to be exercised to ensure that the desired economic effect is really achieved.

In the simple example given in the previous paragraph, let us suppose that the profits of the merged firm were to be split equally between the partners of the two predecessor firms, and it was agreed to allow the partners of Firm B to enjoy the first £40,000 of profit to compensate them for the fact that their work in progress was relatively undervalued. It will therefore be necessary to give Firm B a prior share of the profit of the new firm of £80,000 to achieve the desired result:

	Total £000's	Firm A £000's	Firm B £000's
Prior share to Firm B	80	–	80
Reduction in residual profits of £80,000 shared equally	(80)	(40)	(40)
	–	(40)	40

While the above analysis gives a correct theoretical answer, it should be emphasised that, in a successful merger, there has to be give and take on different issues, and the theoretically perfect answer may not be attainable – and perhaps should not even be sought.

Fixed assets

A brief review of the accounts of each firm will quickly highlight whether there are significant differences in relation to the approach to the ownership of fixed assets. We need to consider in this context both office furniture and equipment and motor vehicles on the one hand, and property on the other, but firstly, non-property assets.

Partnerships are likely to have different attitudes to the acquisition and depreciation, where appropriate, of non-property fixed assets. Some firms will purchase fixed assets on the grounds that the firm's cost of capital is significantly less than that charged by leasing companies or finance houses, while others who are advocates of keeping the partners' capital down to a minimum, will prefer for assets to be acquired by way of leasing or hire purchase arrangements.

However, this difference in approach may not introduce any major inequity between the two firms. If the firm that acquires fixed assets writes them off over a relatively short period of years, there could be some equity in the fixed assets at any time; their 'real' value could be significantly greater than their book value.

The same situation could well arise where another firm leases its fixed assets. It is likely that the lease period is significantly shorter than the economic life of the assets such that, at any time, the 'real' value of the asset exceeds the discounted value of the outstanding lease payments.

Just because the potential merger partners have adopted a different approach to the acquisition of office machinery, this may of itself not justify any financial adjustment in order to be fair to one or other firm.

While 100% first year allowances were granted for tax purposes, some firms adopted the policy of writing-off fixed assets in the year of acquisition. This was a prudent policy which recognised the fact that the cash had been spent and was therefore not available for partners' drawings on account of profit.

However, with the phasing out of first year allowances, most firms now depreciate fixed assets over a period of years so as to recognise in the charge of each year's profit and loss account the value consumed in that year. It is less likely now that the valuation of fixed assets in two firms that have adopted a policy of depreciation will give rise to a need for adjustment on a merger.

If there has been a wide divergence in the depreciation policy adopted within the two firms there may still be a need to re-work the depreciation charge for each firm on a consistent basis in relation to fixed asset additions over the few years prior to the proposed merger date.

Such an exercise will result in the need for the firm that had adopted a more stringent depreciation policy to write up its fixed assets in the final accounts prior to the merger, and to credit partners' capital or current accounts appropriately. The merged firm will then base its depreciation of those assets on the revalued amount. If that adjustment proves to be a significant one, there might be a need, also, to consider the tax implications.

However, it will be appreciated that tax relief granted by way of capital allowances is totally independent of the basis adopted by a firm for depreciating the assets through the accounts and, notwithstanding the adjustments to the book values, a tax adjustment may not be required. This is a further area where the striving after ultimate fairness is not really appropriate and it is hoped that a relatively broad brush approach can normally be adopted.

Freehold property

It is the view of the writer that, generally speaking, professional partnerships are well advised not to acquire appreciating property. While this is not a suitable place for a full discussion of the subject, this view is held because, briefly, such an acquisiton:

1. increases the capital required of incoming partners, and turns the professional partnership, in part, into an investment club which all new partners may not wish to join; and
2. creates difficulties when a partner retires and naturally wishes to be paid for his share of the unrealised appreciation in the value of the property.

It has to be recognised that a significant number of firms do own the premises from which they operate, and the potential difficulties of merging partnerships with different practices in relation to the ownership of property need to be recognised. Basically there are two alternatives; either the new partners will have to join in the investment club or membership of the club may be made voluntary.

If the property-owning firm is content to allow the partners of the other firm to join their investment club this will involve an injection of fresh capital by these partners.

It is likely that the existing partners will wish to revalue the property immediately prior to the merger, and if they do so, there will be capital gains tax consequences since the original property-owning partners will effectively be making a disposal of part of their interest in the partnership property when the new partners are admitted.

Any capital gain made by a partnership is, of course, allocated between the partners in accordance with their interest in the property and treated as part of that individual's total capital gains. Any gain realised on a partnership property transaction may therefore be covered by a partner's annual exemption for capital gains tax purposes.

It is possible that the existing property-owning partners will not be willing for the partners of the merging firm to be allowed to take a stake in their investment property. Alternatively, some or all of the new partners may not wish to invest their personal capital in this way. There is therefore a potential conflict within the partnership between those who wish to own the property and those who do not. Fortunately, this can be readily accommodated.

In these circumstances it is necessary for the capital involved in financing the property to be kept separate from the other partnership capital which is financing the partnership's normal working capital requirements.

The property owning partners will have part of their capital designated as, say, 'P' capital, and in total this will aggregate to the book value of the property asset concerned. Any partnership borrowing to finance the property should be taken on by the property-owning partners as personal borrowings in order to subscribe partnership capital, thereby relieving the partnership as a whole of this indebtedness.

Tax relief will be available to those partners since the funds borrowed are being injected into the partnership to enable the partnership to acquire an asset to be used in the partnership's trade or profession.

The property should be occupied by the partnership rent-free in order to safeguard important tax concessions for the property-owning partners.

Firstly, they will want the property to be treated as a business asset for capital gains tax purposes so that if a partner realises a gain on disposing of his interest in the property on retirement from the partnership when aged over 60, that gain may be covered in whole or in part by capital gains tax retirement relief.

Additionally, if the property is occupied rent-free by the partnership, it will be treated as business property for inheritance tax purposes should the partner die prior to retirement. In that event, his property capital account would be eligible for the 50% business property relief.

If no rent is to be paid, it will be necessary for the property-owning partners to receive a prior share of the profits of the firm in lieu of rent. To ensure that the ownership of the property does not give rise to tensions or inequity between the partners that do and do not have an interest in the property, it would be advisable for the determination of the prior share of profit in lieu of rent to be agreed by an independent property expert for a period of years similar to a normal rental term.

It is permissible, of course, by agreement between the partners, for partnership assests to be owned in different proportions from those in which residual income profits are shared. It is only an extension of this principle for the ownership of some partnership assets to vest in only some of the partners, with others being excluded.

This arrangement distinguishes between the partners' capital contributions required for the essential working capital of the business and that subscribed to on a voluntary basis for investment reasons, thereby easing the potential burden on new partners of subscribing capital to the firm.

Leasehold properties

While the previous discussion has concentrated on freeholds, one partnership in merger talks may enjoy the ownership of a lease which, although nothing was paid for it, now has a significant value through the movement of market rents in the particular area.

If the partners of that firm require compensation for introducing this valuable asset into the merged firm, the compensation should not take the form of a capital payment from the incoming partners since this would give rise to a capital gains tax liability on the recipients with the likelihood of no relief being obtained by the payers (since the lease would be regarded for capital gains tax purposes as a wasting asset).

Any adjustment deemed necessary should be effected by means of a prior allocation of profit in the merged firm to the relevant partners over the remaining term of the lease or until the next rent review.

However, care needs to be exercised to ensure that the lease-owning partners do not obtain a double benefit. If the profit-sharing arrangements for the merged firm are based on the recent profit record of the two firms, the firm with the beneficial lease may already have secured for themselves a profit share in the merged firm which is based on earlier years' profits which have been inflated by the fact that a sub-market rent is being paid for the firm's premises.

It would be wrong, in these circumstances, for any additional adjustment to be made to reflect the essentially short-term advantage derived from the ownership of a beneficial lease.

Nigel Davey is a partner in the chartered accountants Spicer & Oppenheim, having joined them on graduating from Cambridge in the late 1960s. For ten years he has specialised in advising professional partnerships, particularly on taxation issues. In recent years, he has advised on a number of mergers of professional partnerships. He writes and lectures frequently on partnership topics and is co-author with another partner from Spicer & Oppenheim of a book entitled "The Business of Partnerships".

8 Drafting the Merger Documents

The merger will or will not proceed based on the chemistry of the parties on the one hand, and the fact that, after digesting the financial and other information exchanged, it is possible to put together a package which adequately combines the resources of both firms by accentuating the positive elements and minimising or eliminating the negative ones. It is a strange mixture of tangible and intangible items.

A great deal of the progress towards merger will be made face to face and as a result of oral discussions generally. However, much has to be reduced to writing and the purpose of this chapter is to discuss the merger documents which are likely to be needed, and perhaps to try to establish a code of good merger practice.

After identifying the documents themselves, we must consider how they can best be put together. A solicitor in particular is used to receiving instructions to draft an agreement when the terms have been agreed by the parties. This is the typical static situation. However, where merger is concerned a number of the documents will have to be drafted in a dynamic situation, in that negotiations will be proceeding, but the parties will need to see something in black and white on their desks to be able to evaluate effectively what progress has been made at the relevant point in time. In other words, different drafting skills are required, and this chapter will endeavour to deal with those skills.

In chapter 3, I alluded to the need to produce a specification for merger. On the one hand, this deals with the vital statistics of the ideal firm with which your firm would like to merge. It is impossible to draft that document without a proper strategic appraisal of your own firm. In an ideal world, the decision to merge will have arisen out of your own strategic planning process, and you will have your written strategic plan to offer to the other firm at the outset and as part of the merger negotitions.

Among general documentation, both sides will obviously exchange their brochures, if they have them. Resumés of the careers of the partners and other key personnel should be exchanged, although the actual personality of the partners will come across far better in the meetings which must take place. This is not the chapter to discuss the financial documentation which will be exchanged between the parties. Nigel Davey does this elsewhere.

Drafting the Merger Documents

A good deal of paper will have to be perused. I have a particular liking for looking through the other firm's bill book. Many of us have illusions about the nature and depth of our practices. The bill book does not lie, but really gives the flavour of the work done by the firm. One of the statistics which will be exchanged will be the average amount of the bill of each firm year by year. These are documents already in existence and we must now turn to those documents which have to be specifically created for the merger in contemplation.

To avoid doubt, confusion and subsequent recriminations, the merger agreement must be reduced to writing. Dynamic drafting demands that a first attempt is made as soon as possible, but there will be a vast number of blanks in it. What should be included? Some items will be of vital importance while others will merely relate to housekeeping. The agreement or heads of agreement for the merger ought to contain them all.

Obviously, the main part of the document should not be too overloaded and matters which are considered as relating to administration only can be consigned to appendices, or incorporated by reference only. This again is a cultural matter, but the merging firms will have to decide just how much formality they require in their merger documents. Very often, the decision may be that the drafting can be extremely informal, and formality can be reserved from the relationship with the client!

At the personnel level, lists of staff will have been exchanged with a certain amount of biographical and salary detail included. The merger will require an agreed list of the staff of the proposed joint firm with revised salaries and terms of employment generally.

As I have already indicated, solicitors are used to drafting based on instructions. In a merger between law firms the clients are the solicitors themselves, and it might be a good idea to designate one of the partners, known for drafting skills, to act as the scribe to take instructions with a view to the preparation of the written heads of agreement.

As the negotiations continue the 'dustbin' approach is often the best; points will be agreed in rather a haphazard manner; some will be of vital importance; others will be peripheral. They all ought to be noted down in writing and thrown into the 'dustbin' from which the agreement will be drafted.

Some people favour the idea of a spike on which the pieces of paper are put. A more formal approach would be to have an alphabetical card index and put the various agreed points on cards in that index with a view to being extracted and drafted into appropriate wording in the heads of agreement. By using this method, important, or even unimportant points, will not be overlooked. The draftsman will be able to produce a first draft and subsequently variations based on the new information being fed to him, or her.

The culture of the firms may be democratic, so that all drafts are circulated to all partners for their perusal and approval. Frankly, this is a cumbersome method of operating and it would be far more effective to have the drafts approved by small committees of partners on either side, to whom executive authority to make progress in the merger has been delegated. My experience has been that the most effective committee is a committee of one, but this is not always considered appropriate by one's peers.

I have indicated elsewhere that the merger negotiations must not paralyse the work product of the firm. The more partners involved in the committee activities, the fewer there will be available to handle the affairs of clients.

Each committee will inform the other of the limits of their authority and presumably the finished version of the draft will be submitted to all partners for their approval. In an ideal world, once again, this would be a formality. However, we all know of the possibilities of finding minor drafting points in documents. The legal profession, in particular, is well know for being unable to see the wood for the trees.

I have set out in Appendix 6 a draft of heads of agreement which were actually used in a merger which took place successfully. A certain amount of detail has been removed in order not to identify the parties. I stress that this was a document which fitted one particular set of circumstances and two particular firms. The precedent is included for guidance only and other firms will no doubt produce their agreements in entirely different forms with entirely different contents.

I repeat that there are no rights and wrongs in the way to go about a merger and this book can merely indicate ways which have been tried and found effective, by contrast with certain others, which have proved a recipe for disaster. The readers will draw their own conclusions, and no doubt make their own mistakes by using or discarding what they learn from this book. This is not the appropriate place to discuss the terms to be included in the new partnership deed for the merged firms. All the normal principles relating to drafting such a document apply, with the additional problems created by the harmonisation of two different partnership structures. Governance and compensation, to use the American terms, will almost certainly take up a good deal of time during the negotiation stage.

It is highly unlikely that the partnership structures of the two firms will operate in the same, or even a similar manner. This can often be a major cause for abandoning the negotiations.

For example, one firm may operate on a strict 'lock-step' system, whereby partners' profit shares are based purely on seniority. By contrast, the other firm remunerates its partners on a performance basis only. At the very worst, this creates complacency in one set of partners and selfishness in the other.

Two such divergent cultures will be difficult to merge, unless both sets of partners are totally unhappy with their respective compensation procedures, and realise their inadequacies.

Once again, although it is often not the case, the partnership deed for the merged firms ought to deal with the management structure. Here again, no two firms will have the same methods of running their firms and either one will have to be adopted to the exclusion of the other, or a totally new management structure put in place.

The actual drafting and approval of the new partnership deed may be the least of the problems arising. The real difficulties will be created by the merger negotiations themselves on these subjects and the need to reach agreement, where one party, or certain partners, may have to compromise to their own seeming detriment.

Even so, the difficulties in reaching agreement on these points may be reflected by problems in agreeing the draft, as solicitors especially are so well known for expressing their feelings over 'nice points' of drafting. While a normal person will often express their frustration by kicking the cat, a lawyer will often do so by being as difficult as possible over the small print of a contract. Each to his own!

In all probability, if agreement can be reached on terms, then the actual drafting will not present too many problems. There are still far too many firms without partnership agreements. There is always talk of producing something in writing, but it does not usually progress beyond the first draft. A merger must be the ideal opportunity to remedy that omission.

No modern partnership should be without a written constitution. A merged firm requires one as an even greater necessity, if that were possible. To fail to do so reflects an attitude of irresponsibility to one's own affairs, and it does not augur well for the success of the new joint venture.

Michael Simmons

9 Merger Administration

Editor's note

This book looks at merger from most aspects, but not enough has been said to date on the subject of administration. Mrs. Gilda Buckwell, wife of one of the partners at Gates & Co., a Brighton firm of solicitors, was brought in to manage the administration in relation to the merger of Gates & Co., with another local firm, Messrs Fitzhugh Eggar & Port.

She was in the unique position of being entrusted with this particular project and her notes on the subject written for this book are invaluable as we really do see a merger from the point of view of the person entrusted with the administration. This contrasts with the views of senior and managing partners.

By taking some sort of average between the two perspectives, the reader can begin to see the problems of merger, both long term and day to day, in their true perspective.

Fitzhugh Gates merger

When the decision to merge became final a suitable time had to be chosen. It was decided to move on the first working day after Christmas, being slack time with work and staff. Many of the latter were taking extra days holiday at that time and the remaining ones were needed to assist. I became involved about two months prior to the move, working primarily from Gates & Co. who were vacating their premises and moving into the offices of Fitzhugh, Eggar and Port. Both firms had an administration partner to whom I referred for major decisions. Given below is a diary of the jobs required.

1. Sought estimates from removal firms, finally choosing not only a competitive price but those whom we thought most capable and helpful in an office move. Once we had decided on the firm, I met the manager to work out a schedule.

2. Acquainted myself with all staff, their rooms and contents; discussing with them what they wanted to take, what was redundant, etc.
Liaised with administration partner of Fitzhugh's regarding space and positioning of staff in their building; also seeing what surplus

Merger Administration

furniture they had, any duplicating of office equipment, etc.

Checked from time-to-time their schedule of clearing and making space.

We had to do a lot of sorting and disposing of unwanted papers and furniture; making space for our filing; decorating certain unused rooms; putting up shelving, etc.

3. Organised printing of new stationery with new name of partnership, also printing of letter announcing the merger to clients. Christmas cards were printed and these were used for other business associates.

4. Compared the two firms' lists of periodicals, and cancelled from Gates & Co. any duplicated. Compared the two library inventories, and decided what to do with duplications. In our case we were able to dispose of unwanted sets of law books to our other branches (three).

I was also able to offer unwanted furniture and equipment to our branches, and later anything remaining was sold through second-hand shops.

5. Made an arrangement, through a local contact, with the local Council regarding the safes. We heard that they wanted some and gave them about five in return for their collecting and delivering two wanted by our other branches. There is a reasonably easy sale for small safes but big safes are too heavy to move and are therefore a problem. The removal firm would have quoted for them separately had we decided to keep them.

6. Informed British Telecom of the termination of the number of our facsimile machine. This was being moved to one of our branches. A new number had to be applied for, and an engineer booked to reinstall and connect it once it had been moved. B. T. also informed of termination of our rental of their telephone system, with the numbers.

Arranged for the re-direction of calls on the vacated numbers. Fitzhugh's were just able to cope with the extra lines needed, as they had some spare on their number.

7. Contacted the company renting a tannoy system to us. This was moved over to new offices with extra speakers, as they did not previously use a system.

8. Contacted the computer company to arrange time for their engineer to come and move our computer. Not to be done by removal firm.

9. Collected relevant forms from the Post Office for the redirection of post. Fees paid for period to be covered. The Post Office ask for at least one month's notice of this.

10. Made plan for filing, and liaised with Fitzhugh's, regarding space. We were going to use space in their attic but, being an old building, had to limit ourselves to a certain weight.

11. *Two weeks prior to move.* Worked out exactly who would be there on the day of the move (two partners) and I and two helpers on the second day for the packing up of the filing.
Circulated staff with a time-table of exactly what was happening on which day.

12. Contacted the police traffic department to discuss any loading and unloading problem, and ask for three meters to be covered.

13. Cancelled weekly services and rentals.

14. Made plans of each room having furniture moved into it in Fitzhugh's building, having got staff, in some cases, to visit new premises to decide what they wanted.
Numbered each room, essential for removal firm especially with large items such as filing cabinets. Had a last minute liaison to check that all space was ready for us.
Labelled all furniture from Gates with room number in new premises.

15. *Last day before move.* Had packing cases delivered from removers.
Needed even more than they estimated. In afternoon, staff packed their own desk tops, and cupboards.

16. *Removal day.* Three partners and I in old premises checked packing up, which took up morning.
Afternoon unloading in new premises, supervised by a few extras.
Although each piece of equipment and packing case was labelled and there were room plans and numbers, the removal men were still inclined to dump large filing cabinets in middle of the room!

17. *Removal day 2.* Packed up files from old premises. Each packing case was labelled with contents.
The idea was for the latest files to go on to van first, so that the earliest files would go on last and come off first. In practice, the removers were

just not that well organised.

It soon became evident that we could not possibly have 90 packing cases delivered all at once since space in the files department was just not large enough. In this instance the removal firm was quite helpful, and kept back the cases, delivering about 25 a day.

Four helpers were needed to unpack files and sort them on to appropriate shelves.

18. Helped settle staff, making sure they had all their equipment; finding anything missing; seeing that they knew the whereabouts of all personnel files, and copiers, etc.

19. Cleared up old premises, disposed of a collection of books, office equipment and unwanted clutter.

Gilda Buckwell. Trained in London as a secretary, and worked for three years as PA to the Secretary of The Booksellers Association. Marriage and four children kept her busy at home, and this was subsequently followed by a second marriage and three step-children. When her husband's firm of solicitors merged with another local firm, he saw her as the obvious 'administrator'; an otherwise impossible role for the partners trying to carry on their normal full workload. Their interests include ski-ing, sailing and golf, the latter involving playing and administration for the county.

10a Personnel and Remuneration

'Progress is a nice word. But change is its motivator and change has its enemies'
Robert F Kennedy 1925 – 1968

I asked a colleague recently for the name of a good solicitor, and he responded with: 'Go to Bloggs' firm; they are very good, understanding, and have a lovely way with people'.

The implication behind the above statement was quite simply that this firm had not only retained client business but attracted more because it had a reputation for being 'people-oriented' or 'client-centred': professionalism with a human face. However, it does imply more than that, for being 'human' means understanding human beings, whether staff or clients, understanding how they feel and how they will respond or react to any particular environment or situation.

What was even more surprising about the referral to Bloggs' firm was that it had merged in the previous year with another practice and has now some 200 staff.

When a professional office or firm has a high state of staff morale and productivity – which in turn creates efficiency – that same office or firm has a high standard of management and leadership, and ultimately this is reflected in the attitude displayed towards the customer or client. From my experience, the most successful mergers worldwide are those whose management style throughout the merger process has been staff-centred, and where meticulous attention was paid to human relations skills.

Firms who wish for a successful merger can only hope for increased efficiency if a warm and highly generated internal ambience is created. This will then contribute in the new practice to strong staff loyalties and commendable client relations, the latter feeding from the former. It is therefore necessary for all partners to appreciate that it is the art of 'people' management which strengthens the union of two practices marrying.

Developing a sensitive response to staff at times of change is difficult (it is certainly time-consuming) but essential. It cannot be done, as I have witnessed in some firms, with management missives on notice boards saying 'have a nice day', and 'from a month on Monday we at Bloggs are merging with them at Frobishers'.

However, a thoughtful attitude towards staff on its own is not

Personnel and Remuneration

sufficient. It is a matter of leadership and example, with staff being motivated by their respective partner, fee earner or manager to want to give of their best to the new entity.

It is also about marrying the staff's objectives to those being proposed for the firm, with everyone being committed to the end-products of a more potent practice, increased staff performance and client caring service.

Any professional firm is always much more likely to attract and retain work and client goodwill through any merger, if it is both efficient and caring. Yet mergers, and indeed many professionals, have gained for themselves an image of not taking into account the 'human' side of the enterprise. They pride themselves rather on the clinical cultivation and commands of the business factors rather than on the caring required for the people factors of feelings and fears.

Much of the reason for this lies in the fact that many professionals are principally talented in their specialised area of expertise. For example solicitors' knowledge and skills relating to the 'human' side of the enterprise are often less well developed because, up to now, they have had all their pressures from their training and their professional bodies towards further technical expertise and excellence. The time to develop a concern for staff and client-centred accountability and relationship has simply not been available. The need to appreciate what makes human beings tick has not been felt necessary in the legal profession or indeed most professions generally.

Correcting this imbalance forms the foundation of an office climate that is much more likely to have all of its staff within the firm becoming 'client-centred' and indeed committed to the new merger. It is also the best marketing tool any new practice can have!

In business, the earning of profit is something more than an incident of success. It is an essential condition of success because the continued absence of profit itself spells failure. Profitability may be the sovereign criterion of the enterprise, but all business has two basic functions, marketing and innovation. These areas consume a great deal of partners' time and energy especially at a time of growth, merger and change. However we are also in the business of managing or dealing with people and their feelings, as well as facts, figures and files. Any firm that has gone through a merger will endorse that it was essential for their partners, managers and all fee earners to have some basic background on what makes staff tick, their fundamental make-up, qualms and needs.

Education, particularly in the area of human relations and behavioural science, is the first essential step towards acquiring a staff-oriented approach so essential for successful merger practice. The first stepping stone to knowledge is to admit that we are ignorant.

Successful Mergers

Those firms who have sought a staff and client-centred approach during merger planning, and reaped the most success, are those who admitted at the outset that it was a new world and actively sought information and counsel. It is always wiser to investigate how other firms have managed change, and learn from any failures. It is unwise to try to cross a major chasm of new initiative in two jumps!

The important point for any manager (and any professional be it solicitor, surveyor, accountant, engineer and so on who has one or more people reporting to, or working with him or her, is a manager) is to remember that all adult human beings have a range of needs – they may display one or more of these needs at any given moment, but they have them all and are incapable of bringing two into the office and leaving three behind at home!

All human behaviour is determined by the wants and needs of individuals, and all behaviour aims at satisfying one or more of these needs, although one is almost invariably striving for satisfaction of more than one need at a time. If we want to win people, or want people to give of their best, then we must respond to their needs.

Motivation, is in fact, first of all understanding the kinds of needs a person has, and then secondly creating the office climate or practice environment, and providing the incentives, which will allow that individual to maximise his or her fulfilment of all those needs.

In Diagram A there is an illustration of the levels of needs to which a normal adult is subject:

Diagram A

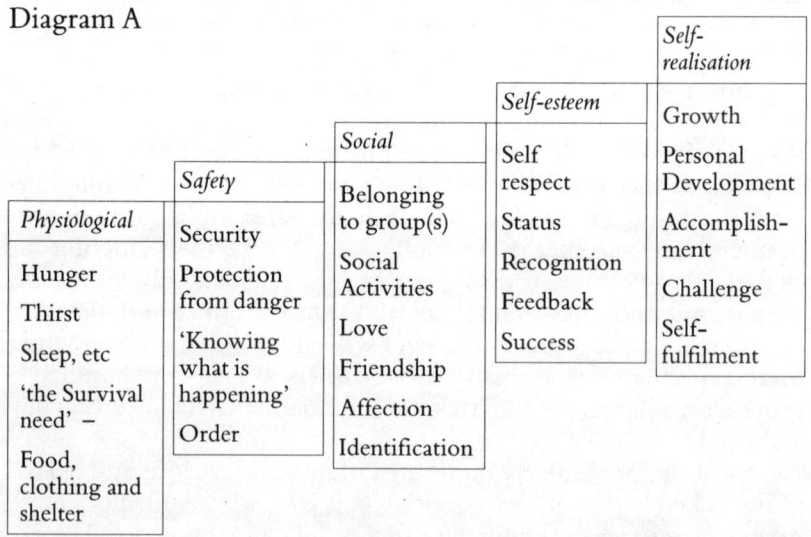

(Adapted from Maslow's Hierarchy of Needs for Lynda King Taylor's book 'Not for Bread Alone – an appreciation of Job Enrichment': Business Books, Century Hutchinson, London)

Personnel and Remuneration

The *physiological* need, basic though it is, does not concern us too much in this book, but the four higher level needs are much more relevant and vital.

Our *safety* need includes assurances that future physical needs will be met, as well as the concern for our present bodily safety. The young child is constantly asking 'why?' not so much in an attempt to understand the surrounding environment, but rather in an attempt to perceive a coherent structure and feel safe. Later on in our lives these 'whys?' become an intrinsic part of our security need for communication; to know what is going on.

We are all aware of people's deep curiosity and the importance they place on 'being in on the thing'. We all have this need – even our support staff! Perhaps, from experience, switchboard operators in firms have this need satisfied much more than anyone else!

The need for safety therefore, is two-fold, both physical and psychological, in that we have to feel comfortable and secure within our immediate environment and job, as well as feeling emotionally secure. Communication therefore plays a vital role in satisfying the *safety* need in any human being. All too often this safety need is under threat when mergers are being discussed in the mahogany corridor.

When any need is put in jeopardy people react with a form of psychological warfare diaplayed by symptoms ranging through apathy and lack of interest to downright resentment and open antagonism to any changes being registered.

Another very important level of need in human beings is the *social* requirement. People need a sense of belonging. We all want to belong and be loved, or at least liked. This sense of belonging, at first within school, but later on in life as part of a team, a firm, department or office, will satisfy this need. The need to share the values of others, and to have satisfactory or convivial relationships with others, is a vital part of the social requirement of individuals.

Imagine walking into the office tomorrow morning and having no-one talk to you, or even being rude: apart from feeling uncomfortable, one's self-respect would have been severely damaged. This should never happen, but alas it does. Often the seniors in a firm do not associate with, or even talk to, those at the grass roots. This causes more demotivation and morale-breaking than any other issue such as the pay and working conditions in the new environment.

When considering a merger situation, the menace posed by size is most alarming. Staff are worried that their existing cosy cliques will become cold crowds. The marrying of people is as much about personalities and their feeling of belonging within the new firm as it is about the politics of their presence within this new empire.

The most mature needs of all, and often the most neglected when

Successful Mergers

planning and executing a merger, are those of *self esteem* and *self realisation*: the need for dignity; status; feedback; recognition; accomplishment and self-fulfilment.

It is vital for us all to appreciate that, although at any one time one particular need will dominate an individual's behaviour, all those working for us come into the office with all of these needs at *Diagram A*.

For example, a member of staff may be feeling apprehension, even fear, over a problem of fitting in with the new department. His security need is under attack. That same individual also has other psychological needs to be met for self-respect, feedback, pride and dignity, and we must recognise that. This means that we must not only attend to his security need, but do so while respecting his need for self-esteem. Put another way, every human being must be treated as unique.

It is going to be much more pleasant and productive to work within the new environment where the staff have a sense of belonging, of caring, have a feeling of self-respect and dignity, and know what is going on and why, and what is going to happen to them next. All this offers them a sense of recognition, pride and feedback – three psychological generators which power human motivation. And remember, when staff care, you have the basis of a client-centred image.

If we appreciate that all people have the needs as outlined in *Diagram A*, then it should also be understood that such needs exist within the working environment of any firm, and that they must be managed, particularly so at a time of major change. If one does not know what is going on in a firm – has minimal feedback – then one feels uncomfortable. When one is uncomfortable, one becomes ultimately demotivated and nervous.

That is why feedback is so vital for staff. It does employees no good at all to leave them as often as we do in a state of suspended animation. How often has one followed the merger rule of 'if you can't convince them, confuse them'? Individuals, staff, other departments and clients alike, must always be told what is happening, how they will be affected, and why.

We have discussed, albeit briefly, the first part of the education process; that is appreciating the needs that all individuals have whether fee earner or tea lady. If one understands and satisfies staff needs, then you gain staff loyalty which breeds commitment to client and firm, and ultimately to the new entity. If full commitment is to be obtained, then such needs must be tended within the firm's climate, and it is therefore the duty of all those who manage others to insist that the personnel climate supports this objective.

A professional can learn the necessary skills for understanding and motivating people on a one-to-one basis. It is, however, also essential

Personnel and Remuneration

that these operate within an office environment that is prone to sensing and meeting the staff's needs effectively. To merge successfully as far as staff interests are concerned, the two ingredients, of personal knowledge in the behavioural sciences and climate development, must be mixed simultaneously.

The most successfully merged firms are those which have taken a long hard look at their existing working procedures, and made them much more compatible with their staff's *human* needs. They have spent a great deal of effort on communicating and dealing with staff on a personal basis, and in creating an atmosphere that promotes an image of wellbeing, and caring, and of being part of the team. This image is as relevant an objective for any internal department servicing other areas of a firm, as it is for the practice as a whole serving the general public and its clients.

The coin of maintaining merger motivation therefore has two sides. On one is the understanding of people, their needs and reactions and on the other is the creation of the climate which will allow individuals to satisfy their needs. Attention must be alerted to *both* sides of the coin if one is to attain a successful approach to merging any two firms' operating styles.

Below is an illustration of what motivates individual staff to work with more commitment, and help to create a more team oriented/client-centred environment. The inner circle is the job content and the motivators, while the outer circle is the job context – the environment in which the work is done.

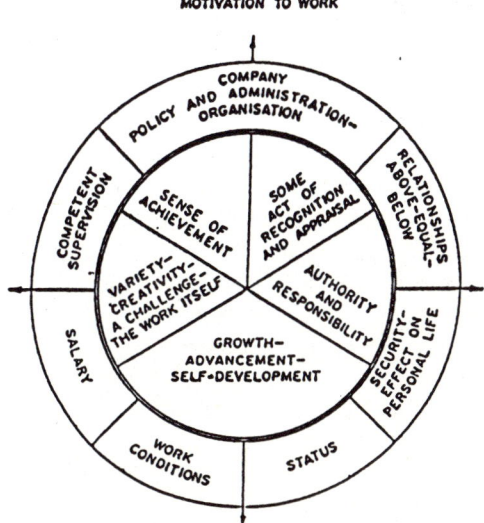

The diagram is reproduced from Lynda King Taylor's book "Not for Bread Alone" published by Business Books – Century Hutchinson London.

Many people in merger management pay a great deal of attention to the factors in the outer circle of *Diagram B* which come under the firm's strategy, proposed merger structure, or within its existing control systems. Usually when a firm wishes to make changes, the odds are that it will reorganise the structure, introduce a new strategic direction or impose a new control system – the latter is a favourite!

Even with those factors in the outer circle, the same *security* need mentioned earlier must be borne in mind. When changes are being made to any one factor people must be informed of the reasons. It is always wiser to seduce individuals in a changing environment, rather than rape them with changes that affect their lives at work. Allow them to have their say – even in their own downfall.

However, seldom is it that much attention is paid by management to those factors in the inner circle of *Diagram B* when contemplating merger. They are, in fact, the very components that give any professional practice its life, for they are all to do with staff, their work, skills and management style.

Such factors satisfy more of an individual's *psychological* needs than the factors in the outer circle, and it is the inner factors that dominate in the building of a new staff and ultimately client-centred environment.

That is not to say that the factors in the outer circle at *Diagram B* are not important; of course they are. Staff will always be questioning such issues anyhow, especially at a time of merger. But attention must also be given to the internal areas if one wants to have a motivated team who are committed to their new firms, its objectives, clients and end-product.

One cannot *buy* staff commitment, it is something which has to be won, and attention to the inner circle will make for greater job satisfaction and motivation, both fundamental elements in building efficiency, effectiveness and client service – all so essential to the objectives of any merger.

It is attention to *all* the factors in *Diagram B* which can help staff give their best possible service to their new firm and its clients, simultaneouly maximising their work load and gross fees delivered.

It is essential for all professionals managing the merger to have a staff-centred approach to change. To acquire this, there is a need for learning more about human beings, and their needs, and understanding how they can be better met and satisfied within both the existing working environment and the new climate of merger.

Conclusion

There is simply not enough emphasis placed in any merger situation on the people aspects, nor on understanding the staff and their feelings and fears. Yet, as professionals, we are very much in the people business, which contributes so much in the competitive market place as demonstrated by Messrs. Bloggs' firm.

A great deal more training is required in these behavioural areas of practice management in order that those faced with the responsibility of managing people will have a competence and confidence to see the leadership of change as a challenge rather than a chore.

When people lack both competence and confidence in any given area of their work, this in turn breeds lack of commitment. One tends to do the job one is trained, or qualified to do, or that one is good at, rather than do a task which must be done but one is not keen or confident to do.

The task of managing people through a merger is often overlooked because of pressing problems elsewhere. In fact the managing of people tends to become a process of prevarication and procrastination, and the hope that by the time the partner or fee earner gets around to it, the problem will have evaporated.

Unfortunately, people problems seldom vanish when not attended to, but rather they fester and become quietly malignant, breeding a militancy and lowering of morale, all of which destroys any element of hope of the successfully merged firm.

Enlightened firms who have merged have discovered that by attending to such areas as understanding human needs, as in *Diagram A*, simultaneous with the improving of staff relations and the job content factors in *Diagram B*, they have encouraged a better working relationship between all management and staff which has resulted in a more professional client-service when the firms have finally merged.

Organisations, institutions and the professions, must go hand in hand with the progress of the human mind. If that human mind of the client is now questioning standards and services the only way forward is to face that reality by offering a client-centred service superior to any competitor, and one that makes the client want no alternative. This is often the major reason why firms merge at all.

However, to live through a merger which ultimately gives a better service to everyone, professionals must understand the human being they are both managing and serving. This sounds like common sense but regretfully common sense is not so common. Without taking into account the 'human' side of the merger, the potential for motivation through change will be lost to the enemies of staff resistance, resentment and ultimate rejection of the goals on the merged horizon.

Successful Mergers

Lynda King Taylor has worked in many types of professional firms, specialising in the 'human' aspects of practice development, and the personnel side of the enterprise. She has written a number of books including "Not for Bread Alone — an appreciation of job enrichment", and is also the author of a variety of books for the Stock Exchange Press. She writes for numerous magazines and papers and is a frequent contributor to radio and audio video programmes relevant to the professions. She has been an adviser to the UK Dept. of Employment, a visting lecturer to the Cranfield Institute of Management, is a frequent conference speaker and a director in Manpower Services Ltd.

10b Personnel and Remuneration: The Practitioner's Viewpoint

Until very recent times, solicitors and most other professionals were notoriously bad employers. It was only market conditions which saved us, in that there was a shortage of jobs and too many people to fill them. Previously we could get away with almost any bad practice and the 'them and us' philosophy flourished unabated.

We have all heard of the partners' corridor and the partners' lift, and little was done to build bridges between partners and the rest. Of course, for qualified staff, there was always the hope, distant or otherwise, that the transition would be made and the caterpillar would overnight become a butterfly.

Lynda King Taylor has been kind to us in her essential view of staff from the outside. This chapter is designed to give a somewhat different view of staff as seen by a practitioner inside the firm.

In recent years increasing competition for good staff has meant that we have had perforce to become much better employers. The hard and soft costs involved in losing staff are now so great that we do everything possible to retain those whom we already have, provided of course that they are satisfactory. Hard costs relate to the sheer expense of replacing staff in terms of cash. These costs include advertising, commissions paid to agencies, and the cost of temporary replacements.

Soft costs relate to the time of others spent in inducting new staff into the firm's practices and the general economic loss and inefficiency experienced until new staff have had time to familiarise themselves with new work procedures and clients and become thoroughly productive.

However, in the merger situation, we have a tendency to regress to our old bad habits. In mitigation, there are some good reasons based on the overall stress and strain of the merger negotiations and the distraction which they provide from our normal activities.

In addition there is the need to preserve as much secrecy as possible during the merger negotiations until such time as they can be made public. In any office, it is always difficult to keep secrets, and this seems to be accentuated in a professional office where the duty to clients on the subject of confidentiality is paramount.

If partners are going into huddles or spending a lot of time out of the office in meetings, the staff will wonder why. No merger can proceed without documentation and, if the documents are created in the office, extremely close-mouthed secretaries are required for the work. We are fighting against human nature, if we do not expect there to be leaks and rumours. After all, while our clients' affairs might seem slightly remote to some staff members, the consequences of a merger affect all vitally and we must expect leaks and rumours to abound and multiply.

It has been advised elsewhere that we should bring senior staff into the picture as soon as possible. Lynda King Taylor dilates fully on the uncertainties created by the merger situation. We overlook them at our peril.

In firms which do not have personnel officers fully trained for the work, one partner in each of the parties to the merger negotiations should be given the task of considering staff relations as paramount work, not only in the firms involved in the merger, but also in the firm to be created after merger. Obviously, the partner given this task must be chosen with care and must be one to whom staff relate well, and who can communicate the desired messages.

It is only humane that those who are not to be included in the merged firm should be told of this decision at the earliest possible moment and their compensation terms negotiated. It is equally, if not more, important that those who are to remain should be reassured that their jobs are safe and told at the earliest possible moment of any increased benefits in their terms of service in the merged entity. This ought to help in ensuring continued loyalty, but is not sufficient by itself. There may well be a sense of grievance that some of their working colleagues are not to be included in the new firm. It may be necessary to explain the reasons and satisfy some rather probing questions.

The main object of the exercise is to achieve acceptance of the merger and cooperation throughout both firms, and ultimately throughout the new firm. The partners will be looking in many directions during the merger, and it is so easy not to concentrate sufficiently on the staff aspect. After all, important and lesser clients have to be considered, and they will be concentrating so much on effecting the merger at partner level that it is vital to delegate the task of staff satisfaction to partners whose main preoccupation it will be both before, during and after the merger.

As has already been said elsewhere in the book at the risk of stating the obvious, a merger of two small firms creates a medium sized firm.

Personnel and Remuneration: The Practitioner's Viewpoint

Similarly, a merger of two medium sized firms creates a large firm. The administrative requirements in each case for such merged firms are much more burdensome than hitherto. Can your administrative staff cope?

These problems need to be considered by the merger committees in advance. Many small firms have felt that they do not have the resources or need to employ a well qualified practice manager. They may well appreciate that the merged firm not only can but needs to employ such a person. It is sensible to make the recruitment before the merger, so that the new practice manager can be vitally involved and take a great deal of the administrative work off the shoulders of the partners.

Many firms find that their accounts personnel are adequate to handle their activities, while their firm is still a separate entity. However, those accounts staff are out of their depth in the merged firm and speedily have to be replaced. If this problem has not been anticipated, there may well be considerable disruption caused by abrupt changeover of staff.

A long, cool look must be taken at the actual and potential capacities and working habits of administrative staff before the merger. Are they capable of raising their game? Those who are to be retained in the long term need to be identified and reassured of their future in the merged firm at the earliest possible moment.

Those who are only to be required in the short or medium term need similarly to be told of their future, to avoid subsequent disillusionment and hence early departure, before they have fulfilled their allotted roles in the merger.

It is often a good idea to offer such future short term employees enhanced contractual terms, which will bind them into the merged firm. While we all know that it is extremely difficult to enforce such a contract against an unwilling employee after the event, nevertheless the existence of a contract of this nature may well prevent early defection.

The common theme of the practical cases of merger within this book is that the interests of staff were overlooked during the merger negotiations, and the partners only became painfully aware of this lack after the event when it was too late to remedy it. This mistake should be avoided in the future.

After the merger has taken place, it is very important to instil in staff the ethic of the new firm. For some time, there is almost bound to be a 'them and us' attitude, but it is important to reduce this to the minimum and focus the attention of staff away from their allegiance to the old firms, on to a new adherence to the merged entity.

This is best done by making staff look outwards at the competition in terms of all professional firms in the same sphere, or the competition generally. If the individual parties to the merger had not run sports teams or had staff activities out of hours beforehand, now is the time to institute them (although this is, of course, only one reason why a social programme is desirable). We need to get to know each other in the new firm both inside and outside office hours.

As time goes on, the original distinctions will become blurred, unless antagonistic spirits try to perpetuate the differences. There are ways of neutralising such antagonism short of removing those responsible, but the ingenuity of the partners and those in charge of staff may be tested considerably before the desired results are achieved.

The merged firm may well be in a position to employ for the first time people skilled in the personnel function. This ought to have an immediate effect on efficiency and morale generally. Once again, this can be one of the beneficial results of mergers and may take the task off the shoulders of the partners, who, as Lynda King Taylor points out, are not trained in staff matters and have plenty of other responsibilities to keep them busy.

It may be possible in the merged firm to introduce, also for the first time, an appraisal system on a regular basis, where staff can find out what is expected of them and how they are meeting those expectations. Appraisal ought to be a two way matter. The employee should have the chance to criticise his or her superiors in a relaxed environment, and the personnel officer should be able to feed back, in an appropriate form, those criticisms constructively to the employee's superior.

The personnel officer can also ease the inevitable problems of adjustment caused by the fact that different management and administrative systems have to be adopted in the merger. If it is a takeover, then very often the systems of the dominant firm will be imposed on the personnel of the target firm. However, in a true merger it may be necessary to produce systems which are an amalgam of those previously in existence in the component firm. Alternatively, entirely new systems and procedures will be adopted to fit the demands of the new and larger entity.

All these changes create uncertainty and it will require sympathetic handling at all levels to ensure that staff are made familiar with the changes and are happy with them.

In any merger it is going to be necessary to have some staff redistribution, in that logic demands that departments doing similar work are merged as well as the firms of which they are component parts.

It is important to settle lines of communication and responsibility very early on before the physical moves take place. This will allow staff to meet their new superiors and become comfortable with them or otherwise. It will also allow those responsible for these aspects of the merger negotiations to consider before the merger takes place whether changes have to be made in their plans.

If certain of their proposals create irreconcilable personality conflicts, it is well to have early warning, so that the plans can be adjusted. On some occasions, it may be necessary to add to the list of those who will not be joining the merged firm, but early communication does leave the partners room for manoeuvre if their plans to do not turn out to be successful in this respect.

The mixing of departments, with consequent changes in responsibilities, requires a great deal of sympathetic handling from the top if the initial impact is going to be one of success. If trouble is anticipated then there will be less unpleasant surprises. It is alarming how partners can still treat their employees as chess pieces, usually pawns, in this situation. We revert still so easily to the old, bad habits.

These changes on merger may also result in the redistribution of work and clients. It is amazing how possessive the average professional becomes over his or her clients or work, even if they are, in fact, not personal clients, but those of the firm.

It will often be necessary to balance the greater efficiency which might be obtained, if certain work and clients are switched from fee earner in firm A to the fee earner in firm B against the damage that this change will do to the morale of the original executive.

If there are plans for retaining that executive in the new firm, it may be better not to make the disturbance. A good deal will depend on the new management style and the importance of the particular executive in the scheme of things. I repeat that it is a question of balance and we have to remember that the merged firm is intended to have a long term future, and any professional firm depends on the continuity of its good personnel to achieve that future.

All firms have a career pattern and plan of advancement, even if they do not recognise the fact or publicise it generally. Staff soon get to know over the grapevine what they can expect in terms of promotion and enhancement of their terms of service during their careers with the particular firm. The better firms today are well aware of their career structures and do their best to make their staff equally aware of what they can expect, as well as what is expected of them.

No two firms will have the same career path progression, and, once again, it is going to be necessary very early on in the merger negotiations to consider how to achieve the best blend from the two differing structures. As has been indicated elsewhere, it may be necessary to scrap what is on offer and start again.

However, it is vital that those interested must be told of the proposed changes at the very earliest moment. It may even be a good idea to pub-

Successful Mergers

lish the proposed changes in the form of a discussion paper so that staff's feedback can be obtained before implementing the changes. The paper can be supplemented by a question and answer sheet and ample opportunity must be given for discussion and explanation on a face to face basis.

All this is time consuming, but, if the merger is to be successful, it must not be accompanied by an exodus of key staff. Unfortunately that has been all too common and we must learn from the mistakes of those who have already been through the merger process. After all, a number of future mergers will involve those who have already merged. The disease becomes contagious! They will certainly try not to make the same mistakes again.

Michael Simmons

11 Integrating the Systems

It would be wrong to complete this section of the book without giving some consideration to the problems which arise in relation to machines. A good deal has already been said about the people involved in mergers and, while people must be paramount, nevertheless the tools which they use must also be looked at in some detail in the merger situation.

A merger requires compatibility of the people involved and, in an ideal world, all office machinery and systems will also dovetail adequately. However, it is not an ideal world, and the sheer variety of the bits and pieces of equipment found in the normal professional firm will almost always produce some misfits.

The first and the most obvious area for scrutiny is the communications equipment. Each firm will have a telephone switchboard but, if the two firms are to be together in the same premises, will it be possible to dispose of one set of telephone equipment without undue problems?

It will be necessary to look at leases and how they can be terminated, and at what cost. Perhaps, if premises are being vacated, the incoming tenant will wish to take over the telephone equipment on the site, and this could be part of the price paid to the outgoing partnership.

Will the existing telephone equipment in the premises where the two firms are to merge be sufficient for the requirements of the enlarged firm? It may be necessary to call in consultants to conduct a survey to see whether there is sufficient excess capacity. It will always be easier if both the firms in the merger are moving to new joint premises, where new equipment can be acquired which will be suitable for the firm's requirements.

As with telephone equipment, so the other communications media will have to be considered. These will include facsimile transmission, telex and electronic mail. Both merging firms may have all three, or there may be gaps. Fax seems to be the rage of the moment and, as the equipment becomes cheaper, so more firms seem to be taking on more fax machines. Some of us think that fax is here to stay, but it might only be a passing fashion.

Once again, equipment which will not be required in the merger will have to be sold, or disposed of under the lease or hire terms. There may be penalties to pay, and this will have to be costed in to the post-merger accounts.

Whatever is done or not done with communications equipment on the merger, it is absolutely vital that any professional firm deals adequately in the merger situation with the accounts side.

In an ideal world, one of the parties to the merger will have computerised accounts with sufficient capacity, not only to take on the accounts of the merging firm, but also to provide room for growth. Furthermore, the transition will be made easier by the compatibility between the two computers, so that one can effectively impart the information stored in it into the other.

If that happy situation does not exist, then probably the next best scenario is for one firm to have the computer with excess capacity, while the other firm's accounts are not yet computerised. The merger can be used to effect the translation.

The most likely situation is that both firms will have an accounts computer, neither of which is nearing the end of its active life. Neither computer will have the capacity to take the work of the other. It is possible that the systems are so compatible that one computer can be 'bolted on' to the other to provide sufficient capacity for the merged firm. However, this is not normally the case, and usually the merged firm will have the expense in money and time of taking on a new computer, which will necessitate the transfer of the information from the present two computers into the new memory.

It is highly likely that this work will have to be done by individuals rather than from computer to computer, which gives a considerable chance of error. Such errors may not be picked up immediately and may be extremely damaging.

If you are told initially that your computer equipment is incompatible with that of the other firm, do not necessarily accept this as the final answer. There are some extremely ingenious computer consultants in the market today, who can find answers to most problems. The 'black box' is very much a box of tricks and all sorts of conversions can be effected. However, these may be short term solutions only, and the answer may be to dispose of both existing computers and buy a new one, especially when excess capacity is required for the planned expansion following the merger.

It is of the utmost importance that this area is addressed at the earliest possible moment and, if necessary, the best outside advice should be obtained.

The other area where systems must be considered in detail is that of word processing. If both firms already have sophisticated systems in place, it will be important to see if they are compatible. Once again, at first impression, a number of the most popular systems will not talk to each other. However, the clever systems engineer can overcome this problem, if indeed it is a problem.

Integrating the Systems

The aim of the merged firm must be to have the most modern network manufactured by the same supplier throughout the firm. This will make bulk purchasing much more effective and will also ease the task so far as maintenance and spare parts are concerned.

However, if both firms have fairly modern equipment, which is not compatible, even if they are moving into the same office, it may be possible to use both in the short term. Different systems can be used in different departments, or, if appropriate, different branches. There will be different leasing arrangements in force and also it will be necessary to deal with more than one maintenance company. This will be a nuisance, but it is often the most effective way of handling the problem.

The cost of terminating a lease prematurely and re-equipping with one system throughout may be prohibitive, and a compromise will often be the best answer on a merger where word processing equipment is concerned. I stress that such a compromise is not normally a practical proposition when dealing with the accounts side of the practice.

There are still arguments in force on whether the accounts computer should be linked to the word processing network. There are arguments for keeping them separate. A merger is theoretically the ideal opportunity to put information about the clients of both firms on to a database. This can be contained within the accounts computer, or not, as the parties think fit.

However, it is not an ideal world, and, as can be seen from the case studies of mergers, there is usually so much to do and such a shortage of manpower available to do it, that it is very unlikely that the creation of a clients' database will have high priority. However, it certainly should be kept on the list of things to do once the merged firm has settled down into an integrated unit.

If one firm already has such a database then it can be used as the foundation and the information from the other firm can gradually be fed into it. If both firms have computerised databases, then we come back to the problems of compatibility. Here it might be desirable to rely on the computer consultants ingenuity to provide an interface so as to combine the two into one. This is a fairly short-term operation, and the other computer can be discarded along with the equipment of transfer.

To use such a linking system in the long-term invites problems, as it is at best a makeshift answer to the problem, which is likely to develop its own problems long-term.

It is a strange fact of life, that almost every professional services firm claims a partner who is interested in computers to the point of mania. It is probably best to use their advice but not to let them have full control of the situation, to avoid the situation where a computerised camel appears rather than the computerised horse which was intended.

There is rarely sufficient expertise in two firms contemplating a merger to deal overall with the problems of office machines, particularly those of a more sophisticated nature. The age of the independent consultant is upon us, and this is one particular area where their services ought validly to be used.

If, after completing this section, the reader begins to think that there is so much to a merger that it is hardly worth the overall effort, it is probably fair to say that the writers have every sympathy with that point of view.

Michael Simmons

Part 3
EXPERIENCES OF MERGER

12 Large firms: Clifford Chance

Before I address some practical details of a merger (and this is what I have been asked to do) I would like to emphasise two fundamental points. The first is; make sure that there are very good business reasons for making the merger and no significant impediments likely to affect it. The second is; ensure that at all stages (before, at the time of and after the merger decision) information is disseminated properly to those who should receive it.

By way of illustration I will briefly comment on the Clifford Chance merger in the light of these two key points.

It was necessary at the outset of the discussions to evaluate that there were good business reasons for merging and that there were no significant impediments to stop it. Accordingly it was essential to ensure, for example, that the people involved in the different firms were generally compatible in terms of personality, philosophy and work style; that remuneration and profit distribution were similar and most importantly that no insuperable conflict problems existed.

The careful handling of information is of vital importance. Before the decision to merge is taken by both firms a detailed analysis has to be made and distributed to and discussed fully by all partners. This analysis results from a great deal of trust, in that information has to be exchanged between the firms in total confidence. Without that information partners cannot be expected to make a sensible and informed decision. It is also necessary to ensure that the matter is kept confidential until the decision has been taken. When it has been taken then time and care has to be taken to provide full and comprehensive information to staff, clients and other interested people. This, of course, also remains of importance for an extensive period after the taking of the decision. It is just one factor but a vital one in the process of the careful management of change that a successful merger necessitates.

In January 1987 all the partners of Clifford-Turner and Coward Chance received a large volume of papers (known as 'The Black Book') which was the prospectus for the proposed merger of the two firms. Tom Johnson-Gilbert and I (as the senior partners of Coward Chance and Clifford-Turner respectively) wrote an introduction and since it could be regarded as the philosophy of our merger I think that the

Successful Mergers

approach which was adopted might be of interest – here it is.

'The proposal and the accompanying papers are the result of extensive discussions between representatives of the two firms. We do not wish to duplicate what is said in the accompanying papers but there are some points which we consider should be emphasised:
1. The new firm will be very large. Size is not a good thing for its own sake, but in the environment in which the two existing firms operate, domestically and internationally, increased size will enable us to improve the breadth and depth of service. This is necessary to meet the requirements of clients and to expand our ability to take on more jobs, particularly large jobs which require teams of people contributing a wide range of special skills.
2. The relative strengths of the two firms are to a considerable extent complementary and they fit together in such a way as to provide a well balanced and very broad based practice.
3. Each firm abroad has a strong overseas network. The new firm will be in an even stronger position with the concentration of resources which will result.
4. The potential for a new firm is immense. The realisation of the potential will require wholehearted enthusiasm and sustained effort on the part of everyone; if we are half-hearted about our determination to suceed, we will fail.
5. Both of us, and the members of the discussion groups of the two firms who have been involved in developing the merger proposals, have, in the course of the development, become more and more convinced of the logic of the merger and the opportunities which it opens up.

We commend the proposal to you and hope that you will share our enthusiasm and our belief that it is the right way forward.'

For some months prior to January 1987 a small group of partners from the two firms had been working away, not in the office but in a flat which we had rented. We decided that when partners voted on the merger it would have to be as a package and therefore the 'Black Book' must cover, amongst a list of other matters, all the points which were material for the operation of a merged firm and for the next two years whilst the partners and staff were integrating. Also of course the partners of Coward Chance had to have all relevant information about Clifford-Turner and vice versa in order to decide whether or not to merge.

I though it might be of interest to set out some of the issues that need to be addressed:

The new firm

1. The new name
2. Immediate and future management
3. People and departments
4. Overseas network
5. Integration of [foreign offices]
6. New partnership agreement
   (a) Profit sharing
   (b) Distribution of profit
   (c) Tax reserves
   (d) Capital
   (e) Decisions
   (f) Holidays and sabbaticals
   (g) Life and disability insurance
   (h) Retirement annuity premiums
   (i) Retirement
7. Financial
8. Premises policy
9. Technology integration
10. Personnel integration
11. Conflicts
12. Transitional matters – financial
13. Transitional matters – new partners
14. Timetable

Information relating to each old firm

1. History
2. London departments
3. The overseas offices
4. The firm's administrative structure
5. Premises
6. Technology resources
7. Summary of financial information
8. Summary of London partnership agreement
9. Retirement arrangements
10. Professional indemnity cover
11. Personnel policies

Premises

So far as we were concerned we had just enough room in our respective buildings for the two firms. We were advised that it would take three years or so before a building would be available which could not only accommodate us all but allow space for expansion.

For the interim period the first step was to decide which departments should be together in one building; which had the closest working connection. For example, we decided that everybody involved in banking should be in the same building as those involved in corporate work.

The operations, conducted at weekends, of moving people and papers from Blackfriars House to Royex House and vice versa, particularly as redecoration was carried out at the same time was a major and difficult exercise. It took about four months but it had to be done. I believe it is an essential step in any merger if the merged firm cannot immediately be housed entirely within one building.

Management structure

The 'black book' stated that there would be two committees. The first would be the 'strategy committee' to be responsible for recommending to partners the management structure for the new firm. The members would be elected by all the partners and chaired by one of the joint senior partners. The committee would be responsible for the strategic issues which would affect the firm.

The second committee, the 'merger committee', would be chaired by the other joint senior partner and the members named in the 'black book'. It would consist of the two managing partners and four other partners. The merger committee, through the managing partners, would be responsible for the management of the firm.

Both committees would be disbanded once the management structure had been approved by the partners with a deadline of 30th April 1989.

In fact the 'strategy committee' beavered away with the result that its proposals for the future management will be implemented at the end of 1988.

An obvious problem which arises immediately after a merger is how to manage the new firm. It was for this reason that we started with the merger committee. This would ensure that there was management until we got to know each other and elections, as well as decisions on structure, would be meaningful.

New partners

In a large firm it becomes increasingly difficult for all partners to know all the possible candidates for partnership: double the numbers and the problem is even worse. For the first year of the new firm it was decided that there was a need to have the process composed of an evaluation of the business needs of the new firm and also an election process targeted on the partners of each historic firm voting on the candidates from that firm only.

At the time of the merger all fee earners were informed that their prospects of partnership would not be prejudiced by the fact of the merger and that at least as many partners would be made as would have been had the two firms remained separate. The new firm has delivered in earnest on this pledge.

Conflicts of interest

We reviewed the list of clients of the two firms and made an assessment of the likely areas of difficulty. We had to take into account not only client relationship but also the rules of The Law Society. There were a number of rules but it was no easy task to apply them to actual situations. During the past months there have been changes and the summary 'E & O.E.' may be helpful.

There are a number of Principles of Conduct (contained in The Law Society's publication, 'The Professional Conduct of Solicitors') which are relevant to the situation arising after the merger of two firms of solicitors.

The first is Principle 2.09. This states:

'Where there has been a material alteration to the composition of the firm, the clients must be notified promptly'.

Commentary number 5 to this Principle extends this. This provides:

'Where two or more firms amalgamate and have previously been acting for clients who are involved in litigation against each other, or who in any other way have conflicting interests, the new firm must cease to act for both clients unless it is able to continue to act for one with the consent of the other'.

The question of when a firm can continue to act for one client where there is conflict between two clients is dealt with in Principle 9.03. This provides:

'A solicitor must not continue to act for two or more clients where a conflict of interest arises between those clients'.

Commentary 1 to this Principle states:

Successful Mergers

'If a solicitor has already accepted instructions from two clients and a conflict subsequently arises between the interests of those clients, the solicitor must cease to act for both clients, unless he can without embarrassment and with propriety continue to represent one client with the other's consent. A solicitor may only continue to represent one client where he is not in possession of relevant knowledge concerning the other obtained whilst acting for the other. Further, a solicitor must ensure that the former client consents to his continuing to act for the other client. The former client should be separately advised before such consent is obtained.'

Where two or more firms merge, the clients of both firms become the clients of the newly merged firm. If there are conflicts between the interests of those clients, Principle 9.03 must, in general be adhered to.

However in the circumstances following a merger, despite knowledge gained, the newly merged firm may continue to act for one or possibly both clients, providing it has erected an effective 'Chinese wall'. This is as a result of a Law Society Statement, published in The Law Society's Gazette, dated 27th May 1987. In order to continue to act in these circumstances the following must apply:

1. there must be no embarrassment to the solicitors involved;
2. both clients must have consented;
3. both clients must have obtained independent advice prior to the giving of consent;
4. the interests of the clients must demand that the amalgamated firm continues to act despite the conflict of interest; and
5. the Chinese wall must be effective. Undertakings to keep the clients confidentiality should be given by the relevant staff; there should be geographical separation between those acting, if possible; and care should be taken over the administrative matters, such as the opening of the post, articled clerk change round, etc.

I have endeavoured to highlight some of the issues which had to be handled in relation to the Clifford Chance merger. More issues will arise in future and will be the subject of the continuing management of the processes of change.

I stress that I have approached the merger in this chapter very much from the senior partners' view point. From other levels within the firm diverse issues have had to be considered and resolved both long term and on a day to day basis.

However wholehearted the approach, there always had to be some initial doubts in the minds of those contemplating what has been in

Large Firms: Clifford Chance

effect a mammoth enterprise; the merger of the two firms to form Clifford Chance. However, signs to date are of considerable success. The merged firm has been accepted by its constituent partners; staff; clients; the public generally and not least the legal profession as a whole.

Sir Max Williams
Joint Senior Partner of Clifford Chance

13a Mid-sized firms: Withers Crossman Block

Withers decided in 1987 that we had to do something about the growth of the commercial department. We had experienced a well-publicised set-back in that a leading commercial partner had gone elsewhere following the takeover of our largest commercial client. We decided that it was best to try to fill the gap and achieve greater growth for the future by merging with a firm which had a strong company and commercial presence.

We considered waiting for organic growth, or recruiting from the City but concluded that, if we could find the right firm, a merger would provide a swifter and more certain solution to our problems.

We therefore needed to target a firm which was not as strong as we were on the private client side, but which already had a substantial company and commercial presence. If that firm had a strong litigation department as well, it would be a bonus.

We made our short list of potential firms and contacted Crossman Block & Keith. We had a preliminary meeting between one of our partners and one of theirs. We exchanged brochures and discussed our philosophies and our thoughts for future development.

Crossman Block came back and said that they were interested in pursuing discussions. We then had a couple of sessions where a large number of partners from both firms met and considered whether they could get on with each other. These meetings took place after hours over drinks. The feedback on both sides was favourable and we therefore decided to start some serious negotiations.

Each firm appointed a team of three, which consisted of two partners on either side and the financial controllers.

We had to examine seriously the commercial logic of the proposed merger and in particular each other's strengths and weaknesses. As our need was for commercial strength, we had to probe seriously to see whether they were as strong on that front as we hoped. Crossman Block were making the transition from being a firm strong on the private client and licensing side into one with strong commercial and litigation departments.

A great deal of detailed work followed, which included the exchanging of client lists, examining each other's major billings and, of course, the exchanging of accounts. There was also a good deal of hard talking about our respective philosophies and where we really wanted the proposed merged firm to be going.

We discovered that we were both happy to act on a broad basic philosophy of combining private client work with company and commercial work. Neither side wanted to jettison the private client department for the sake of commercial growth. This differentiated us from many of the City firms.

Both firms had identified Europe as an area of potential growth Withers had opened a Paris office in 1985 which was specialising in shipping and insurance, and was generally working as a transport orientated office. We were also in process of entering into an association with Michael Soul, who specialises in Spanish legal work.

Crossman Block had been regularly sending assistants to Holland and Germany on a placement basis, but had not felt themselves sufficiently strong in the market as yet to open their own offices there.

Both firms were getting a significant amount of new work from their overseas connections, with Europe and the U.S.A. being the particular areas of strength and each firm also had a partner who had worked in the Gulf. We discovered in talking that our European aspirations very much fitted together.

At this point, we became satisfied that the two firms had unity of purpose and could well merge together into one identity. We realised that there would have to be a great deal more work done on blending our working ethics and general divergencies of practice into one firm, but we were sure that the effort would be well worth it.

However we were now uncovering various problems. On the accounts side, Withers were on a bills delivered basis, while Crossman Block were on a cash basis. Fortunately, our accounting date was the same. We took advice from our respective accountants and made soundings with the Revenue. The problem was solved by both firms undertaking to continue after merger on a bills delivered basis. Crossman Block had the problem that since they were on a cash basis, their unpaid bills did not appear as an asset in the accounts. It was agreed that Crossman Block would have a purge on unpaid bills, but would bring into the merged firm those which they had failed to collect at the merger date.

A good deal of work also had to be done on the question of profit sharing and its structure for the future. We decided that the answer was to be generous and tolerant with each other, as we wanted the merger to work, and we realised that this was a long term relationship. After a good deal of effort, we produced a profit sharing basis with which all partners were comfortable and which provided for a progression to equality based partly on merit and partly on seniority. This was a combination of rather different philosophies in the two firms.

At the conclusion of our discussions the two negotiating teams produced a summary of the proposals for circulation to the partners in the respective firms. It may be of interest to give some information as to the contents.

We started with the reasons and philosophy for the merger. The document then went on to deal with partnership matters and in particular profit sharing.

We then had to consider other matters affecting partners which included life insurance, pensions, partnership capital, drawings, expenses, cars and retirement ages.

The document went on to deal with the management structure for the merged firm. Both firms had managing partners working with financial controllers, and we decided to retain this structure, supported by a board consisting of the heads of department meeting monthly.

We decided on joint managing partners for an interim bedding down period, which was not specified in duration. In due course, we will revert to one managing partner.

It was necessary to agree the senior partner, and heads of department, together with functional partners reporting to the managing partners in relation to staff, practice development, and articled clerks.

All appointments were made for an initial period of two years, which would allow review at the expiration of that time in case it was discovered that mistakes had been made.

The document dealt with the name of the new firm. Perhaps surprisingly, there were no strong feelings, provided that we reached a name which would preserve the goodwill of both firms. There were also no problems about the position of partners' names on the notepaper, although there was a good deal of discussion about the actual form which the notepaper was to take.

Our document also went on to specify the bankers and accountants for the new merged firm and, finally, contained a tentative draft budget for the first year of the merged firm.

We began our discussions in late March 1987 and reached agreement at the end of June 1987. Initially, we thought that we would complete the merger at the end of October or November in that year, but we realised that there was a great deal to do, particularly on the accounts side. We, therefore, put off the merger date to 1st January 1988.

On completion, we found ourselves in four separate buildings. We disposed of one within two months and are currently in three buildings. We have rationalised the departments, but we are still seeking a suitable building to house the firm under one roof.

Post-merger we have had a considerable amount of work to do

beyond what was expected in integrating staff. There have had, perforce, to be considerable changes in relation to administrative systems and working practices. With the benefit of hindsight, we would have considered this aspect of the merger in greater detail beforehand so as to condition and familiarise staff before the merger actually took place.

It was obvious that there was going to be rationalisation needed in the accounts department and support functions but the speed of this was greater than we had anticipated.

We took on a new computer some eight weeks after the merger and the extra work involved has caused disruption. We did however spend a good deal of time before the merger in collecting the requisite accounts information so that we would have have one system from merger date. This was time well spent.

We certainly under-estimated the accounting department effort and time required post-merger in bedding down the new joint firm. This is a difficult problem to solve, as even though we did prepare a manual, which was distributed to administrative and accounting staff prior to the merger, until they were actually working on the new job, the difficulties were not fully perceived.

At partnership level, differences in philosophy and working attitude have materialised post-merger. What we are now seeking to do is to make sure that we pick out the best points from the two firms and merge them together into one coherent philosophy. The differences in attitude relate particularly to client getting and handling, and also to billing and collection practises.

We now have a firm of 35 partners, of whom 2 are resident in Paris. The total staff, including partners, is 250. There are 100 fee earners and 150 non-fee earners. The work already done and still to be done in merging the firm into a cohesive unit has been great, but we consider it to have been well worthwhile.

Tony Thompson. Born 1943. Educated at Haberdashers Askes, Hampstead and Trinity College Cambridge. Articled at Withers and became a partner in Withers in 1970. Specialised in private client, estate and tax planning, particularly offshore tax planning.

Contributor to Tax Case Analysis, Lecturer at London Law Society's Winter Workshops and various seminars.

Head of Withers private client department 1964-1986. Managing partner of Withers 1987 and of Withers Crossman Block 1988.

13b Mid-sized firms: Fladgate Fielder

When I began my articles a third of a century ago the solicitor's profession was about to change and adapt to the greater pressures of the second half of the 20th century. In this chapter I shall attempt to show how the history of Fladgate Fielder mirrored, stage by stage, wider developments within the profession.

In 1955 many firms had a history and tradition going back to the 18th and 19th century and prominent amongst London solicitors were personalities such as Sir Dingwall Bateson of Walters & Hart, John Stanton of Vandercom Stanton and Tony Moir of Fladgate & Co. Equally in many country towns, there were also solicitors who were highly respected members of the local community and John Trimmer in Alton in Hampshire was a typical example.

There was even in 1955 a more leisurely approach to work and this was largely because of the support given to the partners by the old style managing clerks such as Henry Welham at Walters & Hart, Bill Reeve at Vandercom Stanton and Cyril Berry at Fladgate & Co.

All three managing clerks served through the 60s into the 70s to pass their skills on to the next generation and show their ability to adapt to the changing world. The importance of maintaining staff morale during mergers is emphasised elsewhere in the book and this is a practical example of the value of loyalty and continuity over the years.

A firm run in the way these three firms were run in 1955 would have little chance of success in these more thrusting days, but survive they have albeit in a different, merged form to make what is now a successful practice strongly represented in the commercial, private client and litigation fields. The seeds of this reformation had already been sown by 1955.

It was some three years earlier when Walters & Co, a long established old fashioned (in the best sense) Lincoln's Inn firm with a strong private client base merged with the first generation practitioner, L A Hart, who was totally entrepreneurial in character with connections in the merchant banking field (which eventually he took up full time).

It was remarkable that these two could co-exist as Walters & Hart, but they did and it was this merger which was the foundation of our present private client department on the one hand and our commercial department on the other.

Mid-sized firms: Fladgate Fielder

The death of Sir Dingwall Bateson and Tony Moir, both in 1967, had a profound effect on Walters & Hart and Fladgate & Co respectively and both had to go through a period of consolidation before thoughts could turn to expansion. By 1972, the partners of Walters & Hart realised they were in a strong enough position to seek a broader base and were fortunate to be able to merge with Vandercom Stanton.

John Stanton was ready to retire and his son, who was in partnership with him realised the growing disadvantage of being a small firm, so they readily agreed to join Walters & Hart (to make Walters Vandercom & Hart) with John remaining for a few years as a consultant. The merger terms were actually settled over dinner at the home of their senior partner. The thornier points were worked out over the brandy!

This brought Bill Reeve into the new firm which very much boosted the rather weak litigation department of Walters & Hart. His experience was invaluable and the advent of a very good young partner specialising in litigation a few years later produced the third strong department which had been very much needed.

Vandercom Stanton had been managed on a very traditional basis and the Walters & Hart partners were able to inject their own more modern style of management with great effect on the running and efficiency of the combined practice.

We have always considered it necessary for a firm to be active and growing to retain the enthusiasm of its members. As technology becomes important, size itself becomes an advantage. This caused the Walters Vandercom & Hart partners to consider adding to their own organic growth by an appropriate merger and an introduction between two of the partners produced Fladgate & Co as a possible candidate.

Discussions in the ordinary way took place in 1978 and terms were satisfactorily agreed. Fladgate & Co moved from their Whitehall offices to join Walters Vandercom & Hart in Queen Anne Street as Walters Fladgate. Most of the staff at Fladgate & Co were elderly and approaching retirement so it was necessary to reorganise and reallocate work into our strengthened departmental structure.

The merger added to our private clients which we anticipated but at the same time there was an unexpected bonus in that we found our commercial department was considerably enhanced by a number of clients and contacts of Fladgate & Co who found the new firm well able to deal with the commercial aspects of their work.

It was soon after this merger that it became apparent that a radical change of staffing policy had become necessary. Up to then the firm had been manned by partners supported by managing clerks, and assistant solicitors were comparatively rare. In both constituent firms, the remaining managing clerks (by now the proud possessors of the

Successful Mergers

enhanced title, 'legal executive') were rapidly approaching retirement and with few exceptions their replacements were not to be found.

The new policy (as with other firms) was to find good young assistant solicitors. In this we proved to be fortunate and have built a good team and have perhaps not found the extreme difficulty other medium sized firms have in attracting good staff. It may be that our nearness to West End shops is part of the attraction.

Discussions within the partnership became centred on possibilities for growth and expansion and an initiative spoken about was a possibility of hiving off part of our work to a country office where it could be done at a lesser cost without London salaries and rents. At the same time we anticipated that such an office would be in a good catchment area and would obtain local work.

After an appropriate business plan had been produced, this project was put on one side as not being viable until it could be started using an existing base, preferably on the commercial side. It took us a couple of years before an opportunity arose and in 1984 we replied to an advertisement from a sole practitioner in the Gazette.

The advertiser Charles Boundy had a small practice based in central London with a recently opened office near Basingstoke. He wanted to concentrate on commercial work and felt there were great prospects in North Hampshire backed by a strong London connection.

This seemed to fit in with our earlier thoughts so a merger was arranged on the basis that we opened an office in Basingstoke. This was staffed by Charles Boundy and four executives two of whom we sent out to join him. His recently qualified London solicitor joined us to work in our litigation deparment in London.

We sent out some of our work to be done in Basingstoke and it soon produced a volume of its own through local introductions and in 1987 one of our London commercial partners decided that he would like to move to Basingstoke, taking the bulk of his work with him.

A move to new improved offices in Basingstoke became necessary and it was at that time that Charles Boundy introduced Bradly Trimmer, a firm with offices in Alton, Basingstoke and Andover. The senior partner was retiring and we agreed to merge with the four partners of their Basingstoke and Alton offices.

This meant that we could move their Basingstoke office into our new larger premises there, where we now have a mainly commercial practice under the Fladgate Fielder name. The office is now staffed with three commercial partners, one litigation partner, two commercial associates, one other commercial solicitor and other fee earning staff.

The Alton part of the practice continues to work under the name of Bradly Trimmer but is part of the overall firm and concentrates on the

Mid-sized firms: Fladgate Fielder

private clients work with two partners in that field, one associate and one litigation associate.

In a short space of time a good relationship has been built up between each office with all working to keep the approach of a unified firm.

We now find ourselves with a London practice which works in three departments of commercial, private client and litigation. We have a commercial practice in Basingstoke and private client practice in Alton, each with its own litigation back-up.

So far as the management of the firm is concerned, this is dealt with by a management board with partners in charge of each of the three offices, and with partners with specific roles to play as finance partner, marketing partner and resources partner.

We cannot yet say we are in our final form and new proposals are looked at from time to time. What we can say is that our approach to mergers and their negotiations has advanced in recent years and is now organised on a formal basis and in accordance with the firm's business plan. On our last merger with Bradly Trimmer the thornier points were settled not over a brandy but on a Saturday with three partners from each side sitting down to a formal meeting with an agenda.

Times move on and when I started writing this chapter I expected it to conclude with the previous paragraph and use throughout this chapter the name of Walters Fladgate. Now the partnership has changed again, giving the firm a larger interest in the commercial field. Since the merger with Fladgate & Co. (which was essentially a private client firm) our long term plan has been to join with a commercial firm and during the summer the opportunity arose to discuss a possible merger with Fielder Le Riche. Their history goes back to the last century and like Walters & Co. they have moved since the war from the Lincoln's Inn area to the West End.

As from 1st December 1988 we have merged the two practices as Fladgate Fielder and whilst there is considerable sadness on my part in losing the Walters name, it will be fascinating to see the combined firm take such a quantum leap to become a firm of 28 partners. Time and space do not permit me to elaborate on this new merger but we are all reasonably satisfied that our structure set out earlier in this chapter will stand the additional strain although we have decided to divide our commercial department into two separate departments, one emphasising the property side and one concentrating on purely commercial and corporate matters.

Anthony (Tony) Baker is senior partner of Fladgate Fielder where he works in the private client department dealing with landed

Successful Mergers

estate, trusts (large and small) and U.K. and international tax planning.

He read law at Emmanuel College, Cambridge, graduating in 1955, followed by the post graduate LLB (now reclassified as LLM) and the solicitors' finals where he was awarded the John Mackrell Prize.

He was articled to Sir Dingwall Bateson at Walters & Hart and has spent all his working life in that firm. For a time he was Assistant Examiner for the Law Society Finals in "Equity and Succession".

He is married with two children and lives in Norfolk, and London during the week. His interests are mens hockey (he was president of the Bucks County Hockey Association) and golf. He claims to be an 'international' in both since he has represented the Law Society in both sports against the Dutch Bar!

13c Mid-sized regional firms: Taylor Vinters

Taylors was an old-established Newmarket practice. It had a strong private client base having fairly recently opened an office in nearby Cambridge, where it had located its commercial property and commercial departments.

Vinters was a Cambridge city practice with a much stronger litigation side and a larger commercial department than Taylors.

The respective strengths were: Taylors: 8 partners, Vinters: 9 partners and two salaried partners. The staffs were more or less equal in size.

Both firms had come quite separately to the conclusion that a merger would be in their best interests in order to promote the growth necessary to compete with other top local firms. While organic growth was taking place, it was too slow and a merger with the right firm would provide the required boost to make competition that much easier at the highest local level.

The other possibility was to identify suitable niche markets and in fact abandon certain unprofitable areas of work; or to consolidate. However, we found that we both favoured the merger route as the one to achieve our goals more quickly.

The process started with both firms as a result of a 'strategic planning review'. In a changing world, we both realised that organic growth was not sufficient. Both firms wanted to increase their respective shares of the commercial market. The obvious place to achieve this was Cambridge with its high-tech image and its science parks. To be credible in that market, we needed to be bigger in the public eye.

Both firms had already started to be departmentalised, but we realised that what was lacking was back-up and support in depth in the smaller and more specialised departments. This applied very much in the commercial departments. To put it at its crudest, if one partner was not available in the commercial departments in question in either firm, there was effectively no-one of sufficient seniority to cope with a substantial influx of new work.

We feel that one of the great strengths of our two firms' approach to the merger was that we had both reached the conclusion that we wanted to effect such a merger independently.

Once we had made the decision in principle, we had to consider what size of firm we wanted. In the case of Taylors they were fairly open

Successful Mergers

minded, except that they knew they did not want to be taken over by a larger firm. Vinters had some time previously held abortive discussions with another local firm. Both sides reviewed the possible candidates and targeted each other! We considered it very important that at our respective sizes all partners would be able to get on well with each other. Both firms considered that was one of their strengths. It was decided to set up a meeting well away from our normal areas of work and play. We decided that we did not want to be damaged by loose talk going around that our two firms were meeting if the merger did not subsequently go through to completion.

We arranged to meet for a half day at a weekend at a town about forty miles away. The meeting was structured into mixed groups of the partners in each firm, and these groups were changed so that we could all have a chance to talk to each other. The discussions were a mixture of the philosophy underlying the work of our two firms and the practicalities of working together in a merged firm.

We ended with a meal, where we were seated next to the partners in the other firm with whom we had had least contact generally and on this particular occasion. By the end of the evening, we had a fairly good idea of what the others were like.

We then went back to our respective firms, held partners' meetings and voted unanimously in favour of proceeding with merger negotiations. If there had not been unanimity on either side, the discussions would have been abandoned at that stage.

We decided, for the same reasons that the initial meeting was held away from the office, to keep the decision secret, at least for the time being. After all, it was only a decision in principle and, once again, we wanted to limit the damage in the event of the merger not proceeding to fruition.

A merger committee or 'working party' was set up, consisting of three partners from each firm. We prepared a check list of important matters which needed to be cleared before a final decision on the merger could be taken and an announcement made. Meetings took place weekly outside the office, once again to preserve secrecy. The discussions were both general and specific covering a variety of subjects from general philosophy and partnership structure to order of names on the notepaper and motoring arrangements.

The questions of figures and finance were delegated to one out of each side of the working party. Fortunately, as both firms were computerised, the necessary data was readily available. The projections were prepared by an independent firm of accountants and not those who were then advising the respective firms. Those particular accountants have remained as the merged firm's accountants, after making a

Mid-sized regional firms: Taylor Vinters

presentation in competition with two other firms.

Before the merger, both firms were worried about recruitment. We felt that we were not the right size, and that the merged firm would be much more powerful in the recruitment market. To date, that has proved correct.

Both firms were very much run by the partners. Vinters had no managing partner as such, but the various activities of that firm were dealt with by a number of committees. Taylors did have a managing partner and had appointed an office services manager. We viewed the merger as the opportunity to appoint for the first time a partnership executive who would assume overall responsibility for running the accounts and services departments of the combined firm and provide the necessary financial data for management and budgeting purposes. This would relieve the partners from a lot of the day to day work in those respects.

I think that it is now necessary to say something on the subject of timing. The first approach was made in late November 1986 and a preliminary meeting of representatives from both sides was held in December. However, because of Christmas holidays, the initial meeting of all the partners, to which I have referred above, was deferred until early January 1987. The fundamental points on the checklist were cleared by mid March after some eight or nine formal meetings of the working party and numerous informal meetings of individual members.

Most of the really contentious issues were finally resolved at individual level. The pace of the negotiations was hastened at this point by the feeling that certain members of the staff of both firms were beginning to get wind of what was happening. In practice, it is impossible to keep these things secret for too long. We felt that we wanted to combat uncertainty, as we thought that this was something which would be very damaging to staff morale. Added impetus was provided by the fact that we had identified a new building to house the Cambridge end of the operation.

Heads of terms were drawn up at this stage and each of the two firms held partners meetings at the end of March resulting in a final decision by both sides to proceed with the merger. A merger agreement and draft partnership deed were prepared and settled very quickly and the former was signed by all partners on 6th April 1987. The announcement was made that day although no date was then suggested for final completion.

Steps were taken immediately to recruit the appropriate partnership executive and we set up a public relations sub-committee consisting of two partners from Vinters and one from Taylors. Their brief was to deal with press releases and the brochure. Vinters had much more experience of this kind of work and hence their numerical preponderence.

One of our great potential problems was the Cambridge premises. Neither Vinters nor Taylors had sufficient room to accommodate the other firm and we were anxious to avoid split offices if possible. It was, therefore, necessary to find new premises to combine the two Cambridge offices. We agreed this in principle very early on, but in practice finding suitable premises was quite difficult and we had to wait until the right premises came along. Both firms agreed that they wanted to move the Cambridge office out of the centre of town.

Towards the end of the merger discussions we found a suitable new building, nearing completion, on the perimeter of the city. Although the building was far bigger than we required for our immediate needs the location was felt to be ideal and the identification of the premises certainly helped in crystallising the merger negotiations.

However it was important that we should be able to sublet parts of the building on a short term basis with a view to recovering them for our future anticipated expansion. We agreed that, if we could exchange contracts for the lease by the end of June 1987, the merger would be deferred to coincide with the move into the new premises. In fact, we had to revise this deadline, owing to difficulties in the lease negotiations, until September.

From then on we were helped enormously by the fact that we had recruited our partnership executive, who was able to take on a lot of the day to day work. With the benefit of hindsight, it would have been very difficult indeed to have effected the merger before he took up his position.

The question of the search and preparation of the premises was delegated to one partner from each of the two firms serving on the steering committe (being a slightly different version of the former working party). They had to deal with the landlords, the fitting out arrangements and all the other details while the partnership executive was assimilating the different cultures of the two firms and getting to grips with the integration of the accounts departments.

In an ideal world, the whole merged firm would have been under one roof. However, we had to consider our client bases and our introductory sources. These, we decided, were our most important assets. As a result, we felt that we had to keep a separate Newmarket office, while ensuring cross-fertilisation of ideas, clients and work between the two offices and two parts of the new merged firm. We, therefore, located the commercial and litigation work in Cambridge and the probate, trust and private client side in Newmarket, with slight exceptions.

Mid-sized regional firms: Taylor Vinters

Vinters had also fairly recently opened a residential conveyancing 'shop' in a prime position in one of Cambridge's best professional/shopping streets. They did not actually sell houses but they did have a shop-front designed to attract the eye of the public. It was decided that as this office had been set up to serve a particular clientele and purpose it would also be retained as a residential conveyancing centre and shop window for the new firm. However a separate office in one of the outlying villages was excluded from the merger and sold off.

While we wanted the new firm to be commercially led, nevertheless, we recognised the importance of the private client department, both historically, currently and for the future. This had to be discussed during the merger negotiations with a view to achieving the right balance.

Turning now to problems after the merger. With the benefit of hindsight, we should have investigated in greater depth the quality of the back-up staff of both firms, including services. We did carry out this investigation among the partners and senior fee earning staff, but we did not really consider whether the support staff would be of sufficient calibre to deal with the much larger firm following the merger.

Furthermore, once we had identified the staff who could do the job, it would have been sensible to have placed them under contract, at least to cover the merger period and a time thereafter to see us over any difficulties. We anticipated a certain amount of fall-out among staff following the merger, but it did not necessarily take place where it would have been most convenient.

If we were to merge again, we now appreciate that it is necessary not only to keep staff informed about the merger decision, but also to keep them persuaded that the merger is right for their future as well as for that of the partners. It goes without saying that this exercise has been performed among partners on a continuous basis, but a good deal of time and effort needs to be put in to keep the staff fully in the picture and comfortable with the merger.

There has been, of course, much hard work done after the actual merger, and more is required to be done. Integrating the different working practices of the two firms has had its amusing as well as its more prosaic side.

For example, one firm had a rule that women were not allowed to wear trousers and women from the other firm, where there had been no such rule, not unnaturally insisted on exercising their trouser wearing rights. This caused some embarrassment even at partner level.

Where the storage of wills was concerned, we decided to centralise in Newmarket, but found that one firm's envelopes would not go in the other firm's storage cabinets. It is little irritations like this which keeps the partnership executive and office service manager fully occupied!

Successful Mergers

By re-siting the Cambridge office out of the centre of the town, we caused some logistical problems, which were in fact anticipated. It was no longer possible to walk to the bank, nor could the staff do their shopping so readily. The former problem was resolved by concentrating banking in Newmarket and employing a messenger with a vehicle for inter-office deliveries. The latter was solved by hiring a coach for weekly shopping trips for staff.

It has been hard work, and will continue to be so, but we are optimistic for the future. We are one of the biggest firms in the area and, of greater importance, known as such to the profession and the public, as well as to our clients.

We have already had our first retreat as the merged firm, where we discussed a wide variety of subjects. These discussions took place entirely without acrimony and we all came back heartened by what we have achieved, and what we hope still further to achieve.

We feel that we have been able to merge together the diverse personalities and attributes of the partners and our two firms into something where the whole represents more than the sum of the two parts.

If I am to end with a caveat, it is that the expense of merger is far greater than either side will ever anticipate. The inevitable result is that we all have to work just as hard if not harder than before.

Philip Lionel Pardoe Swift

Born: 23rd May 1939 at Bristol

Educated at: Stone House, Broadstairs 1947-1952
Radley College, Abingdon 1952-1957
and Kings College, Cambridge 1957-1960

Graduated with 2 (ii) degree in Classics.

After travelling for a few months in America and Canada articled with Moore & Blatch, Lymington, Hampshire 1960-1963 and stayed with them until 1967 when moved to Taylors of Newmarket where he became partner in November 1968.

Married: 4th April 1964. Perdita Le Marchant Hutchesson with one daughter and two sons.

Interests: Golf, tennis, bridge, walking, ski-ing, water-sports, gardening, music, theatre.

14a Regional Groupings: M5 Group (A critical view)

The M.5 concept provides an interesting variation on merger. An equivalent would be putting one's toe in the water without actually immersing the rest of the body. To elaborate the metaphor, there is always scope to take the plunge later and the idea is obviously to obtain the benefits without some of the burdens and sacrifices that total merger requires.

Will it succeed? The M.5 Group currently brings together in a loose association five powerful provincial firms. There is no doubt that the firms chosen to date are forces in their own right in their own particular areas. It is noticeable that the accent to date is on the provinces and no firm in London has been asked to join.

It is worthwhile analysing whether this omission is a strength or a weakness. It is arguable that a London centre of equivalent strength, if also an independent firm, might draw into itself a lot of the talent and better clientele which currently resides with the constituent firms. For the moment, without a London centre, it could be said that the M.5 Group lacks real fighting power, and this must no doubt be a subject for debate among the partners concerned.

An alternative to linking up with an existing London firm might be for the current five constituent members jointly to establish a firm in London, or perhaps take over an existing one as its London entity. It must certainly be in the partners' minds that, without London, a number of important opportunities for advancement must be lost to the member firms, and hence the group as a whole. The group's current answer is that their firms currently have plenty of excellent commercial work, and who needs London anyway?

The M.5 concept is that the five member firms retain their separate identities and client bases. It is not expressed but presumably they also retain confidentiality about their internal finances vis-à-vis each other.

The group operates as 'M.5 Limited' with a co-ordinator, a recently appointed director of training, an information co-ordinator, and a growing support staff. The overheads must be fairly heavy, but, as the underlying firms are substantial, the contribution payable by each should not currently prove particularly onerous.

The publicised areas in which the M.5 Group is effective are information exchange, training, recruitment and publications.

The idea is to create a computerised database of legal information, which is available at the touch of a button to all members of the constituent firms. This will go considerably beyond the public databases and must obviously be advantageous, but depends on the willingness of those involved to commit their experiences to the computer. The concept goes well beyond the database and includes meetings of specialists within the group with a view, presumably, to providing a harmonised service.

All firms are now finding the need to provide some kind of inhouse training, not only for articled clerks, but also for assistant solicitors. The group has the resources and already lays on residential training conferences. It is obvious that the concepts of training and information exchange are inextricably linked.

The first M.5 Group advertisements for recruitment have now made their appearance. Whether or not these strengthen the appeal to potential employees of the constituent firms remains to be seen. The geographical spread may turn out to be a strength and presumably there will be a homogenity in the nature of the posts offered and the terms of service.

As the requirements of recruitment have already moved beyond mere advertising, the M.5 Group is well equipped to make presentations at universities with a view to attracting the better graduates to join its firms. Once again, recruitment and training go very much together and the group is currently able to present a strong appearance in this respect.

Many firms are currently toying with the concept of the newsletter. A number are deterred by the resources required to produce such a publication on a regular basis. The M.5 Group is already producing regularly its 'Law Review' and produces a number of other publications as well. It seems that these are over-printed or re-packaged in the house-style of the constituent firms and this is an example where togetherness is converted into separation rather than vice versa.

The M.5 Group obviously intends to grow and expand, but does this intended growth contain the beginning of its own downfall? At the moment, there does not seem to be any serious talk of merging the firms comprising the group. As the firms increase in number, so the headquarters staff will be able to spend less and less time servicing the individual outposts unless the size of the staff is increased drastically.

The question of value for money will then have to be considered by the constituent firms. If they continue to grow, then each firm will be faced with the fact that its peers have their own full time training officers, publication officers as well as all the other services which the M.5 Group currently offers its members. At that stage, it may be more economic to withdraw from the Group and provide those services at home rather than on the present shared basis.

In other words, the concept of the M.5 Group seems to be one which can only succeed on an interim basis. It provides part facilities for all its members, where in future they may wish to have a fully integrated service. Growth of the group or of its members may create its own problems. The alternative is the fully fledged merger, but this would demand the subordination of individual personalities, which the group presently allows to flourish.

There is no doubt that M.5 is an interesting experiment and we will all watch to see whether it is the first of a number of similar arrangements, or whether it merely turns out to be a brave but brief episode in the development of legal practice in the latter part of the twentieth century.

Michael Simmons

14b Regional Groupings: Eversheds

Evershed and Tomkinson, a major Birmingham firm, of which I am senior partner, had been thinking for some time about creating links with other firms in similar provincial centres. Our determination had not been very great but we were galvanised into action in the Autumn of 1987 by a number of factors which all suddenly became important at the same time.

1992 and the Unified Market were both looming, and we considered this to be a matter of great importance. The improvements in information technology increasingly made a linking of firms in different provincial centres perfectly viable. Our recruitment problems were growing, and we saw that these would be as nothing when the 'baby boom' came to an end.

Despite the well-publicised industrial slump in Birmingham and the West Midlands, my firm had been doing very well. This was probably at the cost of certain other local firms, and we could see that ours was a finite market. We could not go on prospering forever at the expense of others locally; we needed a larger market.

We decided to seek liaisons with other firms and we had certain parameters. There was no point looking to link too locally, as our market would be too small. We saw that there would be a community of interest with similar firms in other industrial areas. Shortly before Christmas, we started looking seriously.

We formed a planning group of between two and four partners within Evershed and Tomkinson. We looked round at the other major provincial centres to identify firms with a similar mix of work to our own. We decided that it was vital that they had similar high professional standards and they had to be firms which were strong in their own right.

We were targeting firms who were strong in commercial work. With the best will in the world, we did not want to accentuate the private client side. Ideally, we were looking for firms which offered uniform standards of performance to major commercial clients. We were seeking a merger with such firms and not a takeover. This meant that the firms in question had to be more or less on a par with our own.

We reached the identification stage very quickly. We approached Broomheads in Sheffield and with them created a joint committee of three from each firm. That committee prepared a brief concept paper

Regional Groupings: Eversheds

and a draft budget and on the basis of these other contacted firms. Daynes Hill and Perks in Norwich and Alexander Tatham in Manchester soon expressed an interest and it is a matter for comment that they displayed a remarkably similar thought process. In other words we were preaching to the already semi-converted.

It is easy to see for example that Sheffield and Manchester have much in common with Birmingham. Norwich is something of a case apart, but East Anglia had to be recognised as one of the fastest growing areas in the U.K. with strong European links both in fact and geography.

With the nucleus of four firms the announcement could be made. We always appreciated that others would join: indeed since the announcement Dibb Lupton in Leeds (by merger with Broomheads) as well as Phillips and Buck in Cardiff have become members.

In the most unlawyer-like manner, we started without a written agreement. We identified certain areas and issues that would have to be clarified and we set about trying to clarify them. One of the most important was uniform standards of work.

The parallel was that of the large firms of accountants who lay down certain parameters and check lists for all standard types of work. We had to establish that the firms which interested us were prepared to listen to that kind of talk and were, in fact, enthusiastic about adopting uniform standards of this nature. All the firms in question were not only interested, but enthusiastic. It was important that the imposition, for such it would be, would not be treated as a challenge to their virility. The answer was: 'we would welcome it'.

Of course, having established the will, it is an entirely different matter to establish the standards and set them down in writing. It will be done but we regard it as a medium term object – an ongoing enterprise. We found that the young associates and articled clerks were extremely receptive to the idea and they are keen to do it. We all realise how much work is involved in setting down these standards.

In all we identified and addressed about eighteen areas for discussion. One for example was what we feared would be the knotty problem of professional indemnity insurance. In fact it turned out to be the first major issue which was resolved. We made such good progress between the four firms that we decided to make the announcement.

It was made in mid-June and it is an announcement about what we intend to do to create the joint firm, rather than what we actually have done as yet. This shows the confidence which we have in each other and our joint ability to perform. We do not think that we will end up with egg on our faces, although we recognise the danger.

The firms concerned carry on under their existing identities, but we are working towards designing a package which will show our identity as one firm. For example we are all adopting notepaper of a similar design.

Each firm will have to consider local feelings and prejudices. We are all old, established firms in our own localities and it may be a slower or speedier business to move identities to Eversheds. In the first instance, the change will be from, say, Daynes Hill Perks to D H P Eversheds. Ultimately, D H P will be dropped from the name and Eversheds will be the name adopted by the Norwich firm.

The 21st of December 1991 is the final date for the change so that we are ready jointly as Eversheds to combat the challenges of the Uniform Market on 1st January 1992. Of course, the changes may have been completed earlier, but we are leaving the component firms to make their own decisions.

What will be the final moment of unity? The answer is that we do not yet know. Peat Marwick is regarded as a national firm, but it has seven different regional partnerships, which are separate profit centres, as its makeup. Is it any more or less a national firm than Ernst & Whinney, which is one partnership alone? We may well reach the Ernst & Whinney model in time, or we may stay on the Peat Marwick track. We do not know currently, nor do we know the time scale. Our view, frankly, is that it does not really matter. We are one firm whether with one profit centre or a number of profit centres.

At the moment each firm has taken its decision to proceed on the basis of heads of agreement and a quasi philosophical document which is called 'the explanatory memorandum'. This sets out thirteen problems which English lawyers generally and regional lawyers in particular, have to address with a view to finding solutions. It is a cross between heads of terms and a business plan. We all know what we are trying to achieve, and for what reasons. Originally we were unsure in certain respects how we were going to reach those goals; but the means of achieving our ends are being identified rapidly as we progress?

As to London, this will be the first practice which operates under the name Eversheds. We propose to join together the current offices of the constituent firms – there are in fact four. The joint office will consist of not less than 21 fee-earners and appropriate back-up staff.

We have to address the problems of profit sharing within that office and this is being dealt with as a priority.

Our first inter-office committee is the recruitment group. It was necessary to establish this early to achieve a joint policy for the purpose of recruiting articled clerks from the universities, and this has been remarkably successful.

Each firm has its own public relations and marketing activities. However Daynes Hill Perks had recently taken on a marketing manager

Regional Groupings: Eversheds

who so impressed the group as a whole that we asked (and DHP generously consented) for him to transfer and become our first marketing director. He is in fact our first employee.

Alexander Tatham in Manchester have a particular interest in the publication side. They are, therefore, taking on responsibility for training, publications and research. We will shortly be employing a director to co-ordinate those activities.

We also require a administration director to act as a progress chaser and problem solver. He or she will be appointed to work outside the ambit of the component firms. In fact, too much closeness with any one firm would be viewed as a problem.

We also view the harmonising of the information technology of the four firms as very important. In a similar manner, we have to create and integrate the client databases. This will be a task for a paragon as yet to be recruited. In fact, we have not even gone as far as writing the job specification.

In addition to the technical problems, there are professional problems until we merge as one firm. These relate to the Law Society requirements on client confidentiality. Obviously, we do not want one office operating in a conflict situation with another where clients are concerned. We can foresee that the computer in one office will have to interrogate the computer in the other office along the lines of the question which accountants now have professionally to ask of each other when taking on a new client: 'Is there any reason why we should not act for ... ?'

Each firm is taking responsibility for a number of key areas. Cardiff's brief is to define special subjects. We are looking for novel groupings of types of work. An example of this will be the creation of a unit combining pensions and trust work for the businessman. Once we have established the units, we then have to solve the problem of how to market them. We will be seeking a unique selling point. We may consider marketing by cold calling. Who knows? It is far too early to say.

It is going to be important to keep up momentum in order to make sure that the present high morale is maintained. It is all very exciting and novel at the moment, but we appreciate that it will not be that easy. Everybody will have a job to do in the scheme of things in relation to the merging of the four firms, as well as their normal day to day activities.

There will be dull patches, but these will be short, we hope, as we anticipate that there will be announcements regularly, for example about other firms joining us. We also anticipate that there will be other new initiatives which will require a good deal of work and which will

Successful Mergers

be announced regularly in the legal and national press.

Our first co-operation between two component firms took place on the day of the announcement itself. Alexander Tatham are, as most people know, prominent in acting for clients of Barlow Clowes. Their first public meeting at Manchester Town Hall required a good deal of manpower. We received a call at Evershed & Tomkinson to assist, and we sent up two articled clerks for a couple of weeks. They enjoyed their participation and Alexander Tatham were glad to have access to additional people 'within the family' at such short notice. We foresee many more joint operations, which will help to bind us into one unit.

We certainly are living in exciting times and we are confident that Eversheds will be one of the premier law firms in England for many years to come.

Peter Bromage. After education at Queen Mary's Grammar School, Walsall, and St. John's College, Cambridge, Peter Bromage became articled at Evershed & Tomkinson in 1955. He passed his finals in 1958 with Honours and a couple of prizes. In 1960 he became the youngest partner ever appointed at Evershed & Tomkinson. In subsequent years he has mainly been involved with commercial work (patents, trade marks, commercial drafting, building contracts, etc.) and litigation. In latter years there has been added to this security work for banks and other institutional lenders. In 1984 he was elected Senior Partner of the firm.

In such little spare time as his partners and clients allow him he is involved in the administration of cricket and rugby football. In the former, as well as being a member of the Warwickshire Committee he is chairman of the Discipline Committee of the Test and County Cricket Board. In the latter he is a member of the committee of the Rugby Union and currently is concentrating on the problems of re-building Twickenham. He also plays golf and bridge.

15 Mid-sized firm taking over smaller firms: Malkin Cullis & Sumption

I joined the firm in 1961 as a stepping-stone, as I thought, to greater things. Having qualified in 1958, I had my professional progress interrupted by a two-year stint as a National Service officer in the Royal Air Force. At a time when National Service was being phased out, it was hardly the most stimulating of experiences, but I was given (although I did not realise it at the time), some basic management training with particular reference to structure of organisations and how to get the best out of staff.

I was fortunate in being put on the notepaper as a salaried partner on joining, but I found myself with a senior partner/sole proprietor, two secretaries and a part-time accountant. This was hardly a recipe for greatness!

A year later, I became an equity partner, and two years afterwards, at the tender age of twenty nine, sole proprietor of what was a small City firm. My mentor and former senior partner had retired to do, as he thought, better things. He certainly considered that there was a life other than the law! By then, my ambitions were to create the entity in five years, which has, in fact, taken twenty five years to put together.

Whatever other talents I had at the time, these did not include necessarily picking winners so far as partners and staff were concerned. However, in spite of my mistakes, the firm managed to grow. People of better calibre joined, and – of vital importance – stayed.

Geographically, we moved over the years from the City gently westward. Circumstances, in the shape of an insistent developer, caused us to move from our comfortable offices in Trafalgar Square to our present premises in Covent Garden. At the time, we were doing very well, and there was a tremendous spirit of optimism in the firm. The fact that the new offices were twice as big as we really needed did not seem much of a problem. There was some very good work about and we were confident that we would expand to fill those premises.

Within six months of the move, we lost our most productive client

Successful Mergers

in somewhat traumatic circumstances and, after the initial rent-free period, we were faced with the overheads of these far larger and prestigious premises. Rather than sublet part, which would do little more than cover overheads, the answer was to find a suitable merger. As a general practice, we looked for a similar practice of somewhat smaller size.

Almost three years later after much hard searching, I was introduced through a merger agency to Cripps Harries, a relatively small Lincoln's Inn firm. The senior partners had all reached retirement age together, and, of the four equity partners remaining, one wished to leave. The average age of the partners was about thirty four, which fitted nicely with our structure.

The practice mix was very similar and they had the advantage of some large and long established clients. Our own growth rate had been such that we had hardly had the time to develop a constant clientele, and ours was still very much a transactional practice.

Any other twenty-nine year old sole-practitioner, who wishes not only to survive but expand, will tell the same story, that it is necessary to learn and practise marketing skills very quickly. This was one of the Malkin Cullis strengths, which was, in effect, a first generation firm. Cripps Harries, on the other hand, was in the second phase of development with partners doing the work of institutional clients.

The introduction was effected in February 1985 and each side put forward a committee of one. Fortunately, the two of us had a very similar viewpoint and method of working. Points were raised and disposed of with almost bewildering rapidity. Where we did not agree, the matter was put aside for reference back to our partners. Obviously, not everything was simple, and there were points of obstruction in the steady flow towards consensus.

Our respective office managers were put in touch with each to discuss the 'nuts and bolts' of the proposed merger. We both referred back to our accountants and they were put in touch with each other. We agreed that we would not concern ourselves with the post-tax merger situation of the other firm. We had enough to do sorting out our own tax situation as a result of the proposed merger, but we were of course vitally concerned to see that the new merged firm started off on the right foot so far as taxation was concerned.

Initially we exchanged audited accounts covering the last four years together with a written screed of general information. This included a breakdown of fees by percentages. We also exchanged management accounts up to the latest available date and our current brochures.

The first meeting was between the two moving spirits, but was followed very quickly by meetings between all the partners on both sides.

Mid-sized firm taking over smaller firms: Malkin Cullis & Sumption

As both firms were relatively small, in the sense that we had seven equity partners then and they had three, it was possible to move speedily through the acclimatisation stage, and also through the financial aspects.

On the latter front, there was not much which concerned the other unduly. Our year ends differed by one month, while our accounting bases and respective tax situations gave no great cause for concern.

With negotiations being conducted through such small committees on either side, it was important that there should be total communication with the other partners, who were, of course, vitally interested. This was done on both sides by daily, or sometimes twice daily, bulletins in the form of confidential memoranda, supported, where appropriate, by copy documents.

One problem which affected us initially was that one of our partners was on holiday abroad. We decided to make the merger decision in principle very speedily indeed. The absence of one of our number was something of an embarrassment, and necessitated sending one of the longest telexes ever received in Switzerland. Fortunately, he has always been very reasonable and he did not disappoint us on this occasion.

In fact, when I review the file, I see that the merger decision was made within two weeks of our first meeting. Is this a record? It was always understood that this was a decision in principle only, and either side had the right to withdraw without giving a reason at any time up to the signing of the heads of agreement.

Our accountant was asked to look at the projections, which both sides prepared for the coming year, as well as the past accounts of both firms with a view to producing a pro-forma balance sheet and profit and loss account, together with budgetary and cash-flow forecasts for the coming year. Both firms' banks were informed of the proposed merger and the decision was made which of the two was to be the banker for the merged firm.

Concurrent discussions were taking place with regard to the library and insurance arrangements generally. The next few months were a flurry of activity. The principal partner on either side was keen to delegate specific areas of the merger to others, merely for the purpose of remaining relatively sane.

Our best draftsman was given the task of redrafting our partnership deed to take into account the merger and the revised terms of partnership generally, which also had to be negotiated. There hardly seemed to be sufficient hours in the day to deal with all the aspects of the merger and also the day to day affairs of our clients.

I produced the first rough draft of the heads of agreement and submitted it to Iain Harris at Cripps Harries for his views. It came back

Successful Mergers

very quickly looking much more like a legal document!

We left it to our office managers to compare our respective contracts of employment. There were good points in each and a partner was given the task of preparing a new contract which would be acceptable to both sets of staff.

By sheer good fotrune, there was only one piece of litigation current where our firms were acting for plaintiff and defendant respectively. Both clients were informed of the impending merger and advised to seek new solicitors.

Plans were prepared showing the new seating arrangements and the Cripps Harries staff, who were to be joining us, were given conducted tours of our office during the lunch hours. They were introduced to as many of our staff as possible and shown where they would be sitting. Various after-hours drinks parties were arranged for the more senior members of the staff of each firm to get to know each other.

The announcement of the proposed merger was made to the staff of both firms immediately after the partners had agreed in principle to go ahead. This was practical in our firms, but might not be so in larger partnerships.

I have referred elsewhere to the need to have complete disclosure. Very few firms are without their negligence or potential negligence claims. We exchanged details of ours and decided that there was nothing particularly to concern us.

Iain Harris and I were also busily at work on re-drafting the brochure as we wanted to use the announcement of the merger as effectively as possible to market the new firm.

On the financial front, it was agreed that both firms would bill as much of their work-in-progress as possible down to the merger date, which was agreed at 31st May 1985, our year end. This left Cripps Harries with a thirteen month year, but their accountants stated that this would cause no difficulty.

Obviously, some matters on both sides were incapable of billing at that date. In those cases, the work-in-progress had to be valued on each file, so that, when the bill was finally rendered and paid after completion of the matter, the funds received could be apportioned between the new merged firm and the firm from which the work had originated. In the case of Cripps Harries, this meant that a dissolution account had to be maintained after merger, and this was of course provided for in the heads of agreement.

As discussions continued new points kept coming up for consideration; for example storage of deeds and files had to be dealt with and the most economic and practical solution agreed.

Fortunately, there were no problems about the order of seniority of

Mid-sized firm taking over smaller firms: Malkin Cullis & Sumption

the partners, or the promotion prospects of senior employees in both firms. At junior staff level, certain savings were being made with regard to receptionists and others. It so happened that the last in, first out, principle accorded with the relative efficiency of the personnel of both firms, so this was effected almost painlessly and also to the best economic effect.

Meanwhile, the draft heads of agreement were going back and forth as new points had to be inserted, or old points amended.

We then found that we had to consider the change of registered offices of companies which Cripps Harries managed, and notice of change had to be served in all Cripps Harries litigation matters. Where Legal Aid was concerned, we had to put in hand arrangements to inform the appropriate offices.

I have mentioned elsewhere that cars can create a disproportionate difficulty in the merger negotiations. Such problems as there were here were speedily considered and solved.

By the beginning of April, each firms' amalgamation file was enormous. However, there were very few points still to be agreed and Iain Harris and I sat down to prepare the various merger announcements. April was no less busy than March had been and the daily letters and memoranda were continually being overtaken by events.

At the administrative level, we were seeking quotations for the move, dealing with the discontinuation of telephone lines, while ensuring that all calls were appropriately referred. There were sudden panics created by the accountants on taxation, which had to be overcome with a little diplomacy and detachment.

The heads of agreement were in their final form and ready for signing, but somehow we never actually managed to sign! Things were moving at such a pace that 31st May arrived, and the move was effected over the weekend. Circulars and party invitations flew in all directions. As a prudent senior partner should, I made certain that I was as far away as possible from Covent Garden during what must have been a traumatic weekend. I can only speak from second-hand knowledge! Suffice it to say that I walked into my office on Monday morning and, apart from the fact that a number of previously empty rooms were filled with not very familiar faces, work carried on as hitherto.

We 'bedded down' very quickly indeed with our new partners. Some six months later, I was talking to a professional colleague at a cocktail party and he asked me how the merger was going. I was totally at a loss to understand the subject of his question. I thought for a moment that he was talking about the current activities of one of our more prominent corporate clients. It was only after a long pause in the conversation, that I realised that he was referring to our own merger. The truth of the matter is that I had forgotten that the merger had taken place, which must be the proof of its very success.

About two months after merger day, we had a superb garden party, with far too many people present, to celebrate the event. It was obvious that the merger was warmly welcomed by all. I do not think that any of us has ever regretted it. The name Cripps Harries has now been removed from our newly designed notepaper, and we no longer talk about them and us. We are one firm.

Encouraged by our efforts and by the fact that there was still empty space in our offices, we decided to seek yet another merger. However, our brief this time was totally different. The space available was far less, and we reckoned that we wanted to increase our commercial strength by absorbing a small firm with specialist company and commercial work.

Through the same agent, we were introduced to Ralph Haring & Co. Ralph Haring was a sole practitioner with two assistants and two secretaries. He specialises in taxation and construction work. Once again, the courtship was relatively brief. With our past experience and, as this firm was a much smaller entity, the deal was done very simply.

We were able to produce draft heads of agreement using the Cripps Harries model and there was nothing in it which was objectionable to Ralph. Once again, negotiations took less than three months from start to finish and he joined us on 1st August 1986 with his staff, all of whom were absorbed into our building.

He has probably had more problems as a sole practitioner in adjusting to the differences of a larger partnership, than we have had in absorbing him into our midst. It is always difficult for the sole practitioner to concentrate on specialist work having been hitherto a generalist. There are always certain clients who have looked to you for all their legal work in the past, and do not take particularly kindly, at least at the outset, to being passed on to others in the firm. However, Ralph is now learning the art and has integrated fully into our ways.

There is no doubt that the merger, even when it amounts to takeover, does not mean that the philosophy and culture of the dominant firm in terms of size remains unchanged. We have been considerably influenced by the personalities of our new partners and we are by no means the same as we were before either merger. Those changes include a broadening of the partnership base and hence its outlook. This has been for the best.

What does the future hold in store? We have now expanded to the point where we have taken a floor in an office building opposite, but are still two executives to a room. The time will shortly come when we will have to move again.

Mid-sized firm taking over smaller firms: Malkin Cullis & Sumption

We would like to take the opportunity to use that move to find a suitable firm with which to effect another merger. If we cannot find such a firm, we will go on as we are, and we are aware that we must not delude ourselves into thinking that any old firm is suitable, merely to achieve greater size on moving offices. Our ideal specification is a firm half our size with a strong corporate and commercial side. This is probably everyone else's ideal at the moment in this age of merger mania.

While we feel that we know the London scene fairly well, we are also aware of the fact that firms are changing rapidly. Thus a firm which we would have categorised a few years ago as sleepy and uninteresting, may now be a prime candidate. Equally, last year's dynamic market leader may no longer be what we are seeking. The only way to seek a merger partner is in a relatively relaxed frame of mind. Others may be frantically looking, but we are not going to fall into that particular trap, or so we hope.

This chapter may have to be re-written if there is a further edition of this book. I must use a phrase from another professional culture: 'Watch this space'.

Michael Simmons

16 Small firms: Townsend Livingston

When all around are amalgamating, merging or being taken over, it is a brave firm which can ignore the trend. This is not to say that one follows it, but it ought to be examined in order to ascertain if there are benefits to be had from joining that trend.

Before the merger, the constituent partners have to convince themselves that there are to be benefits. The danger afterwards is that these brightly perceived objectives become blurred in the new relationships, methodology and administrative burdens which the enlarged partnership has to face.

Our merger was not to achieve economies of scale, reduce office overheads or acquire expertise in foreign fields. It derived from the long held feeling of a number of the more senior partners that a broader base and more widely spread influence had to be the best way of achieving the continued prosperity of the firm. Our constituent offices very rarely had much litigious conflict, nor did we find any evidence of major clients being in opposition.

To set the scene and perspective, the pre-merger situation was like this:

Firm A consisted of a 4 partner firm, employing some 20 staff (including 4 executive fee earners and one articled clerk) with one office in a busy industrial town.

Firm B was a 3 partner firm, employing the very recently retired senior partner as a part time consultant and 11 staff (3 of these were young, inexperienced executives) again with one office in a busy market town some 8 miles from A.

Several decisions about future working practices and reorganisation were taken in the many meetings between the partners in the run up to Merger (or M) Day. The first decision was the easiest, and preceded M Day by some few weeks. It was to follow Michael Simmons' strong advice that we should employ an office manager. A young graduate in economics, who had opted out of articles to our office auditors and become a local authority manager was duly head hunted and she has proved a gem.

Prior to M Day, partners' meetings had been largely ad hoc affairs, and office administration had been left to delegated secretaries, a senior clerk and crisis response. Now we were being organised into formal and regular meetings, well before M Day, with minutes taken and circulated, jobs allocated to two or three partners or, more often than not, to the office manager. The mechanics of putting office B on to the accounts computer was relatively painless and we were up and running within a week.

The advent of regular management information was, to the new partners, both a revelation and a scourge. It soon threw up the unpalatable fact that, in office B, whilst it seemed that the litigator was busy, the figures did not show it. On the other hand, it helped to provide comfort to the doubting (there must always be some) that the other partners were pulling their weight.

Within four months the junior partner (from firm B) felt he would be better on his own, and off he went, with a secretary and a clerk. We wish him well, but doubt his wisdom.

The benefit of the merger was then proved to the remaining partners in office B. A shift system comprising two partners and a legal executive from firm A took firm B's litigation department into its bosom and got it on to an even keel. It now needs a dedicated litigator in that office, who can relieve the pressure on the other partners who would prefer to be concentrating on other matters. At first we wondered about letting the department run on a default basis, but soon realised that that was not the ethos we had epoused and set about advertising (at the time of writing the first advert has been placed and it remains to be seen whether country can outwoo town).

What sort of decisions did we take before M Day, have they been followed up and have they contributed to success? It is difficult to determine whether the mere fact of amalgamating of itself attracts new work and clients or whether we chose a time of local and national expansion which would have resulted in extra work in any event. Be that as it may, some of the more fundamental decisions which all who tread this path need to take are:

Specialisation

Small country practices seldom have specialist practitioners outside probate, conveyancing and crime. We can now concentrate on upgrading our tax, commercial and litigation expertise. Save for exceptional cases (and a little indulging of existing clients, on a decreasing scale) criminal work has been abandoned.

Supervision

Partners have been given responsibility for supervising the different departments, although it must be said that there has not been an overnight transition of partners into managers. On account of the distance between the two offices, supervisory visits tend to have been from firm A to firm B to assist in the litigation sort out, but otherwise canoes are still being paddled as before. The excuse is always pressure of work, but as the point is always at the top of the agenda for our monthly meetings, as one of the 'matters arising', it will shortly be dealt with properly. Staff leaving, retiring or going long-term sick all contribute to hastening the activation of this decision.

Rationalisation

Computerised accounting being imported into firm B has been mentioned already. Other matters involved assessing the merit of each member of staff and deciding what his or her future was with the firm, centralising the purchase of many of the hefty and expensive annual tomes and equalising working hours and holiday entitlement and salary structures. The changes brought about have been accepted readily by the staff in both offices and at no great cost.

So far we have considered, but rejected a dedicated telephone land line between offices, although it will remain on the agenda. Firm B is now on Fax. Firm A is having to look hard at its probate costing.

Equalisation

At first sight, the equalisation of the several partners' interests seemed quite daunting.

1. Firm A had abandoned goodwill several years ago, firm B had not only retained it but had also contracted to pay a large chunk of it to the recently retired partner, by instalments.
2. The freeholds of the respective office premises were owned by the four partners of firm A and by the senior two in firm B (subject to paying out the retired partner for his share). The value of office A was almost twice that of B.
3. The junior partner of firm B had just paid for a share of goodwill (to the other two partners of that firm) and was contracted in the old partnership to pay for and receive a further (equalising) share

some ten months after the merger.
4. Firm B was taxed on a cash basis whilst firm A was assessed on bills rendered.
5. We employed different accountants and used different banks.
6. Firm A had moved heavily into delegation of much of the routine work, whereas firm B was still partner intensive in its approach.
7. Firm A had been trading with the assistance of a medium term bank loan for a number of years. Firm B had no bank borrowings and substantial partners' capital accounts in consequence.

The merger would not have succeeded if individually and corporately we had not been prepared to bite one or more bullets in order to resolve the foregoing problems, and this we did in the following way.

1. The two senior partners of firm B manfully decided to write off the goodwill for which they had paid relatively dearly, and in the case of the younger one, quite recently. The net profitability of the two firms, per capita, was quite similar, weighed slightly in favour of firm A perhaps, and that made the decision a little easier.
2. Michael Simmons brought logic to bear in dealing with the office values, pointing out that when respectively divided by the number of equity partners, there was not sufficient difference to worry about.
3. The junior partner of firm B had to to agonize over the prospect of 'losing' the goodwill payment he had so recently had to make (in fact it had yet to be made when the merger talks began) but he appreciated that after merger he lost the liability to make a further payment for goodwill. He was told that he would need to make an equivalent payment (by bank borrowing if necessary) to boost the firm's working capital. That he left after 4 months and reclaimed his goodwill payment from the former partners of firm B may, or may not be significant.
4. The differing methods of accounting for costs has caused our accountants something of a headache, mainly because of payments due to the retired partner of firm B. This to me is incidental – the numbers will eventually sort themselves out.
5. The banks presented a more interesting question. We felt, and still feel, that to spread the benefit of our client account is sensible and with a ready made split between the two firms already in existence, neither banker was going to feel that he had lost part of the account or be aggrieved. On the other hand, we were able to take a fresh look at the relationship with the banks and take a more aggressive stance, on the subject of recommendations

particularly, with one of them.

As for the accountants, the two firms continue to wind up the old A & B accounts and agree an opening balance sheet. In this connection our office manager has been of enormous assistance to both sets of accountants in obtaining and preparing the figures and keeping them on the ball. After this exercise has been concluded, firm A's accountants will audit the new firm's books, leaving the old firm B partners to take personal advice from their accountant as they clearly know him better.

6. The delegation of work is often a difficult nettle for a solicitor to grasp. The advantages have been acknowledged by those not previously experienced in this way of working, but the staff training and acceptance of the system have yet to be achieved.
7. The partners of firm B quickly embraced the advantage of freeing their capital for personal use, and arranged a loan to equate with that in place in firm A.

One of our senior members has now produced a first draft of a five year plan, with several thoughts on expansion. With the possibility of incorporation in the near future, this takes on an added interest, not to say attraction.

In fine, the rationale behind the amalgamation of two country practices, from neighbouring towns, has to be one of projecting to the public a greater competence and solidity. Properly executed, it should bring early success, but be prepared to have to recruit extra staff equally early. Seven months into the merger, we recognise that there are many tasks yet to complete, but the first and essential one of trusting and inspiring each other has mainly been fulfilled. Projected costs figures are holding up and we are looking forward to the challenge of the FSA and FIMBRA.

Alan Dunn

Admitted 1958. Practised in Liverpool for 8 years and in Barrow-in-Furness ever since.

Sometime (part time) Registrar of Barrow-in-Furness group of County Courts; sometime assistant recorder.

Now full time partner in recently created 6 partner firm in Barrow and Ulverston.

Married with 5 sons – occasionally finds time for the odd round of golf.

Small firms: Townsend Livingston

"I believe in multi-discipline practices but also consider that an advocate performs better if he does not have too direct a contact with the client. The present system is intended to ensure that the solicitor keeps the daily hassle away from counsel."

Part 4
POST-MERGER

17 Post-Merger Accounts

It will be quite common for a merger to be agreed in principle, for all the publicity to be despatched, press releases issued and in fact a common name adopted well before the accounting systems are integrated and any attention is given to the format of the accounts of the merged firm. This is largely to be expected.

It is frequently unwise for there to be a great deal of delay between the announcing of a merger – to the firm's staff and to the world at large – and its consummation, and there are more important things to attend to than accounts.

Furthermore, a merger commences the day after the two predecessor firms cease and it will be some months until, in the normal course of events, the final accounts of the predecessor partnerships have been prepared, reviewed and presented to the partners. It is therefore likely to be in the period after the merged firm has commenced to trade that attention will be directed towards the accounts of the ongoing entity.

Establishing the opening position

By the time that the merger has been effected, agreement will have been reached by the two firms as to the basis of accounting to be adopted by the merged firm. The implications of the various choices confronting the two firms if they do not already account on the same basis have been discussed fully in chapter 7. Ideally, any changes to be introduced by one firm or the other will already have been incorporated at the relevant firm's last accounting date and the move by either or both of the firms to the accounting date to be adopted by the merged firm will also have been made already.

There may remain, however, the need for the assets of the two firms to be valued on a consistent basis in their final accounts, and for the tax reserves of the two firms to be prepared on the same basis.

We will be concerned here with the valuation of fixed assets. As discussed in Chapter 7, if the depreciation policies of the two firms have been widely divergent, it will be necessary for the fixed asset records of one of the firms to be re-created so that depreciation on recent additions can be charged at the same rate as has been adopted by the other firm and will be adopted within the merged firm. Any revaluation surpluses or deficits arising from this exercise will be credited or debited to the relevant partners' capital accounts.

A common policy for the provision for doubtful debts should be considered. Practice will vary as between firms as, indeed, will their experience of bad debts. While it is always possible, after the merger, to charge a large bad debt specifically against the share of profits of the partners of the relevant predecessor firm, it is to be hoped that these kind of adjustments can be avoided (unless, of course, they are very significant) and this is best ensured by each firm appraising rigorously the collectability of its debts.

Alternatively, if a formula basis of providing for doubtful debts has been used by one firm — for example a provision may be made for all debts older than six months — it may be appropriate to adopt this in the final accounts of each firm. The other most likely area where practice between the two firms may differ is in the tax reserving policy of each firm. A full treatise on the merits of various forms of reserving for the partners' tax liabilities is not appropriate here, but it is likely that variations on one of the following methods will have been used by each firm:

1. the statutory liability basis;
2. the forward reserving basis; or
3. the discontinuance basis.

In the first of these options, the partners' current accounts are merely charged with their share of the firm's statutory liability on the preceding year basis for those parts of each fiscal year which the accounting year spans. Thus if a reserve was required for the year ended 30 June 1988, partners would be charged with 75% of their share for 1987/88 liability and 25% of their share of the 1988/89 liability, with each liability calculated on the preceding year basis. This will give a very minimum reserve and could be regarded as being imprudent. This is because, if profits are rising and a discontinuance was contemplated for any reason — most probably through a desire at some stage to incorporate the business — the amounts set aside would prove to be inadequate to meet the firm's liabilities.

Some firms will recognise the impact of the preceding year basis of assessment by attempting to reserve for the tax liability for the fiscal year, for which the accounting year will form the basis period in the normal course of events. Thus in relation to a year ending 30 April 1988, such firms would attempt to provide for the 1989/90 income tax liability which will be based on that year's adjusted profit.

This is a highly conservative basis and has great practical difficulty inasmuch as the rates of tax, allowances and reliefs — and indeed the partners who will share the assessement — cannot be known for a future year. It is a particularly hard basis to apply to new partners to the firm, and inevitably compromise arrangements have to be worked out, thereby making the reserving policy difficult to comprehend.

The basis recommended by the author is one which assumes that the firm is discontinued at the accounting date so that, when profits are rising, tax is reserved on a current year basis. This basis gives comfort to the partners that there will normally be sufficient reserves set aside within the firm to meet the partners' tax liabilities come what may, and it also has the advantage of charging partners, year by year, tax which is directly related to the share of profit which is being credited to their current accounts. When profits are rising, the amount charged to partners will exceed the amounts which have to be paid away on the preceding year basis, and these 'excess tax reserves' form a valuable source of working capital for the business until they are released back to partners' current accounts once it is known for sure that they will not be required to be paid away to the Inland Revenue.

It will be apparent that the tax reserving policy of a firm will affect not only the amounts set aside in each partner's tax reserve account but also the balance left on his current account which is therefore, hopefully, available to be withdrawn once the accounts are finalised. Firms which have been in the habit of reserving on the first of the bases described, the least conservative one, may find that their current accounts are unduly depleted if they have to move over to, for example the discontinuance basis.

The final accounts of each of the predecessor firms, if prepared on a consistent basis, will show balances due to partners on their capital, current and tax reserve accounts on exactly the same basis, and will therefore enable a comparison to be made of the amounts of capital which each partner is contributing to the merged firm. It will then be necessary to see what adjustments have to be made by one firm or the other in order to move towards the position where partners are contributing capital to the business in proportion to their share in the residual profits.

The capital requirements

Before action can be taken to bring partners' capital accounts into line within the merged firm, there has to be agreement on the amount of capital which the ongoing business is going to require. That capital will come, broadly, from two sources; the partners themselves and the firm's bankers. It is quite likely that the philosophy of the two firms with respect to the provision of capital will be different. How much of the total requirement should be provided by the partners and how much should be borrowed?

Before that question can be answered, an attempt will need to be made to establish the capital requirements of the ongoing business. This will require profit and cash flow forecasts to be prepared showing the movement in the firm's cash position on a monthly basis. This will indicate the peaks and troughs in the firm's cash flow, and the partners then have to decide whether the firm's existing bank facilities are sufficient to cover the anticipated troughs.

This is where the different philosophies of the firms may be in conflict. One firm may traditionally have taken the view that they should never be overdrawn at the bank or else the partners feel they cannot sleep at night. The other firm may adopt the policy of treating the partners as the lenders of last resort, preferring to use, as far as possible, bank overdraft facilities. The capital accounts of the firm with the first philosophy will be relatively large compared with those who prefer to use bank facilities to a greater extent.

Inevitably, the reconciliation of possibly conflicting philosophies will require compromise on each side. In the author's opinion, capital accounts should be kept to a minimum consistent with the efficient running of the business, but should be large enough to ensure that the firm's profits can be distributed in full to the partners (after proper provision has been made by way of tax reserves) within a very few months after the end of the accounting year. The author's preference is for a tax reserve on the discontinuance basis, and once this has been charged to partners' current accounts, the remaining balance should be capable of being distributed promptly to partners. If that is not possible, this is an indication that the partners' fixed capital accounts are inadequate. Indeed balances shown on current accounts which are not freely withdrawable are really fixed capital accounts by another name.

If tax reserves are prepared on a consistent basis and the current accounts of each firm are genuinely withdrawable, the balance remaining to the credit of partners' accounts will be their fixed capital accounts. It will be normal for the firm to require these to be proportionate to partners' shares in the residual profits, and on the amalgamation of the accounts of the two firms, some adjustment will inevitably be required.

Those partners with deficient capital accounts should be able to borrow to supplement these; interest on such borrowings will be allowable as a deduction for income tax purposes. Alternatively – and possibly more rarely – it may prove to be possible for partners with capital accounts in excess of their required contribution, to withdraw that excess.

These adjustments to capital accounts do not have to be made at one go, and by mutual agreement the partners may decide that the move towards the required capital contribution can be phased over a period of a year or two. This would dictate, however, that a prior share of the profits should be allocated to partners by way of notional interest on capital. If this notional interest is fixed at a market rate of interest, partners with capital in excess of their requirement will enjoy a proper rate of return on that excess contribution, while the amount credited to partners whose capital contribution is below the ultimately required amount will be correspondingly small.

In all these matters, the personal cash flow of the individual partners must be sensibly considered. There is nothing more likely to switch off a partner than to be told that an enormous capital contribution is required immediately or, alternatively, that he can expect no drawings for several months! It may therefore take more than just the first year to work towards the ideal capital position as dictated by the firm's budgeting processes.

Management accounts

The discussion so far in this chapter has been in relation to the financial accounts which, by definition, are largely historical. While good disciplines in relation to the preparation of financial accounts are, of course, important, the management of the new firm will require up-to-date financial information to enable sensible management action to be taken. In this area, too, the bringing together of two firms will inevitably require careful co-ordination.

As soon as possible after the merger, a single management accounting function should be established with clearly-defined reporting procedures. The corresponding departments of the two firms should start reporting financial information on the same basis as soon as possible and profit and cost centres incorporating all the activities of the two firms should be put in place promptly.

The merging of departments from the point of view of management accounting will not of itself achieve the integration of complementary departments in the two firms, but it should assist in that integration process which is so important for the success of the merger.

Drawings and other benefits

While the matters discussed in this section do not perhaps fall properly under the heading of post-merger accounts, in the author's opinion, they can assume a disproportionate importance in partners' minds and therefore need to be addressed at an early stage. A drawings policy is, of course, essential for any firm and should be formalised. Proper financial control of a practice cannot be exercised if partners are free to draw on account of profit in an unregulated way. The policy to be adopted within the merged firm should therefore be established at an early stage and should be thoroughly understood by all partners.

There can be no single 'correct' drawings policy, and each firm will determine its own. However, it may be appropriate for relatively modest monthly drawings to be made to enable partners to meet their regular commitments, and for a more substantial payment on account of the profit for the year to be made once the half-year's accounts have been drawn up and approved. A final distribution of profit should be made, as already indicated, once the firm's annual accounts have been approved by the partners.

The most emotive area within partnerships is quite frequently the partners' car scheme. Inevitably if only one firm has a policy of providing partners with cars, the merged firm will need to extend those or similar arangements to the partners of the other firm. It would be rare indeed for partners to volunteer to give up the benefit of being provided with a firm's car even though, in some instances, the tangible benefits of the firm providing the car, in terms of the tax reliefs afforded, are relatively small. The benefits enjoyed by partners from participating in a firm's car scheme may, to a dispassionate outsider, seem more apparent than real. However, if partners of one firm believe them to be real, they will be unwilling to relinquish these rights, and inevitably the car scheme will need to be extended.

In some firms, partners may have some of their personally incurred expenses, such as part of the home telephone bill, reimbursed, or may receive a round sum allowance to cover minor out of pocket expenses. Such allowances will normally have been approved by the Inland Revenue as allowable for tax purposes to avoid the necessity of partners keeping detailed records of minor items of allowable business expenditure.

Following a merger, the partners will look to enjoy the better of the two deals which may have been negotiated with the predecessor firms' Inspector of Taxes on such items. This should normally be possible so long as the benefits provided are reasonable. Some of the benefits provided, such as private medical insurance premiums, have no pretence of being tax-efficient, but again a merger will inevitably mean providing such benefits consistently across the firm.

Nigel Davey

18 Marketing the Merged Practice

There may well be a number of motivations for professional firms to merge but from the clients' point of view they will be seeking selfishly, but understandably, an answer to the question: 'What's in it for me?' Clients buy benefits, not features and their interest in any merger goes very little beyond perceiving how the changes, which inevitably will occur, will affect the quality, in the widest sense of that word, of the service they receive, and of course value for money.

The merging firms must undertake a vital piece of introspection, inspection and auditing. To offer benefits they have to make an objective assessment of any unique competences, resources or advantages which every firm possesses in some measure. They need to satisfy themselves as to the answer to one vital question: 'Why should anyone retain our merged firm?'. Answers such as integrity, efficiency, competence and commitment are simply the basic requirements of all clients. The 'plus' has to be something else that will convince them to stay with the merged practice or which will attract new clients.

Although the main purpose is to audit the combined firms' strengths which, at the very least, will be as great as the individual practices, it should not be assumed that this will be so. A merger can produce weaknesses as well as strengths.

For the purpose of practice development, resources can be grouped under eight headings:

1. People – skills, qualifications, interests and experiences.
2. Information – internal, environmental.
3. Infrastructure and hardware – word processors, computers, mechanised and electronic equipment, premises, etc.
4. Finance.
5. Systems.
6. Clients and referral sources.
7. Images and perceptions of the practice and its personnel.
8. Services available.

There are, of course, others but identifying and evaluating these will be of only indirect value for the purpose of marketing.

The audit will be improved if all members of the firm are involved in undertaking what is known as a SOFT analysis. This is an acronym

Successful Mergers

for Strength; Opportunity; Fault; Threat and simply requires members of the practice to identify single issues under each heading, such as those listed in the figure below, with references, sources and facts and asking for a range of possible action or resource requirements. This will usually produce a consensus of views but even a single issue which has been overlooked can make a valuable input. Any patterning of response should provide action indications to exploit or avoid a situation and can be set out as in the example below.

(One form for each point raised)
The following is one factor in our firm's future

1. Name _____ Job title _____
2. This issue refers to a: (tick one only)

    Strength ☐   Opportunity ☐

    Fault ☐   Threat ☐

    In our (tick one only)
    Fee and/or non-fee earnings staff ☐

    Administration and/or management ☐

    Clients ☐

    Location or physical facilities ☐

    Technology range and/or quality of services ☐

    Other (specify) ☐

3. Description of statement or point
4. References, sources or facts
5. Range of possible action or resources requirements

The next step is the conversion of the features into benefits. That is the message clients and prospective clients are looking for. Examples of the conversion of features to benefits is given opposite.

    This is not quite such a simple exercise as it might seem since the same features may produce different benefits for different types of clients and, conversely, might generate disadvantages. The conversion of features to benefits must be undertaken from the viewpoint of individual clients or client types.

    The last part of the exercise is to establish which clients are most likely to obtain the maximum advantage from the benefits now on offer. This is called 'profiling' and it is not difficult to undertake.

Marketing the Merged Practice

Features of professional service	Benefits to the client
Expertise in tax law	Higher retained profit or income
Financial skills	Problem solution
Excellent relations with other practices (inter- and intra-professional)	Quick results
Interdisciplinary skills	Assumption of responsibility
Commercial knowledge and experience	More efficient business operations
Advanced diagnostic techniques	Reduction of stress

The best clients of each of the merging firms should be identified, 'best' being interpreted by whatever criteria are appropriate. The profile of these clients can be drawn and that is, for example, by size, form or organisation, extent of specialisation, activity (for business clients) and perhaps psychographic factors, location and demography (for private clients).

If a match is now attempted between the benefits which have been identified and the clients' needs and, so far as the information is available for non-clients, it can be seen at once which clients are likely to be retained, those that are at risk and which types of new clients would be attracted. This analysis also permits the merged firms to see what benefits they must generate to hold or obtain clients. For most practices it will be found that a pattern does indeed emerge which helps both the prospect identification and client retention activities. One of the characteristics of all professional services is the high degree of uncertainty which exists in appointing advisers and because of the essential intangibility of the service 'product', that uncertainty is carried forward from one matter to the next although it must be said it is reduced if the experience curve is one of relative satisfaction.

The merger will have created new uncertainties which even the most sophisticated clients will experience. It is as well for those responsible for presenting the practice to existing clients of both firms to understand these sources of uncertainty and not to ignore but attack them.

What are the uncertainties likely to be? They will vary by client type – private or corporate – and by types of matter handled. High on the list will be the fear of the loosening of links with those solicitors with whom clients have previously worked satisfactorily. These are to the client valuable contacts and to the merged firm invaluable. A policy is needed on how a change of solicitor is to be presented to the client.

Successful Mergers

There is worry that 'bigness' means bureaucracy and perhaps perfectly happy and informal contacts will now become rigid.

How will the merger effect the cost structure and thus the fees charged? Will the clients' business once viewed of sufficient size, profitability and quality to be attractive now be seen as unattractive for the enlarged practice? Will any physical move create its own problems? The list is long but must be compiled and each and every item dealt with, not in the fullness of time but immediately. Clients lost through neglect in understanding the source of uncertainty will not easily be regained.

All the foregoing deals with the message which has to be decided before the method for its propagation is decided. The choice is extremely wide. There are at least 35-40 different methods and media to choose from. Which media are clients and potential clients exposed to and perhaps influenced by? Some can be eliminated without second consideration, for example, national press for a purely local merger would be ineffective and wasteful and sponsorship inappropriate, others need careful assessment as to effectiveness and cost.

It is always wise to notify clients about the merger before any general announcement. They do not like to hear at second hand matters which affect them. The obvious way to deal with this is by a personal meeting with major key clients and a personalised letter or a telephone call to other clients. Within corporate client firms contacts should be made with all personnel who have dealings with the merged practice. It is unwise to assume a letter to the company secretary or managing director will be passed through to others in the company.

The merger is a good reason to contact all clients, not just current ones. Even if it is thought a client is lost, under the dipensation of de-regulation, there is no reason at all not to communicate with all clients of the firm perhaps going back 7-10 years. However, it is important not to imply in any message a situation which does not obviously apply. For example, writing to a firm which transacted one small piece of commercial litigation five years ago as 'an old and valued client' is likely to be counter-productive.

The merger could also provide the opportunity to establish the status of old clients. In circulating the information, with or without a brochure, it is always a good idea to ask the recipient to check that the name, address, title, etc are still correct. Those who respond can be assumed to want to maintain contact against a time when legal services are needed. This is also one way of weeding out non-valid names and addresses.

Once the client list has been dealt with, the general announcement is then needed. Here the press media for the geographical area or

Marketing the Merged Practice

business activity involved should be used both for paid advertisements and, if possible, for editorial comment. Although a merger is hardly fascinating and compulsive news, a good copy writer can indeed make even this mundane subject sufficiently interesting to attract editorial comment. Paid local radio and TV slots can be considered but the cost is relatively high.

In order to consolidate the marketing to both existing and new clients, a newsletter after, say, six months to a year is very useful, even if it is only a one-off. It can provide news on progress of the merger and again emphasise the benefits.

Evidence to-date is that mergers do not encourage pro-active marketing. While what has been written deals with the situation at the moment of merger, it would be totally unwise to think that this ends the major marketing effort. Marketing is a constant on-going activity and should never be stopped or held back either because of current pressures or work loads.

Apart from being continuous, it is also the responsibility of every member of the firm from the senior partner to the receptionist. The whole practice has to be client orientated and that is not just a cliché. It means putting the clients' needs and interests first.

The professions have a great deal to learn from commercial, industrial and consumer service organisations on customer care. The odds in the battle for client retention and client acquisition are heavily weighted against the professional service firm. Few people can obtain clients but anyone, no matter how lowly, can lose them. Thus the practice must become totally marketing orientated from top to bottom down.

Given the human element in legal services; territorial imperatives and the inevitable 'them' and 'us' element, which in a merger takes months if not years to break down, there is an unfortunate tendency to treat the other practices' clients in a somewhat cavalier fashion if in doing otherwise means deteriorating service for a practitioner's own clients. This tendency has to be identified and eliminated – not an easy task. The firm has to be marketed as a single entity, not an unhappy cobbling together of two different cultures. Surveillance, and if need be correction, has to come from the top, as indeed does all marketing motivation.

The concept that the clients are clients of the *whole* practice, not of the constitutent firms is a philosophy that has to be promoted within the new firm. This then identifies a further need – to market the merger internally. It may have come from a totally different service area but one major international hotel chain's belief is that 'you can't make happy guests with unhappy staff'. There is much good sense in this view and it is the task of the senior members of the combined firm to ensure that

Successful Mergers

the merger is marketed internally and that the benefits to all members of the firm are identified and are promoted consistently and energetically to clients.

Aubrey Wilson is an independent consultant specialising in the marketing of professional services. He has been deeply involved with the legal profession having prepared and presented practice development courses for The Law Societies of England & Wales, Scotland, Northern Ireland, Western Australia, South Australia, Australian Capital Territory (Canberra), New Zealand, The Law Institute of Victoria, The Association of Law Societies of South Africa and The College of Law (Sydney). He is consultant on practice development to a number of law firms.

19 De-merger: A Strategy For Growth (Egerton Sandler)

In 1986, Egerton Sandler was an eight partner firm with the head office in central London, and five branch offices spread through Kent. The main branch office growth took place in the early 1980s and was based on the expansion of local residential conveyancing at the time.

A considerable divergence arose since the central London practice, while property based, was dealing with a different quality of client, who demanded a more personal approach. The suburban offices existed on the basis of a large number of clients involved, in the main in a large number of small transactions.

By 1986, the situation had changed. Price cutting in the local conveyancing market was emphasising the difference in practice required to run a suburban branch office operation effectively on the one hand, and a central London firm on the other. We were also facing growing recruitment problems in finding new solicitors and legal executives, as suburban practice was considered unattractive by the majority of people coming into the profession.

Personnel in the branches had grown to twice the number of those employed in the central London office. This resulted in those practising in London feeling that the branch structure was actually inhibiting the growth of the London practice. The imbalance was creating a true lack of direction in the firm. The obvious solution was to split the firm into two separate components, but this did not take into account the fact that as partners we were all part of an indivisible whole.

At staff level, however, it was much easier to accomplish, or indeed has already been accomplished, as our employees tended to think of themselves as part of the local operation without much concept of the overall firm. We had tried to combat this insularity, but pure logistics made it very difficult. It was known for a central London partner to phone a colleague in a branch office and to be treated by the telephonist at arm's length as an importunate client.

It was obvious to those in central London that the suburban offices were likely to need far greater resources pumped into them in the future to produce an adequate return. The corollary was that growth in central

Successful Mergers

London would be further inhibited by this diversion of resources.

In the past, we had always worked on a 'swings and roundabouts' basis at partnership level, and imbalances in profit had tended to correct themselves over the years. Thus, if central London was doing badly, the chances were that there would be high profits made in the suburban branches in that year, or vice versa.

The truth of the matter is that it is difficult to hold together a partnership in a genuine community of purpose, when the business activities of the component parts are so divergent, and the people involved are so physically distant from each other.

As a result, it proved far easier than we might have anticipated to achieve acceptance, in principle, that demerger was in the firm's and the partners' best interests, and allowed the partners to practise with those having a common purpose. We were helped by the fact that the profits in the year immediately before these discussions were excellent, and both sides of the firm contributed well to them. Thus, discussions could be entered into without any implication of blame on either side.

The actual details of the de-merger were worked out over a six week time span between two of the senior partners concerned, each representing one of the proposed new firms. Although the firm name was available to both sides, the Kent operation elected to practise under a different name; The Marson Partnership.

The de-merger negotiations were conducted in a most amicable manner, and both parties maintained public links with the other for a period of years by cross-over consultancies. If asked, the partners of both firms would say that the right decision was made at the right time. The central London firm has now grown to six partners and a staff of thirty, while the Kent firm has doubled its turnover and opened another office.

There are lessons to be learned from our experience. It is essential to plan growth and not to allow it to take place piecemeal. Constant monitoring of the business allows you to identify problems early and time solutions with sensitivity.

Tony Sacker

Educated: Owens School, Islington 1951-58
Articled: Ronald S. Friedman, Friedman Fredman & Co. 1958-63
Admitted Solicitor: June 1963 (Honours)
Partner: Friedman Fredman 1964-66
Subsequently Partner: Egerton Sandler 1967 to date

De-merger: A Strategy for Growth (Egerton Sandler)

A general practitioner, but with emphasis on commercial contracts, tax and personal finance. Managing Partner Egerton Sandler 1975 to date. Chairman Management & Technology Committee, Westminster Law Society, President (1987-88) Westminster Law Society, member of Society for Computers & Law.

20 Putting Asunder

Almost as if by some kind of physical reaction, the rush to merge seems to create a similar rush to de-merge. Professional partnerships, particularly among lawyers, used to be noted for their stability. Our industrial clients were always changing their identity and senior personnel with bewildering rapidity, while we remained constant. We have now joined the 'merry-go-round' and it may be worthwhile trying to plot some of the causes.

Partnership used to be a situation where the partners took each other's performance more or less on trust although there were obvious exceptions in extreme cases. The computer has changed all that. Our performance can now be monitored to two decimal places in terms of billings and realisations on the one hand, and introduction of work on the other.

These are the objective criteria, and, now that we have more professional management in place, we are also looking at the subjective criteria of partnership. Obviously this should include firm leadership and management; recruitment and training; marketing activities; service to the community and the profession, and whatever else your particular firm considers as activities which benefit the firm.

We are living in an age where performance and financial rewards are considered more important than for many years. All this is bound to create dissatisfaction and hence promote mobility. The thrusting young partner surrounded by stodgy older partners, who are not prepared to recognise his or her worth, as subjectively perceived, is likely to seek greener pastures. Conversely, the under-performing middle-ranking partner, who seems to be suffering from burnout is not going to be tolerated as hitherto, but will be asked to leave to make room for someone who offers more dynamism to the partnership.

With the best will in the world, merger often creates dissatisfaction. Some of the partners in the merged entity feel that their noses are put out of joint by the new arrivals. There may not turn out to be sufficient work for two principals in a particular department, and one of those partners may decide to try his or her luck elsewhere.

One or more partners in the merged firm may realise after the event that they do not like the change of philosophy which their original firm has undergone as a result of the merger. They may feel uncomfortable with their new partners. A typical example is where the preliminary homework has not been done properly and the partners in one of the original firms suddenly appreciate that they give all their time to the practice and put into the firm's account the earnings from their directorships. Conversely, the partners from the other firm indulge in various outside business activities and retain the proceeds for their own account. Furthermore, those partners are entering into joint ventures with clients of the firm, which their new partners feel to be improper as a potential source of conflict of duty and interest.

I repeat, that this is something which should have been worked out beforehand, and, if found to be an insuperable obstacle, should have prevented the merger taking place. Where mergers are proceeding in great haste without proper prior investigation, problems of this nature arising after the event are going to impel de-merger of at least part of the merged entity.

How can these problems be overcome or minimised? It is most important for all the partners concerned to behave in as adult a fashion as possible and acknowledge their mistakes. Obviously, if the remaining partners wish to keep the firm together, it is perfectly proper to make all reasonable approaches to try to persuade those wishing to leave to change their minds. However, realism is important, and, if there is no hope of changing the settled intention, then the departure should be planned in such a way as to be as amicable as possible.

Is there a partnership deed? If not, we are forced back on the provisions of the Partnership Act, with all the problems of a partnership at will. A notice of dissolution is usually the most damaging way of terminating any partnership. Almost by definition, it will be disadvantageous from the tax point of view and, as it can be of immediate effect, it gives the parties no chance to make proper alternative arrangements. In this particular instance, where there is no partnership agreement, a negotiated de-merger is absolutely vital in the interests of the parties, the staff, and the clients.

If there is a partnership agreement, obviously it must be referred to to see what was agreed to in the event of the impending situation. It is often the case that partners will have entered into such an agreement without seriously considering the impact of the termination provisions. We are all optimists at heart, and we did not anticipate that such an event would ever take place. How wrong we were!

In a sensibly drawn partnership agreement, if there are more than two partners, there will be a normal provision negating the Partnership Act to the effect that the departure of one does not terminate the partnership as between the remaining two or more. There will normally be buy-out provisions so that the partners leaving, if they do not propose to continue in practice, can dispose of their interests in the firm at a proper price based on current valuation of the net assets, or in whichever way the partners have decided to deal with this matter.

If the partners wish to continue in practice, it is necessary to consider the provisions of any restraint of trade clause. It has now been decided by the House of Lords that a reasonable clause with space and time limitations preventing a partner from competing is valid and binding.

Before the recent case of Bridge -v- Deacons, there was some doubt on the point, as, where solicitors were concerned, there was an argument that it was in the public interest for the client to be able to consult the lawyer, and this right transcended any impediment. We now know that this is not the case.

The problem is that the unforeseen and sudden intentions of the parties may not coincide with the provisions in the partnership agreement. Difficulties now arise and negotiations have to take place to try to find some kind of compromise.

At all costs, partners should be able to settle their differences without recourse to the courts. Unfortunately, anger often creeps into the situation and partners have a tendency to shoot from the hip. Writs then fly and, once the parties have adopted adversarial positions, it is often difficult to bring them together again into a compromise situation.

Mediation and conciliation are all the rage in divorce today. The same ought to apply in the partnership situation. Most partnership deeds contain an arbitration clause, the idea of which is to provide a more inexpensive and informal forum for settling disputes than the courts. However, an ill-intentioned party can usually circumvent arbitration and bring the matter to court by alleging fraud or improper conduct.

Arbitration itself normally connotes an adversarial position being adopted by the parties, and it is, therefore, far better to deal with matters more informally through a mediator whom both parties trust. Such a person might be the firm's accountant, or one of that growing band of consultants offering counselling service to the professions.

As has already been indicated, it may be necessary to re-write the partnership agreement to take into account the changed cirumstances. For example, the agreement may provide for a twelve month period of notice for retirement, while those leaving may wish to go more quickly. The restrictive covenant may contain a space limitation, which those departing may wish to abrogate. Everything is open to negotiation and often, as we are talking about commercial transactions, compensation can be paid by way of a lump sum or commission over an agreed period of time.

The de-merger negotiations will obviously be considered first of all from the point of view of the parties. The taxation requirements may be such that a consideration for early departure may be the execution by all partners of the appropriate tax elections for the continuing basis.

In a prudent partnership, a stock of these should be held by the accountants already signed in blank, but this is often not the case. The parties will have to decide how to deal with work-in-progress and receivables in what is in effect a merger in reverse.

The position of the clients in such a situation is obviously of the greatest importance. Which clients are to go, and which to stay? The wording and timing of any announcement must be considered. As little as possible must be done to damage the clients' interests, and those interests coincided with those of the partners, who wish to preserve the connection intact as far as is possible.

Similar considerations apply to staff. If some are departing with the outgoing partners, steps must be taken to ensure that the morale of those remaining is affected as little as possible. Once again, the timing of announcements may be crucial.

In these days of media scrutiny, the public relations aspect of the de-merger has to be considered. How is it to be presented to the profession and the world at large? We are all now aware that opinion can be moulded and it is better to do this in advance than in arrears. One public relations consultant may be called in to advise both sides, or each may feel that separate help is required.

A de-merger following a recent merger is a very sad occurrence, as the machinery which has laboured so hard in forward gear will now have to be put into reverse.

Partnership has been compared to marriage and we all know that divorce is so often a cause for continued acrimony, before, during and after. The relationship between partners is not normally as close as that between husband and wife. It should be possible to avoid a great deal of that acrimony, but reality is often such a disappointment in this respect.

A petition for dissolution of a partnership reads very much like a petition for unreasonable behaviour in divorce. Both should be avoided.

As de-merger becomes more common, perhaps partners will become better able to cope with the difficulties which the situation creates. Maybe the ranks of partnership consultants will be swelled by marriage guidance counsellors, who wish to enlarge their horizons.

Michael Simmons

Epilogue

I stressed at the outset that this was intended to be a practical work. We have been fortunate in the depth and variety of our contributors. This provides a stereoscopic view of the opportunities and problems of mergers.

At the same time, it does of necessity create contradictions. Thus, one writer may well have said something which directly conflicts with the words of another. As I have also already indicated, management, and I am including merger as part of management, is not an exact science. There is more than one way of skinning a cat.

Furthermore, even if it were a science, merger activity is still very much in its infancy so far as the professional service sector is concerned. We all have a great deal to learn and are, in effect, feeling our way. The contradictions may themselves provide a talking and learning point for the reader. So far as I know, this is the first work on the subject on this side of the Atlantic. I researched as widely as possible on the other side, and I think that it may at present be unique in North America as well. I am sure that that situation will not continue for long. Merger is far too important a topic to be left, at least so far as the written word is concerned, to me and to my fellow contributors.

I have already tried to stress the fact that it is very much a moving subject, in that no two mergers are the same. We are all learning as we go along. Thus, I hope that this will merely be the first edition, and that you, the readers, will be prepared to assist in providing some of the revised material for future editions, arising out of your own experiences.

In my view, the heart of this book is the series of chapters giving the experiences on merger of my fellow practitioners. The philosophical and practical parts can only arise and grow out of those experiences. I, therefore, expect that the next edition of the book will change a great deal as a result of diverse and new experiences in the merger situation.

Lastly, I want to thank all my fellow contributors and my publishers for their skills, help and enthusiasm, and particularly Kim Corker, my publishing manager, at Waterlows. She kept me going by her encouragement, when my own was in danger of becoming submerged. The book would not have appeared at all without the work of my secretary, Joyce Russell, who not only typed it, but kept me and it in order. With their help, I hope that we have produced a management tool on the subject of mergers, which will be truly useful for those who seek to employ it.

Michael Simmons

APPENDICES

APPENDICES

Appendix 1a

Merger procedure checklist

Exploratory stage

When two firms begin negotiations for a merger it is unlikely that either will want at that stage to disclose full detailed information as to accounts, clients and other matters which may be of interest and importance to the other party. Nevertheless, it is important that at a very early stage certain limited information is exchanged and we suggest the following:

1. Particulars of all partners, giving age, experience, qualifications, specialist knowledge, health and retirement plans.
2. Particulars of all fee earning and administrative staff, giving age, experience, qualifications, specialist knowledge, health, pay and period of service.
3. A list of the more important clients, particularly those from whom an annual retainer is received.
4. Details of the accommodation occupied by the firm, the rent/value and length of lease.
5. Particulars of turnover, profitability and growth pattern for say the preceding three years.
6. An indication of the percentage of billing of each type of service/speciality.

This information, whilst by no means adequate to reach a final decision, should be sufficient to enable another firm to assess whether the structure in the first firm merits further investigation.

Preparatory stage

Once the two firms concerned have made a preliminary investigation of the possibilities of merging their practices and if they have both reached the conclusion that an investigation in greater depth should be undertaken, it is necessary that a full and frank exchange of the following relevant information should take place: –

Examination of Accounts

It is necesary that each firm make a complete disclosure of their financial

Successful Mergers

position and deliver to the other audited profit and loss accounts and balance sheets for not less than three years. It is not unlikely that the basis upon which the two sets of accounts are prepared will differ. Each firm will no doubt wish to give any necessary explanation of accounts. If, since the date of the last accounts, new factors have to be taken into account, e.g. rent, rates and wage increases, these must also be expressly disclosed as well as any other matters likely to affect future profits.

Examination of Facilities

In most firms these facilities can be summarised as follows:

1. Secretarial and clerical services;
2. Staff control and management;
3. Accounting and accounting services;
4. Stationery;
5. Office equipment-provision and up-keep;
6. Library and information retrieval;
7. Premises;
8. Lighting, heating and power;
9. General management services.

Details of Clientele

Each firm will wish to know precisely the nature and extent of the other firm's clientele. One of the forces motivating the negotiations may be either the absence or the presence in a particular firm of clients generating a particular class of work. It will also be desirable to establish the number of long-standing clients in each firm, the quantity and quality of the work which they bring to that firm and its profitability. Finally, it will be necessary to establish what retainers each firm is paid by specific clients; particularly to ensure that no conflict of interest will arise if the merger being negotiated is put into effect.

Merger Information Checklist

Partners

Names, dates of birth seniority and equity share
Retirement arrangements or plans – dates and financial
Any known ill-health
Profit shares – now and planned future changes; any provision for interest on capital or for "salaries"
Specialisms
Professional activities
Succession arrangements at future retirements

Merger Procedure Checklist

Partners' merger philosophy
Copy of partnership agreement
Particulars of any associations, other merger plans etc; copy of any firm's directory

Staff

Numbers and grades of staff
Names, dates of birth and status of key personnel
Partnership potential, expectations and promises made
Salaries – individually for key personnel and bracket for each grade of other staff
Overtime arrangements
Pension scheme – whether contracted out
               – copy of rules booklet
               – membership
               – copy of last actuary's report
Staff benefits – cars, expense allowances, luncheon vouchers, etc
Students – graduate/non-graduate recruitment policy;
Exam. training programme – particulars and who pays?
Professional training programme
Continuing professional education – policy and programme
Recruitment policy and procedures – copy of any manual, brochure, etc.
Working week; annual holiday allowances; statutory and local holidays

Clients

General nature of practice and any special features
Analysis of fees by types of work
List of largest clients, including all listed companies and subsidiaries of listed companies, showing approx. annual fees
Sources of new work
Any other special connections
Work lost in last three years – approx. fees and reasons for loss
Any work considered specially vulnerable
Location of work outside immediate area of office
Directorships
Any independence problems – now or on completion of merger
Importance of firm name

Technical

Copy of any manuals, brochures, etc
Development and maintenance of work standards and procedures policy and practice
See some typical audit and tax files

Successful Mergers

Specialisations and specialist departments, e.g. tax, computer audit, computer bureau, registration, management services, insolvency, trusts, etc.
Style of accounts — see typical set; type face of typewriters

Office

Tenure — if leasehold; next review date and estimated current rental value
Current rent (if any) and rates
Estimated current capital value
Standard of accommodation — is this adequate; any surplus space
Any restriction on hours of use
Parking facilities
Any substantial repairs expenditure foreseen
Any special problems — e.g. planning redevelopment, road widening, etc.

Insurances

Copy of particulars of current professional indemnity policy; any outstanding claims; any past claims
Partner and staff insurances e.g. life cover, accident, sickness, medical costs etc.
Summary of general insurances; name of broker.

Financial

Copy of last three years' accounts: financial year-end
Entered the inter-firm comparison? — if so, see summary of results
Partners' capital and current account balances
Any borrowings
Name of bankers: any special banking arrangements
Basis of valuation of work in progress — for accounts and tax
WIP (at billing value) and client debtors, both expressed as months of billing
Annual fees handled per partners
Explanation of any special features of accounts
Liabilities to existing retired partners — capital and income.
Schedule of billing rates; formula for calculation from salaries; comparison of actual billings with billing rates
Average chargeable time per month — partners; staff
Partners' drawings
Copy of budget (if any) for current year and any future year

The Procedural Programme

For mergers the following points should also be observed: Arrange an initial meeting between the senior partners. If compatibility exists arrange a full

Merger Procedure Checklist

partner meeting. Draft heads of agreement and circulate for partner review. When a proposition has been agreed meet with solicitors. Appoint one partner in each firm to represent both sides. Agree time deadlines and carry forward in definite stages.

Study taxation, pension and partner equity arrangements.

Negotiate property disposal, acquisition and lease terms.

Agree name of new practice and letter-heading arrangement. When name is agreed co-ordinate stationery and printing.

Inform appropriate professional body of new arrangements.

Rearrange insurance policies and inform each brokerage.

Review previous professional and operational commitments.

Necessary announcements to personnel/clients/press/banks.

Rationalise offices/equipment/services/staff and finances.

Form a committee to review and blend previous policies.

Prepare guidelines for next stage of firm's development.

Advantages of an Association

In the case of an association of one or more firms, these objectives may be achieved by the following means:

1. Centralised secretarial and clerical services, receptionists and messengers.
2. Centralised accounting; perhaps the volume of accounting work engendered by the joint use of the management partnership's accounting service may justify the acquisition of more sophisticated mechanical or computerised accounting devices. It should be noted that the accounting function will deal with records only. Each participant firm will continue to operate its own separate clients' and office bank accounts.
3. Bulk purchase of stationery.
4. Rationalisation of administrative office space, with consequent savings in lighting, heating and power bills.
5. Sharing of office equipment. For example, switchboard, telex, copying machines, telecopier.
6. Provision of a central library.

Successful Mergers

7. More efficient and comprehensive information retrieval systems, arising from the ability to employ more complex accounting methods and from the contributions of management experience from the constitutent firms. This will make financial control, planning and budgeting easier and more accurate.

Aspects of Taxation for Mergers

When two or more firms merge, the following important aspects of taxation and their implications must be carefully weighed:

1. Action necessary to retain the best basis of assessment for taxation purposes and the most suitable accounting date.
2. The preservation of any pre-merger losses including any capital allowances that have accrued.
3. The resolution of problems connected with the two or more firms utilising different methods of accounting for work in progress and debtors.
4. Dealing with capital gains tax on merging the interests of goodwill, property, leases and any shares in service companies.
5. The various problems connected with and arising out of items such as partners' annuities, charitable payments and tax reserves etc.

Appendix 1b

Holborn Law Society's Amalgamation Service

In 1970 the idea of establishing an amalgamation service, i.e. the introduction to each other of firms wishing for an amalgamation, was put to the Finance & Administration Committee. The proposition was approved. The essential feature had to be complete confidentiality. For this it was agreed that it should be conducted by only one person who would not reveal, who had applied for the service even to the Society's president or other officers. The person who conducted the service had to have an intimate knowledge of practices in Holborn. It was also an essential feature that he should no longer be in practice. Applicants for the service would have to give him details of their practices to enable him to make appropriate introductions. These revelations could be made to a retired solicitor without the risk of subsequent embarrassment by, for example, their meeting in the course of a case.

The amalgamation service came into being at a time when it was particularly appropriate. Firms were still having to cope with the effect on their practices of the war period. It had deprived them of the possibility of getting in young partners. Accordingly the average age of partners was higher than normal. There was at that time more work than there were solicitors qualified to do it. As these difficulties were in many cases common to both parties to a projected amalgamation getting together for those cases was no solution.

There were many applications for the service. At one time there were as many as forty firms being assisted. The machinery was for the operator to visit an applicant at his office or on some neutral ground such as the Law Society's Hall. These meetings were often attended by a number of partners. Additionally to providing the operator with the information he required to enable him to make an appropriate introduction these meetings provided a valuable opportunity for an applicant firm to review the situation in which it found itself. It turned out that in many cases being given an introduction was of less value than of getting the advice of an independent experienced solicitor as to what to do for the best. Often amalgamation turned out not to be the best answer.

There were several kinds of introductions required. The ideal was a marriage between two firms of approximately the same size. The advantages sought were widening the scope of the practice and making more economic use of premises and of staff. Another kind was a take-over by a large firm of a smaller one. This often was not what small firms envisaged when applying for the service, or wanted, but was sometimes found to be the only practical course. There was however a wish to be taken over in the case of many of the sole practitioners who applied. They hoped that that would solve their difficulties. This was particularly the case with those of an age when they had proximate retirement in mind. A great deal of success was achieved with this kind of introduction. The operator found a firm willing to take over elderly sole practitioners so long as retirement occurred within a year. It was often found that there was a lot more work to be done than the retiring solicitor realised. Twice the amalgamation service was able to give peace of mind to sole practitioners suffering from terminal illness who were worried that their clients' affairs should continue to be properly looked after. There were other cases where sole practitioners were greatly helped.

After investigating the situation of an applicant in the way described above the operator considered what he had on his books and when he thought he had a suitable match he phoned one of the firms for permission to disclose their name confidentially to a partner of the other. Permission having been given he phoned the other firm for a similar permission. Having got the firms together the operator's work was finished. It was no part of the service that the operator should advise on the bringing about of an amalgamated firm. He always asked to be told how things worked out. He very seldom was.

The amalgamation service was extended to the neighbouring areas of Westminister and the City with the agreement of the relevant local law society. This was necessary because of the broad similarity of practices in the whole of central London. In order that members of Holborn Law Society should have advantage of their membership they received the service free. Members of other societies were charged a nominal fee of £5.25. To preserve the confidentiality the fees were paid to the operator who forwarded them to Holborn Law Society's treasurer without disclosing the names of the firms concerned. The amounts received in this way were £61 in 1970 and £79.75 in 1971. In considering how far this reflects the value of business of the amalgamation service it is relevant that only firms outside Holborn paid anything. These were only a small proportion of the whole.

After two years business fell off rapidly. For effective introductions there has to be a reasonably large number of applicants from whom to select pairs. Falling off was accordingly cumulative. In 1972 the City company set up a working party to consider amalgamation which the operator addressed. The outcome was a pamphlet published by the Law Society entitled "Amalgamation and Your Practice". It dealt with the reasons for and against seeking an amalgamation; what can reasonably be hoped to be gained and what cannot. At about the same time the amalgamation service produced a questionnaire to be completed by those seeking an amalgamation. A copy is attached hereto. This did not prove very helpful. The personal interview was much more productive. The amalgamation service was, and had to be, essentially personal and as such it was a Holborn success.

© **Holborn Law Society**

Holborn Law Society
Amalgamation Service Questionnaire

Name of Firm:

Address:

Branch(es):

Firms for whom applicants act as London agents:

Partners
State ages and subjects in which each partner specialises and intentions regarding retirement:

Work category analysis
Set out the constituent elements of the firm's practice and assess the contribution of each to overall profitability:

Accommodation
Give details of present accommodation, freeholds, leaseholds (by whom held) current rents and dates of rent review. Also particulars of any space for expansion:

Staff
State ages, salaries, pension and holiday arrangements; capabilities and work capacity; ratio of fee earning to administration; details of office administration and accounting systems:

Profit record
Breakdown of firms accounts for five year period giving gross costs per annum, wages and salaries,

overheads, and net profit costs and any recurring retainers:

Partnership constitution

Give the following particulars:-

a) whether goodwill is included in relation to payments on retirement or admission of new partners.

b) What is the capital of the firm?

c) Are there any prior charges on profits for any partners?

d) What are the retirement and death provisions?

e) Are there any existing pension liabilities for past partners or staff?

Future outlook and strategy

State the firm's view of future growth opportunities and plans for meeting new demands for firm's services and generally what are the objectives of an amalgamation, what advantages are sought and what benefits are offered?

The Copyright of this form is the property of Holborn Law Society and neither the form nor any part of it may be used or reproduced without the consent of the Society.

Appendix 2

An Amalgamation Case Study

(reprinted by permission of Gazette Practice Handbook & Stoy Hayward)

Establishment & Co—Slicker & Co

Note: Both the above firms of solicitors practise in Richtown.

Introduction

I must stress the characters, firms and the town are totally fictitious and any resemblance to anyone living or dead is purely coincidental. However, having said that, the characters and firms are stereotypes and amalgams of certain qualities, good and bad, that I have come across in my professional travels or more recently, acting in the capacity of consultant to other professional firms.

In that respect, while the firms and individuals do not exist, we all know firms and partners, probably towns as well, with common features.

There is nothing extraordinary about the firms, their partners and staffs, the town and the situation in which all of them find themselves. I claim writer's licence in combining in this case study a remarkably variety of 'juicy' situations which are likely to be encountered over a few years of looking at various amalgamation prospects. Encapsulation is the order of the day.

Richtown

Situated about forty miles from London, the town has always been the market centre of a prosperous agricultural community. Large new residential estates have turned the town additionally into a dormitory for London commuters. New industry, computer-dominated, is rapidly moving into the area, and the town centre is changing as the multiples realise the potential of the area, so that they either open or expand their operations.

Establishment & Co

Founded in 1845, with their own freehold premises in the centre of the town, two converted Georgian houses, the firm has always has the cream of the business from local gentry and farmers. Its strengths and weaknesses are as follows:

1. *Strengths*
    (a) Conveyancing, trust and probate;

Successful Mergers

    (b) established and prosperous personal clientele;
    (c) a 'will bank' second to none in the locality;
    (d) a speciality in estate tax-planning;
    (e) the partners have excellent local contacts and the firm has a good reputation for solid and reliable work;
    (f) excellent, under-used freehold premises slap, bang in the centre of the town.

2. *Weaknesses*
    (a) Ageing senior partners who are no longer hungry;
    (b) weak litigation – the department has merely been one to serve important clients unfortunate enough to get into trouble;
    (c) no company/commercial capability – the work has always been passed on to London firms in the past;
    (d) static turn-over;
    (e) few new clients and some of the old ones have been lost recently;
    (f) falling (albeit still substantial) profits;

3. *Personnel*
Eight partners, four assistant solicitors, four managing clerks (mostly nearing retirement) and usual supporting staff.

4. *Partners*
    (a) **Arthur** – 62. Rich in his own right with no financial worries or commitments – a good lawyer in his time – the prime business-getter – former high sheriff of the county – related to, at school with, or friendly with just about everyone who has been around for any length of time locally. Senior partner. Share 22%.
    (b) **Bill** – age 61. At school with Arthur but there the resemblance ends. A solid conveyancer in his day, but now running out of steam, with no real need to work. Wants to retire to Ireland to fish. Share 22%.
    (c) **Charles** – age 54. An excellent, technical private client lawyer without much personality – his clients like him and he is largely responsible for the firm's tax-planning reputation/expertise. Partnership share 10%.
    (d) **Dennis** – age 52. Bill's protégé another solid conveyancer – an efficient worker, but a nine to five man. He has no clients of his own. Share 10%.
    (e) **Edward** – Age 48. Divorce and litigation – the only non-public school partner – rather kept down by Arthur but is technically quite good – has built up his own clientele, particularly on the divorce front – spends quite a lot of time socialising in the town, rather than the county and would do more, if not always disparaged. Share 10%.
    (f) **Fred** – age 47. Brought in by Charles and also works in the private

An Amalgamation Case Study

client side at which work he is known to be good – is also admin partner which takes up 50% of his time, leaving him none for practice development, at which he is an unknown quantity though there are glimmerings. Share 10%.

(g) **George** – age 42. Another conveyancer – Bill's nephew and owes his place in the firm to that relationship – has a rich wife and works part-time only though enjoying a full partnership share – frankly does little for the firm. Share 10%.

(h) **Harry** – age 34. A litigator, recruited from a good London firm to knock that department into shape – feels that he has made a mistake and is secretly job-hunting, particularly in view of the attitude of the senior partners to his speciality. Share 6%.

5. *Services*
   (a) Accounting – a serviceable mechanised system is in use, run by a 62-year-old unqualified accountant, who has been with the firm for many years, man and boy.
   (b) Time-costing system – nil.
   (c) Accounts rendered system – nil.
   (d) Management accounts – what are they?
   (e) Office administration – in the hands of a manager aged 59 who has also been with the firm for many years – he reports to Fred.
   (f) Staff relations – good among the older staff, but there is a high turn-over among the younger element who find the firm's atmosphere static and stuffy.

Slicker & Co

Founded ten years ago by Ian and James, who had been articled in the same London firm. Both worked locally for three years before putting up their plate. They started with local court work and residential conveyancing. The firm soon built up a reputation locally. Establishment & Co and the like consider them 'pushy'. The firm has expanded every year and operates from central town offices on a short leasehold, which are serviceable rather than attractive and are extremely cramped. In fact, they are overfull. The clientele is still very much 'town' rather than 'county', though inroads are being made in the new industrial and commercial base in the area.

1. *Strengths*
   (a) Conveyancing – particularly for local developers, litigation (Ian has dragged the firm very much up-market since his early days), company and commercial (both the junior partners are specialists recruited from London).
   (b) Growing and ever-changing clientele with a commercial bias. The

Successful Mergers

firm is picking up this new business even if still ignored by the farmers and local gentry, except where their litigation is concerned.

(c) A practice development programme in which all partners participate. This is considered far too aggressive by the partners of Establishment & Co and their like.

(d) The firm is fully computerised both as to accounts and word processing – the accounts system has considerable excess capacity – regular management accounts are produced and the firm uses time-costing; with a mobile clientele there is a debt problem, but it is being tackled by the firm with typical ruthlessness.

2. *Weaknesses*

(a) The firm does not give a good service to personal clients, and despite every effort has failed to break into the 'country' market.
(b) The firm is unpopular locally in circles where it would like to shine.
(c) The premises are grotty and over-crowded.
(d) The connection is still too transactional-based and thus there are not enough established clients. It still gets too much problem work, for which full charges cannot be made for tactical reasons, and the local bread and butter goes elsewhere.

3. *Personnel*

Four partners, nine qualified staff, no managing clerks, partnership secretary and usual supporting staff.

4. *Partners*

(a) **Ian** – age 38. Heads the litigation department with five assistant solicitors – department deals with everything up to heavy commercial work in London – with James responsible for the firm's aggressive marketing policy and growth. Joint senior partner. Share 30%.

(b) **James** – age 37. Heads the conveyancing department with four assistant solicitors – has very good reputation for heavyweight work, and has just landed the South-East England conveyancing of the Northern Public Property Company who are carrying out the largest development in the centre of the town. Joint Senior Partner. Share 30%.

(c) **Kenneth** – age 32. Articled with Price Slaughterhouse in the City, then four years' commercial experience with a smaller central London firm; joined as an assistant and became a partner after two years; business start-up specialist and brings in a lot of commercial work. Share 20%.

(d) **Leonard** – age 30. Followed a similar path to Kenneth with the advantage of being born and raised locally – by coincidence, he is

Arthur's nephew, being the son of his much poorer younger brother, though the brothers are not on speaking terms; specialises in raising commercial finance, he is helping Kenneth build up the commercial department very quickly. Share 20%.

5. Services

Ian and James took on a well-qualified partnership secretary about two years ago to run the firm's management and administration and to relieve them from the necessity to be involved themselves except on an advisory basis. Under his control, the management and financial affairs have been kept in good order and credit control is now becoming much stronger. Staff relations are excellent.

NB Both firms share the same auditors, a prominent firm of chartered accountants.

Commentary

Until relatively recent economic events, this as a potential merger would have been a classic non-starter. While it is true that both firms have a lot to give to the other, nevertheless, the cultural and philosophical differences would have been too much for merger talks even to begin.

Even now, the road towards merger will not be smooth, but adversity makes strange bedfellows.

Establishment & Co is on a downward path, which is going to accelerate. I would have hoped that certain of their partners would be aware of the fact, and would be worried about it, and would like to take corrective action. Conversely, Slicker & Co have no real need to merge at all. They are doing very nicely, and it looks as if their progress will continue. They have the good sense to concentrate on the commercial market, and I would have thought that their next move would have been to have recruited some well-qualified assistants, probably from London, to help Kenneth and Leonard build up that department still further and take off more of the day-to-day work, so that the two partners can concentrate on marketing.

It is true that Slicker & Co lacks a partner to do the kind of work well which has build up Establishment & Co's reputation, namely, private client work with an emphasis on estate tax-planning. However, it is not too late to recruit someone from another country firm who is well qualified and personable.

With Slicker & Co's reputation for aggression, it would not surprise me if they made a direct approach to Charles or Fred at Establishment & Co, even if the current earnings of a partner, particularly on a lower tier at Slicker & Co, are no greater than those at Establishment & Co, the trend looks good, while partners at Establishment & Co must be quaking in their shoes wondering how they are going to cope with the inevitable drop in drawings.

If there is indeed to be a take-over here, it is, in fact, going to be a reverse one with Slicker & Co providing the leadership, the management and the dynamic for the future. They have sensibly organised such departments as they have and their gearing of partners to assistant solicitors in their two more settled departments, litigation and conveyancing, is excellent and is obviously producing very satisfactory profits.

Slicker & Co has good management. In fact, one of their worries must be that their high-powered partnership secretary might become bored with running what is quite a small firm, even if it is allowed to expand by natural progression. To keep him happy, they have to give him a greater challenge and a merger with Establishment & Co would provide just the right type of challenge.

Furthermore, their computer equipment is currently underused. They have obviously paid for equipment, quite prudently, which will cope with their present and future expansion plans. A merger with Establishment & Co will take up that slack immediately.

So far as premises are concerned, Slicker & Co obviously cannot go on for any length of time in their present premises. Their expansion plans are inhibited and the image conveyed is not correct. From the case study it is impossible to say whether Establishment & Co's premises are really suitable for housing a modern firm. There is spare room, but those old Georgian houses converted into offices often are merely rabbit warrens and do not provide a coherent office system.

Establishment & Co owns the freehold, which must be extremely valuable. We are not told whether the premises are subject to a preservation order. If not, as they are in the centre of the High Street, they must be ripe for development.

The management personnel of Establishment & Co is reaching retirement age. Even if no steps are taken toward a merger, Establishment & Co will have to replace them. At partner level, the two partners with the largest shares are fast reaching retirement ages. They are very different characters. Unfortunately, they both currently share the characteristic that they have run out of steam. Bill seems to be a dead loss, and ought to be pensioned off as soon as possible to go and do what he wants to do, fish. Arthur might well respond to a challenge. If the firms are to merge, Ian and James are the logically obvious managing partners. Status demands that Arthur should be asked to stay on as senior partner of the combined firm for the next three years. Slicker & Co's marketing skills are such that they ought to be able to harness Arthur's talents, while relieving him totally from any work responsibilities. This might provide the cosmetic front, which saves the face of the Establishment & Co partners. On the merger, the larger firm provides the senior partner, although the joint managing partners come from the junior firm, Slicker & Co.

If Arthur cannot be persuaded to stay on in this role we are faced with a problem. Neither Charles, Dennis or Edward seem to be the men for the job. They are not personality lawyers, and a merged firm of this type in this particular environment requires such a figurehead. Fred might have the talent, but he is not really senior enough.

If the merger is going to proceed, just as Bill has to go, I can see no scope

An Amalgamation Case Study

for retaining his nephew, George. Fortunately he does not need the money, but I would have thought that the Slicker & Co partners would want to make it a prerequisite of continuing with the merger discussions that George is not part of the merged firm.

If it is decided to sell Establishment & Co's High street premises, then a large capital sum will be unlocked. This can be used for paying off partners who are surplus to requirements.

Ian, particularly as the senior litigation partner, will want to look at the case of Harry. Once again, he may be surplus to requirements, as Establishment & Co's litigation is weak by definition. However, as the old Blues has it 'a good litigator is hard to find'. It may well be a good decision to persuade Harry that his future is assured in the combined new firm.

I would have thought that Slicker & Co would be prepared to defer on the choice of name. Establishment Slicker & Co sounds very satisfactory.

I can see problems on the order of partners shown on the notepaper. If Arthur stays on for three years as senior partner Bill and George having retired, I would have hoped that Charles, Dennis, Edward and Fred would be prepared to recognise the talents and achievements of Ian and James and allow those two to precede them on the combined firms' notepaper. If there is any problem about it, Ian and James may well be men enough to allow professional seniority, to have themselves placed in age order. After all, they can console themselves with the fact that they will have the powers of management and it would be a good idea if the combined firm's constitution provided for them to become senior partners jointly on the retirement of Arthur in three years' time.

There is no doubt that the combined firm would have a certain synergy. We are not told in the case study about competing firms in the area, but a well-organised ten-partner firm, with good management and adequate premises, ought to be something of a powerhouse and, under Ian and James's leadership, I see no reason why turn-over and profits should not continue to increase.

However, having said that, I still see those basic philosophical differences as a problem. Establishment & Co is seen to despise Slicker & Co for their pushy and aggressive methods. I sense that this is based on jealousy, but can the partners of Establishment & Co, at least those who are to be included in the merger, swallow their pride and allow themselves effectively to be taken over by a smaller and more recently established firm? Furthermore, can the outgoing partners, Bill and George, be sufficiently unselfish as to co-operate in their own removal and is Arthur prepared, as he must be in the new régime, to accept a reduced partnership share, particularly bearing in mind that he does not really need the money? The prospects are interesting, and as I said at the beginning of this commentary, I would not have given the negotiations for merger much chance of success as recently as a year ago. However, the needs of Establishment & Co are pressing and Slicker & Co may feel sufficiently flattered, and the partners involved on both sides may be sufficiently adult to allow matters to proceed to their logical conclusion.

In a way, it is a pity that this is only a fictional situation. It would be fascinating to know the answers!

Index to Financial Information

Schedule

A. Establishment & Co – five-year trading record and notes.

B. Establishment & Co – balance sheet at 30 June 1986 and notes.

C. Slicker & Co – five-year trading record and notes.

D. Slicker & Co – balance sheet at 30 June 1986 and notes.

E. Post-merger balance sheet at 30 June 1986.

F. Adjustments to be effected on merger.

G. Revised capital accounts.

H. Forecast post-merger trading record and notes.

An Amalgamation Case Study

Establishment & Co
Income and Expenditure Account

Schedule A

Year ended 30 June:

	1982 £	1982 £	1983 £	1983 £	1984 £	1984 £	1985 £	1985 £	1986 £	1986 £
Partnership Income		758,500		763,700		776,350		781,150		771,950
Less: Expenditure										
Wages and Salaries	304,920		306,785		305,500		300,245		297,000	
Light and heat	4,365		4,410		4,330		4,360		4,395	
Insurance	11,390		11,500		11,640		12,100		15,250	
Telephone	12,980		13,120		13,135		13,200		13,155	
Postage	3,695		3,750		4,615		4,720		4,745	
Printing and stationery	12,640		13,400		13,850		13,975		12,250	
Travel and entertainment	8,055		7,850		8,170		7,010		7,350	
General Expenses	8,205		7,600		7,875		7,375		8,505	
Professional fees	8,890		7,975		8,760		7,580		7,900	
Bank interest and charges	1,615		1,710		810		1,900		1,980	
Accountancy charges	4,200		4,700		4,750		5,000		5,250	
Repairs and renewals	4,660		3,450		3,780		3,990		3,630	
Depreciation	21,375		23,510		27,050		32,450		35,350	
Subscriptions	2,175		2,280		2,300		2,470		2,520	
Bad debts	1,040		860		850		2,250		1,300	
Equipment hire and maintenance	4,695		4,900		7,235		7,275		7,870	
		414,900		417,800		424,650		425,900		428,450
Excess of income over expenditure attributable to partners		343,600		345,900		351,700		355,250		343,500

Establishment & Co
Notes on the Income and Expenditure Account

Schedule A.1

	%	1982 £	1983 £	1984 £	1985 £	1986 £
Partnership income:						
Conveyancing		230,220	228,480	234,300	233,000	228,500
Litigation		48,820	48,500	49,700	50,800	55,450
Trust, probate, wills and estate tax		334,880	332,300	340,800	354,100	356,500
General advice		83,780	83,070	85,200	87,100	91,800
Fees		697,700	692,350	710,000	725,000	732,250
Interest received		21,150	28,750	30,150	26,250	17,300
Commission		39,650	42,600	36,200	29,900	22,400
		758,500	763,700	776,350	781,150	771,950
Excess of income over expenditure attributable to partners as follows:						
Arthur	22	75,592	76,098	77,374	78,155	75,570
Bill	22	75,592	76,098	77,374	78,155	75,570
Charles	10	34,360	34,590	35,170	35,525	34,350
Dennis	10	34,360	34,590	35,170	35,525	34,350
Edward	10	34,360	34,590	35,170	35,525	34,350
Fred	10	34,360	34,590	35,170	35,525	34,350
George	10	34,360	34,590	35,170	35,525	34,350
Harry	6	20,616	20,754	21,102	21,315	20,610
	100	343,600	345,900	351,700	355,250	343,500

Establishment & Co
Balance Sheet at 30 June 1986

Schedule B

	£	£
Fixed assets		163,140
Current assets		
Debtors and prepayments	251,270	
Clients ledger bank accounts	370,745	
Cash in hand	4,115	
	626,130	
Current liabilities		
Creditors and accrued charges	80,825	
Office bank account	27,610	
Clients ledger balances	370,745	
	479,180	
Net current assets		146,950
		310,090
Represented by:		
Partners' capital accounts		310,090

Establishment & Co   Schedule B.1
Notes to the Balance Sheet at 30 June 1986

Fixed Assets

	Freehold property £	Fixtures, fittings and office equipment £	Motor Vehicles £	Total £
Cost				
At the beginning of year	65,000	34,530	131,900	231,430
Additions during year	—	—	27,750	27,750
At end of year	65,000	34,530	159,650	259,180
Depreciation				
At beginning of year	—	9,570	51,120	60,690
Provided in year	—	3,420	31,930	35,350
At end of year	—	12,990	83,050	96,040
Net book value at 30 June 1986	65,000	21,540	76,600	163,140

An Amalgamation Case Study

Establishment & Co
Notes to the Balance Sheet at 30 June 1986

Schedule B.2

Partners' capital accounts

	Arthur £	Bill £	Charles £	Dennis £	Edward £	Fred £	George £	Harry £	Total £
Balance at 1 July 1985	91,735	88,020	54,945	46,985	50,510	45,275	40,285	28,355	446,110
Deduct:									
Drawings	68,160	73,750	29,010	30,350	30,775	31,750	29,850	17,125	310,770
Taxation	37,125	37,125	16,875	16,875	16,875	16,875	16,875	10,125	168,750
Add:									
Profit for the year	75,570	75,570	34,350	34,350	34,350	34,350	34,350	20,610	343,500
Balance at 30 June 1986	62,020	52,715	43,410	34,110	37,210	31,000	27,910	21,715	310,090

185

Slicker & Co
Income and Expenditure Account

Schedule C

Year ended 30 June:

	1982 £	1983 £	1984 £	1985 £	1986 £
Partnership Income	424,070	530,665	707,905	1,013,400	1,298,530
Less: Expenditure					
Wages and Salaries	159,145	215,895	300,045	447,050	597,655
Rent and Rates	119,950	125,180	138,785	158,690	165,840
Light and heat	7,280	7,650	8,030	8,900	10,600
Insurance	12,975	14,825	17,150	18,220	21,390
Telephone	21,460	23,600	28,300	33,920	39,530
Postage	9,545	10,020	11,760	14,700	16,250
Printing and stationery	16,320	17,950	16,410	26,275	29,685
Travel and entertainment	2,580	2,930	6,440	19,720	23,600
General Expenses	6,190	11,430	13,045	22,690	28,360
Professional fees	11,220	13,460	16,160	19,390	24,250
Bank interest and charges	2,325	5,515	8,610	11,710	16,425
Accountancy charges	5,500	7,000	9,250	25,000	26,500
Repairs and renewals	5,445	8,620	10,360	14,980	16,110
Depreciation	8,010	9,620	11,540	13,850	39,000
Subscriptions	2,320	2,650	3,320	3,390	3,980
Bad debts	3,075	—	5,885	18,120	38,650
Equipment hire and maintenance	2,810	4,760	10,635	23,525	25,495
	396,150	481,075	615,725	880,130	1,123,380
Excess of income over expenditure attributable to partners	27,920	49,590	92,180	133,270	175,150

An Amalgamation Case Study

Slicker & Co
Notes on the Income and Expenditure Account

Schedule C.1

		1982 £	1983 £	1984 £	1985 £	1986 £
Partnership income:						
Commercial		80,200	105,250	146,520	213,615	281,700
Conveyancing		126,700	158,780	210,230	308,730	281,700
Litigation		173,100	205,000	259,300	379,010	483,900
General advice		42,100	57,470	85,750	99,405	107,500
Fees		420,100	526,500	701,800	1,000,760	1,276,000
Interest received		875	1,190	2,125	3,465	3,515
Commission		1,095	2,255	3,980	5,110	5,960
Movement in work in progress		—	—	—	4,065	13,055
		424,070	530,665	707,905	1,013,400	1,298,530
Excess of income over expenditure attributable to partners as follows:	%					
Ian	30	8,376	14,877	27,654	39,981	52,545
James	30	8,376	14,877	27,654	39,981	52,545
Kenneth	20	5,584	9,918	18,436	26,654	35,030
Leonard	20	5,584	9,918	18,436	26,654	35,030
	100	27,920	49,590	92,180	133,270	175,150

Slicker & Co Schedule D
Balance Sheet at 30 June 1986

	£	£
Fixed assets		100,500
Current assets		
Work-in-Progress	17,120	
Debtors and prepayments	410,500	
Clients ledger bank accounts	557,980	
Cash in hand	410	
	986,010	
Current liabilities		
Creditors and accrued charges	196,550	
Office bank account	54,645	
Clients ledger balances	557,980	
	809,175	
Net current assets		176,835
		277,335
Represented by:		
Partners' capital accounts		277,335

An Amalgamation Case Study

Slicker & Co
Notes to the Balance Sheet at 30 June 1986

Schedule D.1

Fixed Assets

	Short Leasehold Premises £	Fixtures, and fittings £	Office Equipment £	Motor Vehicles £	Total £
Cost					
At the beginning of year	16,300	15,690	31,140	88,270	151,400
Additions during year	—	5,310	5,060	46,905	57,275
At end of year	16,300	21,000	36,200	135,175	208,675
Depreciation					
At beginning of year	7,335	9,865	7,785	44,190	69,175
Provided in year	815	2,100	9,050	27,035	39,000
At end of year	8,150	11,965	16,835	71,225	108,175
Net book value at 30 June 1986	8,150	9,035	19,365	63,950	100,500

Successful Mergers

Slicker & Co   Schedule D.2
Notes to the Balance Sheet at 30 June 1986

Partners' capital accounts

	Ian £	James £	Keith £	Leonard £	Total £
Balance at 1 July 1985	104,020	100,275	50,960	45,970	301,225
Deduct:					
Drawings	45,700	43,100	18,750	18,850	126,400
Taxation	21,700	21,800	14,550	14,590	72,640
Add:					
Profit for the year	52,545	52,545	35,030	35,030	175,150
Balance at 30 June 1986	89,165	87,920	52,690	47,560	277,335

Debtors and prepayments — Office ledger accounts balances includes a provision of £20,550 against debts which may prove to be irrecoverable.

An Amalgamation Case Study

Establishment Slicker & Co   Schedule E
Post-Merger Balance Sheet at 30 June 1986

	Establishment & Co £	Slicker & Co £	Management Adjustments Establishment & Co £	Management Adjustments Slicker & Co £	£
Fixed Assets	163,140	100,500	A 80,000 B (4,750)	G (8,150)	330,740
Current assets					
Work-in-progress	—	17,120		J 17,120	—
Debtors and prepayments	251,270	410,500	C (2,250)		659,520
Clients ledger bank accounts	370,745	559,980			928,725
Cash-in-hand	4,115	410			4,525
	626,130	986,010			1,592,770
Current liabilities					
Creditors and accrued charges	80,825	196,550	D 60,600	H 17,750 K 15,780	371,505
Office bank account	27,610	54,645		G (13,350)	68,905
Clients ledger balances	370,745	557,980			928,725
Owed to former partners	—	—	E 105,443 F 29,150		134,593
	479,180	809,175			1,503,728
Net current assets	146,950	176,835			89,042
	310,090	277,335			419,782
Represented by:					
Partners' capital accounts	310,090	277,335	A 80,000 B (4,750) C (2,250) D (60,600) E (105,443) F (29,150)	G 5,200 H (17,750) J (17,120) K (15,780)	419,782
	310,090	277,335	—	—	419,782

Schedule F
Adjustments on merger of Establishment & Co and Slicker & Co

1. In Establishment & Co

A. Revaluation of freehold property, previously included at cost, from £65,000 to £145,000.
B. Old fixtures and fittings included in accounts at £4750, but no longer worth anything, so written off.
C. Debtors on office ledger account show balances of £2250 relating to old debts, previously considered recoverable, but not.
D. Three clerks nearing retirement age to be made redundant since on merger with Slicker & Co, their services are not required. Redundancy costs of £60,000 to be paid.
E. Since Bill is no longer keen to work and has no real need to, it was decided to pay him a lump sum on retirement of £50,000 and repay his capital account.
F. George, being an 'extra' conveyancer and part-time only, will not be needed when the two firms merge so his capital account will be repaid.

2. Slicker & Co

G. Slicker & Co will move into Establishment & Co's premises so will no longer require their rented offices, which can be sold for £13,350 to give a profit of £5200.
H. Removal expenses will be incurred of £17,750.
I. Work-in-progress to be written off against capital accounts to bring accounting policy in line with Establishment & Co.
J. Two members of the supporting staff will be made redundant at a cost of £15,780.

An Amalgamation Case Study

Establishment & Co
Capital Account Adjustments (on Merger)

Schedule G

	Arthur £	Bill £	Charles £	Dennis £	Edward £	Fred £	George £	Harry £	Total £
Balance per accounts (Schedule B.2)	62,020	52,715	43,410	34,110	37,210	31,000	27,910	21,715	310,090
Freehold revaluation	17,600	17,600	8,000	8,000	8,000	8,000	8,000	4,800	80,000
Write off old fixtures and fittings	(1,045)	(1,045)	(475)	(475)	(475)	(475)	(475)	(285)	(4,750)
Old debtors written off as irrecoverable	(495)	(495)	(225)	(225)	(225)	(225)	(225)	(135)	(2,250)
Redundancy costs for three clerks nearing retirement	(13,332)	(13,332)	(6,060)	(6,060)	(6,060)	(6,060)	(6,060)	(3,636)	(60,600)
Pension for Bill to retire	(16,156)	50,000	(7,379)	(7,739)	(7,739)	(7,739)	—	(4,328)	—
	48,592	105,443	37,271	27,971	31,071	24,861	29,150	18,131	322,490
Pay off Bill and George	—	(105,443)	—	—	—	—	(29,150)	—	(134,593)
	48,592	—	37,271	27,971	31,071	24,861	—	18,131	187,897

193

Slicker & Co
Capital Account Adjustments (on Merger)

Schedule G.1

	Ian £	James £	Keith £	Leonard £	Total £
Balance per accounts (Schedule D.2)	89,165	87,920	52,690	47,560	277,335
Profit on sale of short leasehold	1,560	1,560	1,040	1,040	5,200
Removal expenses	(5,325)	(5,325)	(3,550)	(3,550)	(17,750)
Work-in-progress written off	(5,136)	(5,136)	(3,424)	(3,424)	(17,120)
Redundancy costs	(4,734)	(4,734)	(3,156)	(3,156)	(15,780)
	75,530	74,285	43,600	38,470	231,885

NB Note capital gains tax liability arising to individual partners continuing in Establishment & Co on part disposal and whole disposal in respect of Bill and George's shares.

An Amalgamation Case Study

Establishment & Co/Slicker & Co   Schedule H
Forecast Income and Expenditure Account

Year ended 30 June:

	1987 £	1987 £	1988 £	1988 £	1989 £	1989 £
Partnership Income		2,109,220		2,323,050		2,743,600
Less: Expenditure						
Wages and Salaries	939,300		1,033,230		1,136,550	
Light and heat	17,770		25,210		27,100	
Insurance	44,500		45,150		48,240	
Telephone	72,685		84,315		102,180	
Postage	30,400		43,290		50,220	
Printing and stationery	127,780		98,720		107,255	
Travel and entertainment	52,730		34,230		47,540	
General expenses	45,200		48,980		54,560	
Professional fees	36,880		47,720		49,190	
Bank interest and charges	16,075		14,065		10,190	
Accountancy charges	31,000		17,500		18,000	
Repairs and renewals	28,950		18,875		21,425	
Depreciation	69,350		75,980		81,230	
Subscriptions	10,640		11,170		11,395	
Bad debts	25,200		27,460		29,520	
Equipment hire and maintenance	26,560		27,890		29,980	
		1,575,020		1,653,785		1,824,575
Excess of income over expenditure attributable to partners		534,200		669,265		919,025

195

Establishment Slicker & Co   Schedule H.1
Notes to the Forecast Income and Expenditure Account

		1987 £	1988 £	1989 £
Partnership income:				
Commercial		228,900	318,100	378,800
Conveyancing		667,700	691,100	802,800
Litigation		458,500	545,900	665,000
Trust, probate, wills and estate tax		472,600	473,700	547,600
General advice		230,700	240,900	291,050
Fees		2,058,400	2,269,700	2,865,250
Interest received		21,750	22,850	25,100
Commission		29,070	30,500	33,250
		2,109,220	2,323,050	2,743,600
Excess of income over expenditure attributable to partners as follows:	%	£	£	£
Arthur	16	85,472	107,082	147,044
Charles	7	37,394	46,849	64,332
Dennis	7	37,394	46,849	64,332
Edward	7	37,394	46,849	64,332
Fred	7	37,394	46,849	64,332
Harry	4	21,368	26,771	36,761
Ian	16	85,472	107,082	147,044
James	16	85,472	107,082	147,044
Kenneth	10	53,420	66,926	91,902
Leonard	10	53,420	66,926	91,902
	100%	534,200	669,265	919,025

Michael Simmons

Appendix 3

Partnership Bust-Up Case Study

Case Study 1

Wordbender & Co. is a well-established, fifteen partner, firm operating in Bishops Wells in the prosperous South Midlands.

Of the partners, twelve are equity and three salaried. The age span of partners ranges from 59 to 30 among the equity partners and to 28 among the salaried.

The partnership affairs are governed by a somewhat old-fashioned deed for life with a provision for notice of twelve months ending at the termination of the financial year (31st December) in case of a desire to retire. There is a provision for expulsion, but only in extreme cases and unanimity of all except the proposed expellee is required.

There is a fairly stringent restrictive covenant preventing equity partners from practising for three years within a ten mile radius of Bishops Wells in the event of termination for whatever reason.

The partnership sharing arrangements are fixed on percentages based on seniority on the lockstep principle.

The firm was established at the turn of the century and has always been one of the premier practices in Bishops Wells. During the swinging seventies, the partnership expanded from five to ten equity partners on the back of a very substantial residential conveyancing boom in the South Midlands. The firm acted for a number of prominent residential estate developers and also for a large number of individual purchasers.

During this period, Frankie and Johnnie were made up to partnership. Both of them joined the firm after undistinguished university careers and following articles stayed on as assistant solicitors, through to salaried partnership, and then to equity partnership.

They are both residential conveyancers and they really reached equity on the basis that nobody could think of a good reason why they should not be so admitted. Both of them are competent craftsmen, but neither has ever introduced a client in their lives, nor seems likely to do so.

Both Frankie and Johnnie are typical work horses. Give them the files and they will process them. They will more or less keep their clients happy, but, if asked, most clients would be pushed to be able to put a face to the name.

The problem is that the firm has very much changed direction. The three latest equity partners are all commercially biased, one in litigation, one in property and the other in company work. The whole firm is very much billings motivated and the problem is that local cut-price conveyancing competition from both the qualified and unqualified has meant that Wordbender & Co. has had steadily to reduce its conveyancing prices from

Successful Mergers

scale fees one per cent, to half a per cent, to whatever it can get.

Furthermore, the developer clients, who are extremely active, have really begun to appreciate the strength of their position, to the extent that the firm now has to act at no cost on the acquisition of new sites, and the fee per sale unit is the subject of very tough bargaining indeed between the clients and the firm.

As neither Frankie or Johnnie has any ability at delegation, they do not have assistants and do all their work themselves. While the volume has held up, the fee income from the work is dropping rapidly and shows every likelihood to go through the floor.

In fact, neither Frankie nor Johnnie is really covering their overheads any more. The younger partners, who are pulling their weight, not only in terms of billings, but also in relation to introductions, are getting extremely restive.

The senior partners see the possibility of losing their bright young partners, Flanagan, Allen and Knox, and being left with Frankie and Johnnie, the middle range under-achievers.

Various informal and semi-tactful discussions have taken place between the senior partners severally rather than jointly, and Frankie and Johnnie. Flanagan, Allen and Knox merely tend to ignore or avoid them!

One suggestion put to the offending couple was that they learn new skills. They both replied to the effect that they were extremely busy and, to be fair, they are both working an average of ten hours per day with time spent at weekends as well. In other words, they could not afford the time off to re-train, and neither of them has the confidence to feel that he has the aptitude for anything else. Commercial conveyancing is beyond them, except in the simplest forms.

Another suggestion, which was put with the greatest diffidence, was that the partnership deed should be re-written so that Frankie and Johnnie take a lesser share. An alternative, scarcely disguised, was to replace the present lockstep system with a points system. Patnership changes of structure under the deed require unanimity. Not surprisingly, both Frankie and Johnnie in these discussions showed unexpected firmness and refused to budge.

Morale in what was a once happy partnership is disintegrating. The senior partners feel isolated and face the prospect of the firm breaking up around them, having spent so long building it. Flanagan, Allen and Knox compare their net drawings with their peers in other firms and find the comparison unfavourable, while Frankie and Johnnie feel bewildered, threatened and generally unhappy. The problem is that both Frankie and Johnnie are at rock bottom. They are thoroughly likeable chaps, who are working long hours and doing their conscientious best. It is hardly their fault that the firm chose badly and, with the benefit of hindsight, should never have made competent assistant solicitors into fully sharing equity partners.

As consultants, you are called in by the senior partners to advise them as to what should be done. As fully rounded specialists, you will of course put yourselves in the position of the prudent general and consider the points of view of Frankie and Johnnie as well, and also of the young Turks, Flanagan, Allen and Knox. As taxation specialists as well, and not being solicitors, you can, of course, hold yourself out in that capacity, you will consider those aspects of the problem.

Case Study 2

Facts are as in Case Study Number 1, only the senior partners do not have the foresight to bring you in as consultants. Another nine months pass and no steps are taken to resolve the situation.

Flanagan, Allen and Knox meet regularly for a drink after work on Friday evenings. Their rumblings of discontent start to take concrete form.

A new town centre is being built in Bishops Wells and a developer client offers the three of them very favourable terms indeed to take a modern suite of offices in what is likely to be the new focal point of the town.

The conversation starts on a theoretical basis, but they soon realise that between the three of them they represent all the appropriate talents for founding a vital and dynamic new legal practice.

Furthermore, they are all locals and well connected. In fact, they have brought in a lot of business and seem likely to bring in a lot more. On a few occasions, their clients, among the more go ahead in the area, have asked them why they associate professionally with such deadbeats as Frankie and Johnnie.

The proposed new office is about half a mile down the road and they are seriously tempted. Once they start sketching out the scheme of things on the back of an envelope, they realise that they carry between them sufficient clientele to provide a viable practice from year one. The father-in-law of Knox is one of the local bank managers, who pledges his support.

They also receive word that certain of the fast growing new businesses in the area will bring them work as a separate entity, but they are not prepared to go to Wordbender & Co. because of its rather stuffy image.

All three feel very torn and they turn to you as a consultant to advise them in their situation. It is now January 1988. Once again, you will give thought to the position of the firm, the seven senior partners, and Frankie and Johnnie in their different situations.

Michael Simmons

Appendix 4

Anatomy of a law firm merger

(Reprinted with permission from the ABA Journal 'The Lawyer Magazine')

Before two law firms merge, lawyers from the small firm, in particular, often become anxious about how the merger will change their lives, how they'll have to adjust, compromise and perhaps even give up a lifestyle they enjoy.

And for them, just like for a person planning to wed, the question that looms largest seems to be, "Is giving up my independence worth what I will get out of the union?"

For the five lawyers in the Beverly Hills, Calif., firm of Pollard, Bauman, Slome and McIntosh, who gave up their autonomy last September to merge with the 35-lawyer Los Angeles office of Chicago's Seyfarth, Shaw, Fairweather & Geraldson, the answer, so far, is yes.

They gave up their name, their power to make compensation decisions, the freedom to control work activity, and the flexibility inherent in a small firm. In exchange, they received more time to practice without administrative distractions, vastly expanded possibilities for new clients, and easy access to the expertise of labour, litigation, government-contracts and ERISA lawyers.

Mergers are now as common-place in the legal profession as in the business arena. Law firms are merging to help attract and keep high quality associates, to expand their client base and areas of expertise and to get a foothold in other cities and states.

But what sounds like a good idea in theory doesn't always work in practice.

The rapid growth of New York's Finley, Kumble, Wagner, Heine, Underberg, Manley & Casey, once the nation's fourth largest firm, came about largely through mergers. But its string of associations was also a factor in the firm's undoing. And the shaky state of Chicago's Isham, Lincoln & Beale – with fewer than 35 of its original 125 lawyers left – is largely a result of its 1986 merger with Reuben & Proctor, an 80-lawyer firm.

This story, though, is an anatomy of a successful law firm merger, about how and why this one worked. And the size of the two firms involved – fewer than 10 lawyers joining with much larger forces – is the most typical combination going.

PBS & M, as it was called by the five partners, had been practicing corporation, securities and business law since 1982. Before that, the five had been the heart of the corporate department at the 80-plus lawyer entertainment-law firm of Kaplan, Livingston, Goodwin, Berkowitz & Selvin in Los Angeles, which broke up at the end of 1981.

After a few years of operation, PBS & M found itself unable to attract and keep the caliber of associates it wanted. The partners watched helplessly while its associate population dwindled from three to one. The firm could barely handle all the work it had, let alone expand its practice.

"We were feeling the 'small-firm crunch,' " said Henry Pollard, the firm's senior partner. "We were in competition with the larger firms for the high-quality associates and were having trouble getting them." Despite the pressure, the firm didn't want to lower its standards, still hoping to find quality associates with two-to-four years' experience, even though it couldn't pay them as much as the large Los Angeles firms.

Pollard admitted it was a gamble for an associate to go with them because they were a relatively new firm with no real track record.

Partner Stephen Bauman put it more bluntly: "This is the big law-firm era. Lawyers are more concerned about big bucks and long-term security and they're not as entrepreneurial as they used to be.

"I think the word 'loyalty' is gone from the law firm dictionary."

PBS & M finally sought help from various headhunters, including Keyth Hart Inc. of Glendale, Calif. Hart and other recruiters sent them a number of associate candidates.

Early in 1987, the firm offered a job to one man they thought would be perfect. "We were delighted," said Pollard. However, when the 'perfect' candidate delivered the news to his own West Los Angeles firm, it made him a counter-offer he couldn't refuse.

"That broke out hearts," Pollard said. It was the last straw in their search for top associates.

After that, the firm began to think about some kind of merger. At first, they considered merging with a firm of three or four lawyers, and pursued that option without success. They soon decided to look for a larger firm instead and give up their firm identity.

Pollard said that giving up their firm name wasn't a problem for the partners. "None of us had any kind of ego need to see our name in a law firm," he said. "What we wanted was to continue doing quality work in a congenial atmosphere."

But PBS & M didn't simply peddle themselves to any and all potential suitors. It wanted to fill a void in another firm's practice. And that empty space had to be in corporate work.

Meanwhile, Seyfarth, Shaw – originally a labor and employment law firm on the management side and still the largest of its kind in the country – had diversified substantially. But its Los Angeles office remained weak in the corporate area five years after five of its lawyers had left to join the newly opened Los Angeles office of Skadden, Arps, Slate, Meagher & Flom.

Looking to develop its corporate practice, Seyfarth's Los Angeles managing partner Joseph Herman had paid for the services of Keyth Hart, who doubles as a merger consultant. "We spent basically five years looking," said Herman.

But Seyfarth, Shaw had had its eye on PBS & M as far back as 1981. During the last six months of Kaplan, Livingston's existence, Seyfarth, Shaw lawyers approached Pollard – head of that firm's corporate department – and some of his fellow partners to see if they were intrested in joining.

Herman had worked with Pollard and Bauman and was impressed with what he saw. There was also a personal connection: Fred Gerard, a partner in Seyfarth, Shaw's New York office, had attended law school with Pollard.

"We contacted Henry and the others on several occasions," Herman said.

"But they weren't interested. They wanted to be independent."

But the problem of finding high-quality associates finally overwhelmed the Pollard firm's reservations about merging. The impetus to merge also came from the fact that being small had handicapped PBS & M in competing for big transactional work.

"We'd done a lot of financing work for particular clients only to see them get to a stage in major private placements where they would have qualms about whether a small firm would be able to service them," said partner Daniel McIntosh. "In a couple of instances, we lost those transactions to competing firms."

So PBS & M finally tied the knot with Seyfarth, Shaw on Sept. 1, 1987. "We spent a lot of time and energy interviewing other groups of lawyers, but none of them measured up to these guys," Herman said.

By expanding through a merger, Seyfarth, Shaw enhanced its own ability to attract the best associates. "We can now offer a broader range of practice areas," said Herman in his spacious and sunny Century City office overlooking West Los Angeles. "If you are just a labor law firm, it, it's much harder to get someone right out of law school saying, 'I want to be a labor lawyer,' to the exclusion of everything else. Having the Pollard firm with us makes recruiting easier."

The merger has also resulted in an increasing number of clients for both parties. Seyfarth, Shaw is now doing employment law work for PBS & M's corporate clients; Pollard, Bauman, McIntosh and partner Edward Pierce are beginning to take care of the business needs of Seyfarth, Shaw's labor clients. (After the merger, the fifth partner, Ansel Slome, went to South Africa on personal business. He was expected to become of counsel to Seyfarth, Shaw when he returned.)

But five months into the merger, Herman said they'd hardly scratched the cross-selling surface.

Guaranteeing that this merger would be a win-win proposition was no easy matter, however. At least 40 hours over a three-month period were spent in discussions before the two firms agreed to the deal.

In those early discussions, PBS & M tried to ascertain Seyfarth, Shaw's style for determining partner compensation. Was it done fairly, uniformly?" "We were satisfied that it was," said Pollard.

It was decided that in their first year, the four new partners would receive compensation equal to what they were earning in their last year at PBS & M. Although the amount is confidential, Bauman did say, "I'm earning more money than I know what to do with, even though I'm putting two kids through college."

After the first year, they are to be evaluated like all other Seyfarth, Shaw partners — by a 10-person elected compensation committee made up of partners from the firm's five offices in Chicago, New York, Washington, Los Angeles and San Francisco.

Each firm shared information on its revenues, expenses and distribution of partnership income. Seyfarth, Shaw, whose Los Angeles Office has 12 partners, gave the incoming group copies of the firm's partnership agreement and described the firm's management and administration style.

They also had to exchange client lists to see if there would be any potential conflicts of interest. "There were a couple of situations which might have been viewed potentially as conflicts of interest," said Herman. "But those were resolved by talking to the clients. They had no objection to our continued representation of them."

Neither firm lost clients as a result of the merger.

Office lease considerations, typically a major headache in a merger, were worked out easily because PBS & M's lease was up by the time they moved over in September. If Seyfarth, Shaw had to assume the lease, it would have needed permission from the partnership as a whole.

Secretarial salaries proved comparable and all five of PBS & M's secretaries came with the merger. A slight hitch did develop in negotiations over the lawyer-per-secretary ratio. At Seyfarth, Shaw, two lawyers share one secretary. At PBS & M, each partner had his own. "Part of our understanding when we joined forces was that they were going to work toward the same secretarial ratio that we had," Herman said.

"But part of the reason they needed one secretary per lawyer," he explained, "is they didn't have the other support people. They didn't have a word processing group, a law librarian and other, more specialized, services."

Before a final decision was reached, PBS & M met with Seyfarth, Shaw partners over a whirlwind weekend in April 1987, spending Friday in Chicago, Saturday in New York, and flying home by way of Washington, D.C., and meeting with those partners at the airport.

At Seyfarth, Shaw's quarterly partnership meeting in June, the merger was put to a vote. The decision to merge was unanimous. (Before an associate can be made partner, the firm requires an affirmative vote by 85 percent of its partners. It has 109 partners nationwide, 135 associates and 18 of counsel).

Once on board, administrative details proved significant but not insurmountable. Seyfarth, Shaw's office administrator, Karen Anderson, had already managed two mergers at another law firm.

One of the first items on Seyfarth's agenda was to upgrade its Wang computer system to accommodate the increased number of users, Anderson said. And all the secretaries from Pollard's firm had to be trained to use it.

Enough space had opened up on the 33rd floor of the One Century Plaza Building to accommodate five more lawyers and five more secretaries. But the latest equipment and furniture had to be ordered for them. And not just any furniture either.

"Their prior collection was eclectic and we wanted continuity to fit with the modern look of our office – grays, pinks and blonde wood," said Anderson. "So we offered to buy them new furniture and they went for it."

Less active and closed files also had to be culled before the move. And because the two firm's file systems were different, new files had to be created for every PBS & M client and each individual matter before the merger occurred. "There were lots of unhappy secretaries filling out forms," Anderson said.

"We also asked them to transfer to our benefits plan. That can be a big problem if one firm's benefits are a lot better than the other's." That wasn't the case here.

The two law libraries had to be consolidated and an inventory of all books and periodicals taken to eliminate any duplication. The PBS & M furniture and older office equipment had to be sold and some of its files put into storage.

Looking much like wedding announcements, news of the merger with the new partners' names and areas of specialty had to be sent out to clients. Martindale-Hubbell had to be notified, as did Parker Directory of California Attorneys. The California Bar Association had to be informed that Pollard and his partners would now have access to Seyfarth, Shaw's trust account.

Documents had to be transferred from IBM displaywriters to the Wang systems. Some were converted by using an optical scanner while others had to be keyboarded.

"We started converting information six weeks before the merger," said Anderson. "And five months into it, we are still at it."

But before these administrative details arose, before the final decision was made, partners at the small firm still had unanswered questions of their own. What, they wondered, would they be giving up going to a big firm?

"The idea of losing the identity that I felt in connection with PBS & M bothered me a little bit," said McIntosh. "I was proud of what we did there and I liked practicing law there. So I did have reservations about that." Even now, he said he sometimes gets nostalgic about the old firm.

Pierce, at 37, the youngest of the five PBS & M partners, worried about strangers making decisions about his welfare. "At PBS & M," Pierce said, "the people making all the decisions were the people I worked with all the time. I knew them, trusted them, and after I became partner, I participated in the decisions too.

"And now, suddenly, people I meet a couple of times a year would be deciding policy firm-wide and for this office, too. And that made me apprehensive."

Pollard was also apprehensive "Seyfarth's management is centralized," he said. "Billings and collections are done through Chicago and all the important decisions are made there. So that was a little strange, somewhat like going to work for IBM."

But after meeting with many of the Seyfarth partners who would have a say about the amount and quality of their work and their level of compensation, they felt more relaxed. "I'm confident my work will be evaluated fairly," Pierce said. "Much of the information evaluated is objective anyway – number of billable hours, how good your clients are at paying."

Seyfarth, Shaw partners average between 1,750 and 1,800 billable hours a year. Before the merger, billable hours at PBS & M were running between 1,600 and 1,700 per partner. Since the merger, Bauman thought their billable time was still within that range. McIntosh, however, said he thought their billable hours were "collectively greater" now than they were at their old firm.

Now that the merger has been completed, everyone is singing its praises. Indeed, Seyfarth, Shaw is so pleased with the merger that it is "actively pursuing" another small Los Angeles firm.

Anatomy of a law firm merger

Seyfarth, Shaw's Mitchell Whitehead said he's in "hog heaven" because of the merger. Before Sept. 1, he was handling the firm's corporate clients by himself. Now he has four new partners and one new associate, Larry Backer, to help him.

"Now I can provide much better service to the corporate clients I already had," said Whitehead. "So if someone has a real estate problem now, I can say, 'Hey, I'd like you to meet Dan McIntosh, he's got 100 years of experience in this area and he can change your life.'

"One of my clients had been scratching his head about how to raise some financing through a public offering. Henry Pollard has a tremendous amount of expertise in the corporate securities area, so he's very interested in Henry's expertise.

"And I have a client, a wealthy individual, in need of estate planning and tax advice and Steve Bauman has provided invaluable help with that.

"Now we've reached a critical mass," said Whitehead. "Without delving too deeply into the subatomic physics of law-firm growth, let's just say there are enough guys here so when we recruit at law schools, people who want to do corporate law are much more interested. And we've already noticed this with lateral recruiting."

He insisted they would not have been able to recruit associate Backer "in a thousand Sundays" if the merger hadn't occurred. Formerly with Irell & Manella in Los Angeles, Backer was hired in November, two months after the merger.

PBS & M lawyers also credited the prospect of the merger with snaring Backer. "Backer is a terrific lawyer," said Bauman. "If we'd been able to find that kind of lawyer when we were a small firm, we might still be a small firm."

Twenty-eight-year-old Backer is very content with his situation. "At a bigger firm, there's more information in the collective legal consciousness," he said. "And being with all these other people makes me more sensitive to litigation, labor relations or environmental issues when I do deal.

"For instance, when a client is buying a piece of property, it might be subject to a host of environmental requirements for the removal of hazardous waste or liability about what was dumped there. And that's the kind of thing you may not think about," he said. "So, it's helpful in drafting agreements to sit down with these guys and figure out what the universe is instead of saying, 'Oh, gee, there might be some liability here,' "

Backer spends about a third of his time with Whitehead and the rest of his time working for Pollard and the other new partners. "Dan, Steve and Henry were considerate enough to offer me some of Larry's time," Whitehead said. "They could have claimed him as their own guy and have him doing nothing but their stuff."

Cooperation of this kind helped avoid a potentially explosive situation. In some mergers, where a group of lawyers come in to strengthen an existing department at another firm, those already there can feel slighted, that the value of their expertise has been diminished.

That didn't happen here. "Some people might say, 'Aren't you upset about no longer being the top dog in the corporate department?' " Whitehead said.

Successful Mergers

"And if they had been jerks – aggressive, pushy, territorial kind of guys – they could have made it unpleasant for me. They could have set up their own little shop and excluded me, but they didn't. They're nice guys."

"A lot of things can go wrong in a merger," Herman said. "But if you know the people, have confidence in them, trust them, believe they are competent lawyers with good judgment and character, then everything else pretty much takes care of itself."

Nancy Blodgett
(staff reporter with the ABA Journal)

Appendix 5a

To merge or not to merge

There are many reasons law firms merge – increased competition; the U.S. Supreme Court decisions in *Goldfarb v. Virginia State Bar,* 421 U.S. 773 (1975), and *Bates v. State Bar of Arizona,* 433 U.S. 350 (1977), that effectively deregulated law firms; the growth by merger and acquisition of corporations that are law firm clients; the worldwide geographical expansion of corporations; the desire for economies of scale; and the rapid growth of other law firms by merger.

Law firms are spending considerable time and money to court prospective merger candidates, with varying success. Ill-considered merger courtships can consume thousands of dollars and hundreds of hours that might otherwise be directed toward practising law.

Even successful courtships often lead to unsuccessful mergers – causing the dissatisfaction and departure of key partners, client migration to other law firms, disorganization, and the deterioration of financial performance. On the other hand, some very successful and profitable large law firms have emerged by this route.

To achieve a successful merger, a firm must first identify potential areas of synergy that can make the whole greater than the sum of its parts. Then, and only then, should a law firm actively seek out merger candidates or position itself to invite merger overtures.

If the "whole" of the merged law firm is not greater than the sum of its parts, the merger will result only in a larger, less successful firm that is more difficult to manage.

All of the valid reasons for a law firm to consider merger as a route to growth involve strengthening the firm through the addition of previously unavailable resources or capabilities. Here is a summary of solid reasons to consider merging.

1. Filling gaps within the firm.

This is the classic reason to consider merging. Merger objectives might include acquisition of key people – rainmakers, managers or technical specialists – filling age or experience gaps, or replacing departed partners with experienced lawyers.

2. Acquiring new specialties.

This is a valid merger strategy where (1) existing clients need specialized services that either result in unfulfilled legal needs, or expose the firm to potential liability by working in areas where it is not qualified; (2) clients are beginning to take specialized legal business elsewhere; or (3) growth potential in identified specialties is greater than that projected for the existing firm.

3. Gaining access to a broader client base.

This is a reason to consider a merger if the firm has expertise that is needed by clients of a firm that doesn't provide service in that area. A classic example would be the merger of a litigation firm with a firm representing corporate clients in need of litigation services.

4. Geographical expansion.

This can occur when existing clients need services in a remote location. It is often easier to begin building a self-sufficient legal presence in another location by merging with a firm there. In merging with a law firm with a good reputation and an established client base, synergy arises through the ability of the expanding firm to provide more highly specialized services to clients of the acquired firm.

5. Acquiring or maintaining market dominance.

This is a valid reason to consider merger where differentiation on the basis of market dominance is critical to firm marketing, as in a transactional practice fed by referrals from outside the community. Positioning as a dominant firm in the marketplace can be a legitimate strategy; positioning as just another, larger firm may not be.

6. Merger for survival or preservation of client base.

A defensive merger can be pursued as a strategy if the partners don't panic. Defensive merger might be justified where failure to negotiate with a prospective suitor might lead that suitor to merge with another firm with similar capabilities. It might also be appropriate where merger is inevitable, and the firm wants to affiliate with the best of the prospective suitors rather than be forced into a less desirable match in the future.

Not all firms pursuing merge as a route to growth are doing it for the right reasons. Consulting experience has shown that merger for the following reasons can be ill-conceived and unsuccessful.

1. "Everyone else is doing it."

This is usually a bad reason for doing anything. However, it is frequently the reason given for premature atttempts at defensive merger. It's only a justification if the fact that "everyone else is doing it" might diminish one's client base.

2. "We need to get bigger."

This is a legitimate reason to merge only in the "market dominance" strategy scenario described above. There are no economies of scale in law practice – larger law firms spend more, not less, on overheads, even when measured on an average per-attorney basis. Law firm mergers calculated to achieve size alone, without an overriding strategic purpose, are destined to fail.

3. Overcoming substandard profitability.

A firm considering a merger with a more profitable firm in order to improve its own profitability is unlikely to find willing candidates. It is the rare successful law firm that will volunteer to share its profits with a less profitable group. Law firm profitability problems should be overcome before embarking upon merger strategy.

4. Ego.

Rapid growth by merger, simply to fuel the ego of senior partners, rarely succeeds. The same ego considerations driving such growth usually result in dissatisfaction.

Firms considering merger as a strategy, either proactively (approaching other firms) or reactively (responding to overtures from other firms), need to make an initial evaluation that leads to a "go/no go" decision. Entertaining every merger overture or blindly pursuing prospective mergers can be disastrous.

Because intense merger activity is a feature of the consolidating legal profession, it is likely that many firms have been, or will be, approached. Even if a decision has been made not actively to pursue a merger, every firm should consider the circumstances under which it would consider a merger opportunity.

Positioning the firm is a first step in this process. This involves an evaluation of the firm's strengths and weaknesses – finances, personnel, clientele, areas of practice and reputation – combined with an assessment of the marketplace.

This marketplace assessment should focus on competitor strengths,

Successful Mergers

weaknesses and activities, client, industry and economic developments, and prospects for regulatory, legislative or judicial change. If the assessment of the firm discloses that economic performance is substandard or that there are productivity problems or a declining client base, those problems should be corrected before a merger is considered.

If the positioning process reveals no significant financial, organizational, management or client problems, the firm should develop a profile of ideal merger candidates. The profile should be characterized by significant factors; age and experience of partners, partner-to-associate ratios, areas of practice, size, geographical focus, financial performance and client mix. This profile can then be used to evaluate merger alternatives.

Even if another law firm meets the general criteria of the profile of prospective merger candidates, a successful merger is not guaranteed. Further consideration should be given to a host of factors that could abort a merger negotiation or cause an unsuccessful merger despite the potential for synergy.

1. Firm name.

Although rarely identified as a potential problem, this single factor probably scuttles more mergers than any other.

2. Conflicts of interest.

Lists of significant clients of each firm should be evaluated for potential conflicts that could obviate any synergy which otherwise might arise.

3. Present or future liabilities.

This should include a review of unfunded retirement obligations and potential professional liability claims.

4. Relative size.

Successful mergers of firms of like size and resources are the exception, because there is no dominant party whose culture, systems and organization will be imposed upon the other. No matter how approached, the merger of firms of disparate size and resources are almost always acquisitions of the smaller of the two firms by the larger.

5. Capitalization.

Law firm capitalization and contribution policies can present particularly difficult problems. Accounting methods must be conformed to enable balance sheet comparisons.

6. Financial disparities.

Disparities in intangible assets of proposed merger firms (work-in-process and accounts receivable) can also pose difficult problems. Different time commitments and disparate salaries for lawyers at comparable levels of experience are often insurmountable hurdles.

7. Leverage and partnership policies.

Dramatic differences in associate-to-partner ratios and disparities in policies regarding admission to partnership are rarely reconciled satisfactorily.

8. Firm culture and management philosophy.

As important as anything else is the management philosophy and culture of each of the merged firms. The balance between central firm authority and individual partner autonomy is a significant factor. Management styles and environments must be compatible. People in both firms must be compatible.

Although it is the fastest way for a law firm to grow and fill gaps or weaknesses, the merger route is fraught with pitfalls.

Firms looking to improve their financial performance may want to consider less risky alternatives, including (1) affiliation or association with other firms, (2) development of reciprocal referral networks, (3) lateral hires of hand-picked partners and associates, (4) adding new associates, staff attorneys or paralegals, or (5) narrowing and upgrading one's practice to become more selective, thereby enabling time to be charged at higher rates and improving overall profitability.

Ward Bower
*(Principal of Altman & Well Inc.
Law Firm Management Consultants from Pennsylvania)*

Appendix 5b

Law firm merger evaluation information

1. Firm partnership agreement and all amendments.

2. Any other agreements, formal or informal, such as employment agreements, retirement agreements, deferred compensation agreements, etc.

3. Copies (or summaries where appropriate) of all lawyer and staff benefits plans, including retirement, medical, insurance, and the like.

4. Organizational charts (administrative and substantive practice) depicting lines of authority and staffing of each entity. *All documented position descriptions and a description of the duties and authorities of all standing and ad hoc committees.*

5. Firm policy and procedure manuals, e.g., office manual, lawyer manuals.

6. Financial statements for the most recent period.

7. Fiscal year end financial statements for the past three years.

8. A list of income distribution *by partner* for the past three years.

9. The income and expense budget (accrual and cash, if available) for the present fiscal year.

10. Any internal memoranda, management reports or other reports prepared by the firm's independent accountants during the past three years.

11. Any documentation of specific or general interest that will provide a further understanding of the firm, including any documentation prepared with respect to firm expansion.

12. A list of clients from whom the firm has received an average per year of $10,000 to $20,000 in fees over the past three years; $21,000 to $30,000; $31,000 to $40,000, etc.

13. A list of clients with whom the firm has a retainer relationship.

14. A list of any major clients (fees of $30,000 or more) that have become clients in the last three years.

Law firm merger evaluation information

15. A list of major clients that have been lost in the last three years.

16. A list of partners providing the full name, age, date first admitted to the bar, year of employment with the firm, number of years to retirement, and a notation as to the practice area of each partner.

17. A list of all partners and associates who have left the partnership during the last three years.

18. An explanation of the firm's method of determining capital account balances in total and by partner.

19. An explanation of the buy-in process of new partners.

20. An explanation of the withdrawal process of departing partners.

21. An explanation of the process for admission of associates to the partnership and a list of the criteria utilized for evaluation for admittance.

22. A list of associates providing the full name, age, date first admitted to the bar, year of employment with the firm, current salary and a notation as to the practice area.

23. A description of the methods by which *associate* lawyers are compensated (including salary increases, bonuses and frequency of adjustment).

24. A list of all payments made by the firm on behalf of lawyers, including CLE programs, bar dues, etc.

25. A copy of documented long range plans or goals.

26. A list of all fee earners (partners, associates, paralegals and law clerks) depicting the client chargeable hours for each fee earner for *the last three years*.

27. A list of administrative positions (i.e. administrator, secretaries, word processing operator, runner, etc.), position descriptions, the number of individuals employed in each position, and the highest, lowest and average salary of each position.

28. A *list* of all (manual and automated) management reports produced.

29. Current aged unbilled time report.

30. Current aged accounts receivable report.

Successful Mergers

31. A list of hourly rates by partner, associate, paralegal and law clerk.

32. A list of owned or leased office equipment (make and model), including computers, word processors, photocopiers and the like, the date of purchase, approximate purchase price, and any equipment stated for acquisition. Please indicate software used, where appropriate.

33. A list of all outstanding loans, if any, specifying amount and terms.

34. Has the firm had any problems with EEOC or similar laws?

35. Has the firm had or does it now have any malpractice suits, pending or threatened? If so, for what reason and what is the potential liability?

Altman & Weil, Inc.
Management Consultants, Ardmore, Pennsylvania,

Appendix 6

Draft Heads of Agreement

Dated   **198**

Parties: –

                                                  (1)
                                                  (2)
                                                  (3)
                                                  (4)
                                                  (5)
                                                  (6)
                                                  (7)
                                                  (8)

                                                A Partners

                                                (9)
                                              (10)
                                              (11)

                                                B Partners

Draft/Heads of Agreement

Recitals (1)   The A **Partners** are at present in practice as solicitors at under the name of

(2)   The B **Partners** are currently practising as solicitors under the name of

(3)   As at   198   , B will be dissolved.

(4)   The B Partners will be joining with the A Partners in Practice with effect from   198   under the name of A at

Agreed

1. As from   198   ("the Commencement Date") the A Partners and the B Partners shall join in partnership as solicitors under the name of A (Incorporating B) at
under the terms of the draft Partnership Deed, a copy of which is attached to these Heads of Agreement as Appendix 1.

Staff

2. The following staff of B shall be joining A with effect from the Commencement Date: –

(a)   – Salaried Partner. Salary £   per annum plus vouched car allowance of £

(b)   Assistant solicitor –   – Salary £

(c)   Legal Executive –   – Salary £

(d)   Office Manager/Accountant –   – Salary £

(e)   Word Processor Operator –   – Salary £

(f)   Secretary –   – Salary £

(g)   Secretary –   – Salary £

(h)   Secretary –   – Salary £

(i)   Articled Clerk –   – Salary £

(j)   Articled Clerk –   – Salary £

(k)   Articled Clerk –   – Salary £

(l)   Articled Clerk –   – Salary £

All staff shall enter into A Standard Form of Contract, which shall make clear that all the above staff shall be entitled to take four weeks holiday at such time as shall be agreed.

There is attached to this Agreement as Schedule 1 a list of the staff of the combined firm together with current salaries and terms of employment generally.

Draft Heads of Agreement

Premises

3.(a) The responsibility and cost of disposing of their leasehold premises at   shall be to the account of the B Partners personally who shall also be entitled to retain any sums received from the disposal.

(b) Prior to the Commencement Date, the A Partners will capitalise, or otherwise appropriate the sum of £   at present designated as a reserve against rent, and shall treat it as credited to them in the proportions that they enjoy as profits immediately prior to the Commencement Date.

(c) Those partners of A holding the lease of shall as from the Commencement Date hold it as trustees for the parties.

Consultants

4. B has a number of consultants who will have no involvement in A as from the Commencement Date and B Partners will bear responsibility for taking out purchased life annuities to dispose of their interest.

Machinery, fixtures and fittings

5. The B Partners will arrange to bring with them for use in the combined firm the following items: –

(a) One Olivetti TES 121 Word Processor.

(b) Three leased and three purchased IBM golf ball typewriters.

(c) Six to eight Phillips System 800 dictating machines and six approximately Phillips hand dictating machines in the 295 series.

(d) One Rank Xerox Copier owned by B.

A will pay the B Partners personally such sum for the above items as shall be agreed in respect of the purchased items.

Library

6. The B Partners will bring with them such part of their library

as shall be agreed.

Furniture

7. The B Partners will bring with them such part of their furniture and shall be agreed.

Moving

8. Moving arrangements shall be made in co-operation between the B and A Partners or is delegated by them. The expenses of the move shall be for the account of the B Partners.

Storage

9. For the time being, the B Partners shall retain their existing storage space at   as well as their Deeds Strong Room at   , until such time as the Deeds can be placed in the A storage space at   and the files can be sent to the A store at   .

Banking

10. Unless   , the present bankers of B, are prepared to offer as favourable terms, as well as undertake to provide a flow of substantial clients on a regular basis, the combined firm will bank with the present bankers of A.

Professional indemnity insurance and claims

11.(a) The annexed Draft Partnership Deed contains the current proposals for top up cover for the combined firm.

(b) The B Partners and the A Partners jointly and severally agree to indemnify each other for claims in respect of the excess of loss not covered by either the basic Law Society Indemnity Scheme, or top up cover arising prior to   198 , irrespective of date of discovery of such items.

Draft Heads of Agreement

Permanent health insurance

12. All Partners will participate in a group scheme to cover two thirds of basic drawings.

Work in progress as at   198

13.(a) B are currently on computerised time costing. All current matters as at their dissolution date will be valued on the basis of the time ledger plus a 25% mark up, and that figure will be treated as either work in progress in the accounts of B as at   198 , or included in an account of post-cessation recepits. When such matters are eventually billed by the combined firm the amount attributed as work in progress at   198   shall be paid into the dissolution account of B maintained with

(b) A do not currently operate a centralised time costing system. Therefore all current matters will be billed or valued on an interim basis as at   198   so as to achieve equality. The basis of billing will be calculated as closely as possible with that employed in subclause (a) above. The reason for the difference in treatment is that the parties wish the combined firm to continue its present accounting basis of bills delivered, which might be prejudiced by the insertion of a large work in progress figure as at   198

Debtors

14. Any sums received from debtors on or after the Commencement Date in respect of bills delivered but written off beforehand shall be credited net to the dissolution account in respect of B debts and to the accounts for the year ended   198   in respect of A debts.

Capital

15. The partners in the combined firm will contribute capital as follows: –

All partners will take out new pension cover prior to   198 and preferably prior to budget day 198   which will provide sufficient by way of a lump sum on retirement to allow the combined firm's bankers to make appropriate loans available for the purpose of providing the capital referred to above. The partners will pay their own premiums in respect of the pension policies and also the interest in respect of the loans secured on the policies, except that the combined firm will be responsible for the interest in respect of the last £   of each such loan.

Life insurance cover

16.   Each partner will cover his own life to the extent of £ and all premiums shall be paid by the partners personally.

Drawings

17.   The drawings and expenses of the partners shall be in accordance with Schedule No. attached to this agreement.

Cars

18.   Subject to the financial situation of the firm at the relevant time being able to support the appropriate borrowings, new cars for the partners use shall be purchased in accordance with Schedule 2, credit being given for net proceeds of sale of any car or cars disposed of at the same time.

Michael Simmons

Appendix 7

Dealing with the library

Books are very much a professional's tools of trade, but most firm's libraries are a disgrace. In the smaller firm, a partner is usually delegated the chore of looking after the library, but he or she has far too many things to do, and the work is almost invariably neglected. This is particularly so in relation to those ever arriving supplements for works of reference. It is a fiddly job to find out which pages have to be removed, and where the replacements need to be put. Most partners have better things to do! A proposed merger is an ideal time to take a long, hard look at your libraries.

Initially there will be duplications to consider. Somebody must go round both libraries and find where the duplications are. Unless the second set can be disposed of at a branch office within the new merged firm, then it will be necessary to consider a disposal of what is not required.

There are a couple of specialist book-sellers in the legal profession who are prepared to take on individual books or whole libraries. They are in business themselves and need to make a reasonable profit. As a result, they will normally only give you about a third of market value.

The alternative, for a solicitor, is to advertise in the legal press, particularly the Law Society Gazette, which has a few book-selling announcements in almost every issue. The seller in that instance can normally expect to obtain a better price.

There are more and more computerised databases in operation, and if each merging firm has one, the company supplying will normally be prepared to allow one contract to be cancelled, and will refund any unexpended portion of the relevant annual subscription. The same situation will normally apply where sets of books are being purchased on subscription.

For solicitors, it is worthwhile approaching one of the major law publishers at the early stages of the merger and asking their representative to come and look at the libraries of the firms in questions. The publishers obviously have an interest in seeing that the firms in question do things in the right way.

Once the merger has taken place, the partners should give serious thought to employing a professional librarian, if there has not been one before, on a part or full-time basis. This really is not a job for partners, who have far too much to occupy their time elsewhere.

While each smaller firm could probably not justify the expense, even though the need was there, the combined firm is a different entity altogether. Even if the partners decide not to employ a librarian on a continuing basis, then it is worthwhile considering taking on a qualified librarian on a project basis to put everything in order and set the merged firm on the right road for the future.

All professional firms spend a great deal of money on books, and we should make sure that we obtain the greatest benefit from that expenditure.

Michael Simmons

Appendix 8

Law Society Rules relevant to merger

(Reproduced from the Professional Conduct of Solicitors by permission of the Law Society.)

2.09 Principle

Where there has been a material alteration to the composition of the firm, the clients must be notified promptly.

Commentary

1. The Law Society must also be notified if the alteration results in a change in any solicitor's practising address (see above Principle 1.02 and Solicitors Act 1974, section 84(1)).

2. Where a new firm takes over from a firm which has ceased to practise or an existing firm is dissolved and the partners divide into two or more entities, the clients affected have a choice of which solicitor or firm to instruct (see Solicitors' Practice Rules 1987, Rule 1(b) (Chapter 6)). It would not be proper for the new firm to take over clients' business, including papers or money previously held without the clients having first been notified. Notification promptly by circular letter is therefore essential as is an agreement between the solicitors concerned as to the contents of such a letter.

3. The letter circulated to clients should inform the clients of the position and it is a useful practice for the letter to state the amount standing to the credit of that particular client's account. The letter may add that, unless he is instructed to the contrary within a specified time, the writer will deal with the client's affairs in accordance with instructions given to the previous firm. It is a matter for the new firm to decide whether to notify clients for whom no current work is in progress and for whom no money or original documents of value are held.

4. Where the partners disagree about the arrangements for notifying clients of a material change in the composition of the firm, one or more partners may separately circularise all the clients of the firm. This circularisation should be a short factual statement informing the clients

Law Society rules relevant to merger

of the change as a result of a dissolution and may give the new practising addresses of each partner. Because of the effect of the Solicitor's Practice Rules 1987, Rule 1(b) (see Principle 6.01), there should be a statement that the client is free to instruct any solicitor of his choice. (For a specimen letter see Appendix C2).

5. The same principles as stated in the three previous commentaries apply where a firm amalgamates with another firm; the clients should therefore be notified of the amalgamation. Where two or more firms amalgamate and have previously been acting for clients who are involved in litigation against each other, or who in any other way have conflicting interests, the new firm must cease to act for both the clients unless it is able to continue to act for one with the consent of the other. (See Principle 9.03; 3). The Law Society has published a handbook on the subject of amalgamations which can be obtained from the Publications Department.

9.03 Principle

A solicitor must not continue to act for two or more clients where a conflict of interest arises between those clients.

Commentary

1. If a solicitor has already accepted instructions from two clients and a conflict subsequently arises between the interests of those clients, the solicitor must cease to act for both clients, unless he can without embarrassment (see Principle 9.02; 1) and with propriety, continue to represent one client with the other's consent. A solicitor may only continue to represent one client where he is not in possession of relevant knowledge concerning the other obtained whilst acting for the other. Further, a solicitor must ensure that the former client consents to his continuing to act for the other client. The former client should be separately advised before such consent is obtained.

2. A solicitor acting for two or more co-defendants in criminal proceedings whose interests became conflicting must cease to act for all of them.

3. Following the amalgamation of two or more firms, the clients of the individual firms will, as a result of an express or implied change of retainer, become clients of the new firm; care must be taken to ensure that the interests of the clients of the new firm do not conflict. If they do, the firm must cease to act for both clients unless they are able, within the terms of Commentary 1 above, to continue to act for one. In certain

Successful Mergers

exceptional circumstances the amalgamated firm may continue to act for one client after erecting a 'chinese wall'. Further guidance can be obtained from the Law Society.

Specimen letter – material change in composition of the firm

A. B. Smith & Co
64, High Street
Craxenford

Partners: Mr A
         Mr B
         Mr J

Dear . . . .
We/(I) write to inform you that Mr J is/(I am) retiring as a partner of this firm on 31st May 198 .
Mr A and Mr B will be continuing to practise from this address as A.B. Smith & Co.
From 1st June 198   Mr J/(I) will be practising at 25 Market Street, Craxenford under the style of J & Co.
Now that there has been a material change in the firm A.B. Smith & Co you are invited to indicate as soon as possible which firm/(solicitor) you wish to instruct in future. You are, of course, free to instruct any solicitor of your choice.
It would assist the smooth running of your affairs if you let us know, preferably before 31st May next, who you would like to instruct. To help you there is attached to this letter a form setting out the alternatives for your signature and return to the above address. Please strike out the alternative you wish to reject.
Your papers will be either retained here or handed over according to your written instructions.
We have £ . . . . standing to the credit of your ledger (Optional Paragraph)

Yours sincerely,

Note: The foregoing wording may be varied according to the circumstances. However it must be clear to the client that he has freedom of choice.

Appendix 9

"I married a myth"

(Reprinted with permission from The American Lawyer.)

It looked great on paper. Take one established Chicago law firm with institutional clients and a history going back to Robert Todd Lincoln. Mix it with a young, flashy litigation firm with lots of name-recognition clients and plenty of pizazz. *Bingo:* Instant Success.

Or so Richard Ferguson and Don Reuben seemed to think on May 20, 1986, when they first met to talk merger. Ferguson was the senior partner and star utilities lawyer at Chicago's 120-lawyer Isham, Lincoln & Beale, a venerable Chicago establishment, and ace litigator Reuben led the 80-lawyer pack known as Reuben & Proctor.

The two shook hands on the deal less than four weeks later. Obviously both sides were anxious for the merger. Both wanted it bad. Both wanted it fast. As it turned out, they got it bad, fast.

Reuben's firm – which he had founded in 1978 after being kicked out of Kirkland & Ellis – had reached an awkward size. It had grown quickly and developed a solid litigation reputation. But Reuben and his partners had set their sights on large-scale corporate transactional work, and that had not materialized. "We were known as litigation tough guys," says Reuben partner Gary Elden. "It was hard to project the image that we could also do sedate deals."

Ferguson maintained that Isham's motivation was simple. "We were looking for . . . a litigation firm, because that's where the action was," he was quoted as saying in a winter 1987 article in *Sullivan's Review,* a Chicago quarterly. (Reached at his home in Florida, Ferguson declined comment and declined to listen to questions from *The American Lawyer.*)

There's no denying that Reuben & Proctor was full of action: It did sexy, high-profile work for such clients as the Tribune Company, Michael Jackson, the Catholic Archdiocese of Chicago, and the Chicago Bears. Isham rarely drew a call from the media, but it did respectable work for a stable of clients ranging from the Commonwealth Edison Company to the Illinois Housing Development Authority.

What Reuben didn't know as he dreamed the big-time dream was that Ferguson was a man without a firm to deliver. His control of Isham had disintegrated. He was acting without the consent of his partners. They were, in fact, trying to kick him out of the firm. Reuben's meeting with Ferguson can be likened to Mikhail Gorbachev's meeting with Ronald Reagan the day after the 1988 elections.

The result: disaster. The merger that was supposed to catapult both firms into the national spotlight has done just that. But the attention hasn't been drawn by booming revenues, burgeoning client lists, or remarkable management. Many on-lookers and participants are shaking their heads at the spectacle with sudden hindsight, muttering the inevitable, "I told you so."

As of this writing, 39 of the original 49 Isham partners have abandoned the new firm, taking most of their clients with them. On the Reuben side, partner defections have been minimal, but the Tribune Company, once the firm's biggest client, has relocated its corporate and tax work.

The two firms' practices were not so much compatible as combustible. Associates sneered at one another. Cross-selling was at a minimum. Partners fought over where to move. Profits impressed no one; neither did the firm's leaders.

Reuben's view now is that "it could have worked, it should have worked, and it would have worked – had they been, when we merged, a law firm. They were not a law firm. You'll never pick this up fast or slow unless you're lucky . . . . The rule is, if it walks like a duck, quacks like a duck, it's probably a duck. In Isham's case it wasn't, although it walked, talked, and swam like one."

Reuben left a significant amount of the financial detective work to a few partners, particularly managing partner Alfred Spada, who has since left the new firm to set up his own international consulting company. Spada says he was well aware that there was some discontent at Isham, and that profits were lagging. The extent of the troubles did not become apparent, however, until after the merger.

Most Reuben partners had even less of an idea of what they were getting into. "It was like going to a Greek tragedy and not knowing what had happened in the first two acts," says James Klenk, co-managing partner of the new firm.

Here, then, is the full story. If the drama sounds familiar – with Reuben as Oedipus, the king who finds out far too late that he has married badly – one of its mysteries also has a familiar ring: Who knew what when?

At Isham grievances against Ferguson had been festering for years. Younger partners were struggling to get out from under his autocratic rule, and a faction was urging drastic action. "Ferguson *had* to merge," says one former Isham parter. "We were going to kick him out."

A brilliant regulatory lawyer, Ferguson, 62, had led the firm's biggest client, the Commonwealth Edison Company, through rough times in the early 1970s, when utilities came under heavy attack from environmentalists. "Dick Ferguson was the best lawyer that that firm had for as long as I'd been there," says Laurence Lasky, who worked at the firm for 22 years before leaving for Sidley & Austin last December.

Ferguson was less successful as an administrator, although he has been in power for over a decade. "A lot of people resented his style of management, which was essentially one of dictatorship," says litigator Richard Phelan, a partner at Isham from 1970 until 1975, when he left with two other Isham lawyers to start his own firm, Phelan, Pope & John.

The senior partner had an almost reverential regard for Commonwealth Edison; the people who did work for Edison were hand-picked and well rewarded. At peak periods, up to 12 partners and eight associates handled Edison matters full time. "He played favourites in terms of compensation," says one former Isham partner. Another ex-Isham partner says. "If you didn't work for Edison you were a nonperson."

In 1979 Ferguson further alienated younger partners by insisting on a partnership agreement that called for a three-tier managing council of A, B, and C partners. The A partners – Ferguson; Richard Ogilvie, a former governor of Illinois; and Frederick Carson, a corporate lawyer and Ferguson supporter – were appointed for life. They in turn appointed three B partners, leaving two C positions open for general election. This arrangement locked Ferguson into power and eliminated whatever semblance of democracy that had existed in the firm.

For years Ferguson rejected younger partners' desire to discuss expansion opportunities and business development. "What we're talking about was whether he would permit the firm to move into a modern age or not," says one partner.

Perhaps because of the common bond against Ferguson – who was called "The Great White Father" and "The Prince of Darkness" at various points in his reign – the partnership displayed signs of collegiality and closeness but lacked any real institutional unity. "Before the merger, the discontent at Isham was such that partners' psychologies were less and less 'this is the firm,' and more 'this is my client,'" says one former Isham partner. "What you had was a trend toward a client-oriented environment, with everybody positioning themselves to leave if necessary."

At the time of the merger, at least 50 of the 120 lawyers worked in litigation. While the firm was at the top of no one's list of great litigation firms in Chicago, Isham nonetheless handled some major cases, representing the Chicago Board of Education in a desegregation matter that resulted in the federal government's having to pay $117 million to the board. Isham also represented one of the contractors for the MGM Grand Hotel in litigation resulting from the Las Vegas fire and counselled the Northbrook Excess & Surplus Company in suits involving the Hyatt Hotel skywalk collapse in Kansas City, Missouri.

Yet Ferguson had a tendency to act as if the litigators didn't exist. "In my judgment he had a vision of the law firm that was no broader than the utilities practice itself," says one former Isham partner. "He clearly was not amenable to an expansion of the business because it would dilute his own authority."

Ferguson's contempt for the firm's litigators and his unwillingness to expand beyond the utilities area were nothing new. In 1973 Richard Phelan, who had just won a case for Nitrin, Inc., that brought in almost $5 million in fees, proposed expanding the litigation practice. Ferguson rejected the plan. "He was having no part of that because I think that would have interfered with his running of the firm," says Phelan.

In the summer of 1985 Ferguson and the firm received a clear signal that his power was slipping. Ferguson tried to fire an outspoken litigation associate, but failed. Then he tried to force the associate out by lowering his compensation. Several young partners, including Paul Schroeder, James Fletcher, and Hugh McCombs, Jr., stood up to Ferguson and protected the associate.

The senior partner was enraged. "Ferguson viewed it as his firm, and here it was he couldn't get a goddamn associate fired, " says a former partner.

According to several partners, Ferguson tried again to push some of the ligitators out. This time he had partners on his hit list, particularly one young partner who was very well regarded in the firm but had been one of the principal lawyers on a complicated Edison case that the firm had lost. The matter involved an attempt to cancel Edison's obligation to buy 15 million tons of coal, then valued at $450 million. It was a virtually unwinable case, and one that Ferguson had not followed closely; one partner says that when Ferguson heard the bad news, he was furious that he had not been kept closely informed about the status of the cases.

Ferguson enlisted partner Michael Miller to try to oust the hapless Edison litigator. They were unsuccessful. "It was clear Ferguson sought to make [the partner] a scapegoat to atone for his lack of direct involvement," says one former partner. "It was a transparent attempt to cover his ass is what it was."

After the loss of the Edison case, Ferguson began to show a new interest in upgrading litigation. He hired two laterals – Robert Hallock, a veteran of Kirkland & Ellis and Levy and Erens, and Gregory Jones, a former first assistant U.S. attorney. Both litigators were well received. No one dreamed that Ferguson would bring abroad dozens of Reuben litigators just nine months later.

Although Ferguson did discuss the hires with the B partners, he rarely brought all of them in on major decisions. In the winter of 1985, the B partners resolved to give him some unasked-for advice. Corporate partner Jon Lind, regulatory lawyer Michael Miller, utilities lawyers David Rosso and Robert Yolles, and public finance partner C. Richard Johnson proposed that a committee be set up to look into a possible merger or acquisition, and to come up with a more businesslike approach to running the firm.

When the plan was presented to Ferguson he became very upset and said he had his own ideas. "He told us, 'No, keep your noses out. We have some hot prospects,' " says one partner. "It was typical. He wouldn't let us do anything because he was convinced we'd screw it up." Ferguson never let on what those prospects were, but partners say they have since heard that Ferguson was considering either a merger or a departure, with Edison in tow.

Isham: What price freedom?

The firm became further polarized after a managing council meeting in March 1986. Ferguson was pushing for additional partnership points for several partners, including some who were working on the Edison account. It was nothing new for Ferguson to make such a demand, but this time the B and C partners resisted. Ferguson warned them that the council was losing collegiality and lectured them about the need to respect the recommendations of a senior partner.

Ogilvie agreed with Ferguson and called for a vote. Ferguson's proposal was voted down. Announcing he had a train to catch, Ferguson quickly adjourned the meeting. It was the last time the managing council officially met.

"I married a myth"

The B partners, however, continued to meet to try to overcome the deadlock. According to three former partners, it was agreed that the main problem was Ferguson. The solution? Edge him out.

Under Ogilvie's leadership, Isham had recently been awarded $2.3 million from the reorganization of the bankrupt Chicago Milwaukee St. Paul & Pacific Railroad. The money was to be distributed among the partners, but one partner suggested offering Ferguson a substantial lump sum in exchange for his retirement. The idea took hold. Someone else even argued that it would be worth the whole settlement to get rid of Ferguson, recalls another partner.

Johnson, Yolles, Rosso, Lind, and Miller discussed this idea and worked out a general proposal. According to a former Isham partner, Miller went to Ferguson with the idea in early May.

Ferguson did not respond, but by the end of the month he was meeting with Reuben. Less than a month after that, a shocked partnership was being told that Isham, Lincoln & Beale would be merging with Reuben & Proctor. (Miller declines comment for this article.)

"It frankly never occurred to me that Ferguson, in an effort to regain control, would go out and embrace a merger," says one former partner, echoing the reactions of many.

But apparently Feguson had been speaking to other firms long before the face-off over his retirement. He told *Sullivan's Review* that he "had been conducting a serious merger study" for two years. Therefore, he cannot be accused of merging his firm as a mere stratagem.

As a power play the merger makes little sense, anyway. "Ferguson is a pretty smart guy," says one of his former partners, "but I cannot begin to fathom what he thought at the time he was getting out of this . . . . . If he thought he was going to consolidate his power with Don Reuben at the firm, that is a bunch of foolishness."

When Ferguson announced the merger, he told partners that the deal would, among other things, bolster Isham's litigation practice. Yet with almost 50 lawyers, the area was obviously much stronger than Ferguson seemed to recognize, and the suggestion was bitterly resented. "Half the firm were litigators!" says one former Isham associate. "How they could think we needed Reuben to bolster *us* illustrated how out of touch they were."

That comment touches on what would turn out to be the chief irony of the merger: that *neither* side found in the other what it really needed – a corporate boutique.

Confessions of a necrophiliac

Nine months after the merger, Reuben wrote a piece for this magazine called "Why I married Isham, Lincoln & Beale" [March 1987]. His cheeky and upbeat piece (known as "Confessions of a Necrophiliac" by some Reuben associates) makes intriguing reading now, given what proved to be the precarious health of the bride.

Reuben on the speed of the deal: "We all agreed that if we got involved in any great detail on the myriad of questions good lawyers could always raise, such as questions about specific individuals or office space, we would merge, perhaps, in the fall of 1994."

Just why he was in such a rush is hard at first to understand. Profits per partner at Reuben & Proctor averaged about $245,000 in 1985, competitive with the top Chicago firms, according to "The Am Law 75." Profits per partner were much lower at Isham, averaging $190,000.

Reuben says that Isham's profits were not a concern. "I was led to believe they were very close to ours by Mr. Spada," he says. "I didn't look at the numbers. I let him look at the numbers." According to Spada, the importance of the profit difference has been exaggerated in the press. Asked whether Reuben knew about the gap between the two firms' performance, Spada says, "Oh, sure. . . . All the partners knew, because all the financials were distributed ... This was probably the most significant fact we had to deal with. Nobody in his right mind, particularly an aggressive litigator, would not have known."

Revenue per lawyer at Isham was also on the low side, since the Edison work – which made up 20 to 30 percent of the firm's revenues – was billed at a flat rate of $97 an hour and was done largely by partners. (This flat rate would prove to be a divisive issue in the merged firm.)

But Reuben, impetuous as he may have been, seems to have had logical reasons for embarking on a merger. Internally the firm was no longer the tight group of rebellious go-getters it had been in 1978, but it had not grown big enough or diverse enough to attract strong corporate work, either. About half of the 28 partners were litigators, but nearly two thirds of the revenue was from litigation. In Isham Reuben thought he would get a strong corporate firm with a white-shoe reputation and a name that spelled instant credibility. Former governor Richard Ogilvie was an added attraction.

The reality was more pedestrian. "In fact," says former Isham partner Hugh McCombs, who left in September 1987 to join Mayer, Brown & Platt, "we had in my judgment one of the weakest tax departments in the city of Chicago. Our corporate practice was quite limited and narrow in its focus, and we had a very limited bank practice."

It was only several months into the merger that Reuben lawyers began to find out that the Isham corporate practice was not all it was cracked up to be. "It was supposed to have a hell of a lot more breadth and scope," says a Reuben partner. Former managing partner Spada now says, "It was more limited than we wanted it to be . . . but it was a start."

As for morale, Reuben & Proctor had its own problems. "There was a feeling that what had attracted people had changed," says a former associate, describing the firm in the year before the merger. "The excitement of joining this group of pirates, of bandits. . . had been lost." Reuben no longer shared real power with this pirate crew. He was "simply the Oracle of Delphi sitting there in his office issuing commands," says this associate. "In that sense there were no real politics."

Demanding and abrasive, Reuben can humiliate without fear or favor. Neither his partners nor his clients are spared; one former associate says Reuben often summons several lawyers to his office at once so they can cool their heels until he is ready to see them. (Reuben denies this.) An associate who left before the merger observes. "A lot of [Reuben lawyers] are afraid to make decisions for fear of pissing off Don. Nuns have a way of giving you a look that strikes you dead on the spot. Don had a nun look."

Reuben is far from saintly in his speech, which tends to the scatological. "A lot of his metaphors deal with sex or bowel movements," says one associate who is no longer at Isham. "He likes it down in the gutter." ("I don't think that describes me," says Reuben.)

While Reuben tempered his manner somewhat with his new Isham partners, he continued in his old ways with his Reuben colleagues. "I saw acquiescence in the [Reuben] partners to a degree I found astonishing," says one former Isham associate.

The parallel with Ferguson and Isham seems obvious. But where Ferguson's paternalism alienated people, Reuben's hard-charging, beat-the-pants-off-them-at-any-cost attitude excites his troops. He can inspire loyalty even in those whom he humiliates. "He was tough on me, but who cares? I can take that," says Gerald Lutkus, a Reuben alum now at Barnes & Thornburg in South Bend, Indiana. "He's an unbelievable attorney."

But other Reuben admirers, like Steven Bashwiner, who worked with Reuben for nine years at Kirkland & Ellis, found his tactics tiresome. "He is someone who is an acquired taste," says Bashwiner, a partner at Katten, Muchin & Zavis. "After you've been practising law for ten years, you think, 'Hey, I'm not the office boy'".

Given the power relationships at both firms, it isn't surprising that Reuben would write, in 1987. "As Ogilvie, Ferguson, and I talked with our respective partners and major clients, we found no serious impediments or objections to the merger." At Reuben & Proctor, however, the news wasn't sprung on the partnership as a fait accompli – as it was at Isham.

Shortly after his initial dinner with Reuben, Ferguson involved Miller and Yolles in the deal. He also brought in partner Paul Hanzlik, who handled much of the firm's administrative work, to go over details with Reuben & Proctor's managing partner Spada. A few days before the deal was announced. Rosso and Johnson were also summoned.

Both were skeptical. "It wasn't the firm that jumped to mind immediately," says Rosso. Rosso and Johnson met with Spada and were persuaded that he would be able to make it work. "Since some of my partners were pretty hot for it, and since I was impressed with Spada, I ended up going along with it." says Rosso.

Rosso did not, however, go along with the way the merger was being presented to his colleagues. On Friday, June 13, 1986, a partnership meeting was called at Isham. Ogilvie, who rarely spoke at such meetings, announced the merger. He talked confidently about catapulting the firm into the twenty-first century, and warned that midsized firms would go the way of the dinosaur, recalls a partner who was at the meeting.

The partners sat in stunned silence.

Then partner Philip Steptoe ventured the comments that the deal was rather sudden, and that the firm seemed to be sailing into uncharted waters.

Ogilvie was not sympathetic. "Son," this partner recalls Ogilvie replying, "I've been in this business a lot longer than you have, and if you think we're in uncharted waters, you can get off the boat."

"This sent the message loud and clear that this was a done deal," says the partner.

Nevertheless, someone asked about partnership structure at Reuben & Proctor. Yolles explained that it was a two-tier system. "The obvious question was, 'What's going to happen [to Isham partners]?'" says this partner. "Yolles's approach was to answer only the question asked. . . .Then there was this silence. The silence was a challenge."

Once again, Steptoe spoke up – "Even after being stepped on and squashed like a bug," marvels the source. Would all the Isham partners be equity partners? Yolles said no, but gave no explanation of the ground rules. (Nine Isham partners eventually became non-equity partners under the two-tier system.)

Yolles says it was not his "inclination to go on and explain every twist and turn." Steptoe declines to comment about his reaction to the announcement. Ogilvie did not return phone calls.

"I was not only surprised, but I was deeply offended," says one former Isham partner, apropos the decision. "What offended me was the arrogance, the presumptiveness, that two or three people could make a decision of that magnitude without consulting the partners."

Welcome to the Big World

On Friday the thirteenth of June, the same day that the Isham partnership got its shock. Reuben & Proctor held its own meeting. If the actual announcement surprised no one – most partners had been informed about the merger during the week before its official announcement – the firm's choice of partner certainly did. Most partners had assumed Reuben would seek a smaller, less traditional firm. "From outward appearances it didn't seem to fit the criteria we were looking for." says Reuben partner Philip Stahl, who says he felt strongly that the merger was happening too fast. "Others felt it was worth the risk and we should try it."

At a later meeting for associates, Spada fielded a volley of questions: Will we have to do regulatory work? How many litigators does Isham have? Why pick such a vastly different firm? One especially outspoken associate, Katherine Rakowsky, pointed out that several Reuben associates had turned down offers at Isham. She also reminded Spada of a meeting only two months earlier during which Spada had told the associates no merger would take place without their involvement in the process.

"Welcome to the big world," Spada said. When that flip response died, he explained that he hadn't considered a merger of this scale and that there was no way to consult with everyone *and* accomplish the merger. "I didn't at all have in mind that kind of merger at that time." Spada now says. "And there would have been no way to discuss it with everyone."

"I married a myth"

Getting to know you getting to hate you

Lawyers on both sides predicted darkly that the cultures would not so much mix as clash. Reuben associates pictured the Isham lawyers as uptight and stodgy: they, in turn, viewed their counterparts as flighty. "They think like one-shot litigators," says one former Isham partner of the Reuben partners. "They have no sense of an institutional law firm that represents institutional clients. These are two different kinds of animals."

A few weeks after the merger had been announced, the Reuben lawyers held a golf outing at a nearby resort and invited a few Isham partners out of courtesy. The agenda included a day of sports followed by a barbecue and dancing – complete with complementary cowboy hats – to a country-western band. Several Reuben associates were wearing jeans.

The Isham lawyers arrived wearing coats and ties. "Oh, my god!" was Gerald Lutkus's first thought.

"Here we go. This is exactly what we heard. They're a bunch of starched shirts."

The Isham partners tried to make the best of their too-formal attire. No one had told them it was a barbecue, says Paul Hanzlik, who even tied a bandana around his neck.

The first combined associates meetings were filled with hostility, especially among litigators. Both groups tried to be friendly, but there were strains. "Each side considered its practice to be cream-of-the-crop," says one former Isham associate. "The reaction was one of condescension on both sides. . . . It was surprising to discover that they hated us as much as we hated them."

Some Reuben lawyers say they encountered hostility when they asked Isham lawyers, particularly litigators, about their practices. "Their litigators felt by this merger they were being told they were no good," says Reuben associate Rakowsky. "I think they felt we were trying to find their best work and take it from them. We were just asking questions because we were curious."

Within two months of the merger, most Reuben associates quit trying. "We weren't the most mature people in the world" admits Lutkus, who left last May. "When it appeared to us early on that it wasn't working, we just said screw it."

The Isham contingent didn't take to the style of the Reuben & Proctor lawyers, either. "The bottom line was that these people were incredibly intense and took themselves very seriously, and the Isham people were just much more easy going," says one former Isham associate.

A few of the Reuben associates came to be know among the Isham lawyers as the "Sex Police." The Reuben lawyers objected to what they saw as outrageous sexism on the part of Isham partners and associates. During a litigation training session, for instance, an Isham partner displayed a poster of a busty model in a tank top to illustrate the maxim that a picture is worth a thousand words. One Reuben associate complained to the partner about the incident.

Nor did Don Reuben go over well. His popularity among some Reuben associates — some of the Isham people refer to it as a cult — did not impress the Isham associates. "When they ran out of things to say," says one Isham lawyer, "they told stories. 'Don. Don. Don. Don.' So that Don spelled backwards is nod, as in nod off to sleep."

There was no money

After the first few months, a deeper sense of frustration and impatience began to set in among the Isham lawyers. Ferguson was showing up for work less and less, although his retirement was not announced until a year later. Reuben was not playing an active role in working out logistics and many felt Spada's efforts focused too much on back-office merging and not enough on firm direction and business development. Some also felt that deadwood wasn't being cleaned out fast enough.

Reuben partners were getting impatient too. Dissatisfied with the flat-rate billing on Edison and the preference the Edison partners still received, they started to grumble. "The partners who had the Edison work were used to being the big kids on the block, and we kind of viewed them as a burden," says William Schmidt.

Billing rates were raised. (For Isham, where rates had been lower, the increase was nearly 20 percent.) Even Edison's discounted rate went up from $97 an hour to $107 an hour. But the Isham lawyers — with many clients in regulated industries — were reluctant to bill at the higher rates. Billable hours also rose more slowly than had been expected. In both October and November 1986 revenue was $500,000 under budget, partly because of slow adjustment to a new billing system.

It became obvious that Spada's budget projection of $3.5 million in income a month had been overestimated. "The budget was a goal," says Spada. "The partners did not deliver the kind of income I thought they could deliver."

A billing binge in November brought in enough cash to allow a distribution of profits in January 1987. But for the ensuing eight months no profit was distributed. "The worst thing had happened is that there was no money," says Schmidt bluntly.

Though both sides made some efforts to cross-sell, territorialism took hold. "You suddenly found yourself in a firm where there wasn't enough to go around," says Schmidt. "So are you going to share?... I think that we were as territorial as they were."

In November 1986 and January 1987 the Isham partners received their shares of the $2.3 million Milwaukee railroad settlement. Within two months two of them gave notice: Richard Johnson and James Mann announced they were leaving to join Schiff Hardin & Waite. In June Isham partner Paul Schroeder left for the Chicago office of Jones. Day. Reavis & Pogue.

"I really didn't like the direction the firm as merged was taking" says Johnson who calls it "an unlikely match." He was a member of the new executive committee: when he left his partners were shaken. "He would come to executive committee meetings, and then two days later he was gone." says co-managing partner James Klenk.

Johnson's departure highlighted the deeper troubles at Isham that Reuben partners had begun to discover. At the same time Isham lawyers began to question their own commitment to the venture. Johnson was considered a thoughtful, intellectual lawyer. If he thought the merger wasn't working, maybe he was right.

In June the first Reuben partner walked. William Schopf gave notice that he was leaving with three associates to form his own firm: he says dissatisfaction with the merger influenced his decision.

Reuben called a dinner meeting for his old partners and asked them to be candid about their fears. "It really was a pep-rally-slash-gripe session." says William Campbell. "The gripes were based on the feeling that there was lack of communication that an effort should be made to push this merger." The partners agreed not to meet separately again.

Recipe for disaster

"So, as time goes by," Reuben wrote in his 1987 *American Lawyer* article, "a good barometer for us is whether old relationships and alliances dissipate and fold into one common Isham, Lincoln & Beale tent."

By midsummer the barometer showed that at a time when the year-old merger should have been moving ahead full force, it was unraveling. The firm was still weak in tax and real estate. It was also hampered by being divided between two offices, and partners were having difficulty agreeing on a single location. Ferguson announced his retirement in August, but continued to haggle over terms with Reuben and others. Spada had resigned as managing partner in early summer. Reuben appointed Paul Hanzlik from Isham and James Klenk from Reuben & Proctor to replace him as co-managing partners, a move that didn't sit well with some of the Isham partners.

"Hanzlik was viewed as a guy who had been Ferguson's gofer," says one former Isham partner. "He had maneuvered himself into the same position with Reuben."

Hanzlik responds. "That's incorrect.... I've acted independently as a co-managing partner to make decisions and recommendations to the executive committee."

Several Isham partners felt Reuben was pushing decisions on them both directly and indirectly. "The feeling that things were being forced down our throats was the reason a lot of people left," says one Isham defector. While antipathy to Reuben was undoubtedly a factor in some departures, another former Isham partner warns that "it really would be unfair in my view to characterize [Reuben] as the evil genius or in any sense to attribute the breakdown in communications to Reuben or Reuben alone."

In August 1987 a deepening note of doom sounded when Commonwealth Edison retained litigation partner Dan Webb of Chicago's Winston & Strawn to assist in a rate case. Webb a former U.S. attorney, had handled some general Edison litigation in the past, but it was the first time since the late 1960s that

Successful Mergers

utility had called someone outside of Isham for a rate matter.

The case – a proposal to increase rates by $1.4 billion required political savvy, which was Reuben's speciality. "If you have Don Reuben as your senior guy and you cannot market him as a litigator, something's wrong," says one Chicago lawyer. "If they weren't really pushing the Reuben people, you've got recipe for disaster."

Edison general counsel Harlan Dellsy maintains that Edison wanted someone outside of Isham. "It was not a question of whether they could or could not market Reuben," says Dellsy. "We were not turning down Don Reuben, we were hiring Dan Webb." Reuben says he was not angling for the business and did not feel rejected. Ferguson and Miller, who would have been the logical people to push Reuben, decline comment.

At the end of August Isham partner Ronald Jacks gave notice that he and two other partners were moving to Mayer, Brown & Platt. A fourth Isham partner, Hugh McCombs, followed a week later. Jacks, whose 1987 billings topped $2 million, had built a substantial insurance and reinsurance practice. Jacks says a move for him was probably inevitable since be needed a bigger, more international base.

Around this time an old proposal by Spada to relocate the firm to the Northwest Atrium Center downtown was revived and quickly contested. "The bottom line was too low," says one former Isham partner. "We no longer had the revenues."

One alternative to the Atrium was relocating the firm in Reuben & Proctor's offices. Isham partners were ambivalent for several reasons: It was Reuben domain; the offices didn't have the gorgeous views they were accustomed to; and several Reuben partners had a financial interest in the building, a situation the Isham partners regarded as a conflict. Also, the Reuben offices at 19 South La Salle have space for about 115 lawyers. By now it was mid-October and the firm had 155 lawyers. A move to La Salle would require more paring down, and some thought the proposal itself was meant to test partner loyalty.

More for me, less for you

This whole scenario was an unfortunate prelude to what proved, two weeks later, to be the ultimate divisive issue: compensation. Co-managing partners Hanzlik of Isham and Klenk of Reuben & Proctor drew up a points list for the executive committee, which had 11 partners – Reuben, Ogilvie, Ferguson, and four partners each from Reuben and Isham. Other executive committee members, including Rosso, came up with their own lists. "In this volatile circumstance, no one, not even God himself, could have created a points list that would have made everyone happy," says a former Isham partner.

The committee met every night for a week, sometimes until midnight, going line by line over the proposed list. The discussions were rancorous. "Some of these allocation differences were quite small," says Reuben's Theodore Grippo. "[Some Isham partners] objected to any attempt to modify anybody they had put forward in any way, shape or form.

"We came up against tremendous resistance whenever we would try to adjust any Isham partner," Grippo charges. "When Reuben partners were adjusted downwards nobody objected .... They were being unfair." According to another Reuben partner who heard about the meetings, Rosso "was probably one of the prime examples of 'If you don't give me what I want, I'll hold my breath 'til I turn blue.'"

"That's the way we felt about *them*," responds Rosso. "I suggested several compromise positions. It was they who sandbagged them every time."

The younger Reuben partners were lobbying hard, too. "The demands of the younger people just got to the point where they just wanted the older people... to take a cut," says one former Isham partner.

Finally a vote was taken. The compensation range going into the meetings was $125,000 to $450,000. Many partners, including Reuben, took cuts. (His draw decreased from $450,000 to $400,000.)

"The points list, came out and things were disquietingly quiet," says a former Isham partner. The Edison people were no longer at the top, but many Isham partners felt that was fine. "A lot of people felt they had historically been overpaid," says this partner.

An eerie calm ensued, lasting two weeks, until November 20. Michael Miller informed his partners he was quitting and didn't yet know where he was going or whether Edison was going with him. Eventually most of the Edison work, as well as three partners, did go with him to Sidley & Austin. (A total of 13 Isham lawyers have gone to Sidley.) By the end of December Rosso, Yolles, and four other partners had announced they were leaving for the Chicago office of Jones, Day, which now counts 13 Isham lawyers in its ranks.

The killing fields

The rumors mill, of course, was working furiously. Tales about the firm's future and its leaders sprouted daily. Many were intriguing. Most were dismissed. One even had it that Ferguson – who by this time was rarely seen in the office – had threatened to shoot Reuben. His supposed motive: fury that his partners were resisting his retirement demands.

By the end of this month, the firm expects its 104 lawyers to be relocated back at 19 South La Salle. Klenk estimates the size of the firm will stabilize at 115. The Isham name may eventually be discarded. With only 10 of the 49 Isham partners left the new Isham looks very similar to the old Reuben & Proctor – except for the loss of some major clients. The most devastating was the departure of some of the Tribune work. In January the Tribune announced it was relocating its corporate, tax, and employee benefits work. Tribune general counsel Lawrence Gunnels, himself a former Reuben & Proctor partner, denies the merger had anything to do with the change. "We would have liked to see them deeper and broader, [but] we didn't say expand or else," he says. "I really couldn't pinpoint any particular one reason why now. It's the new year?"

Major corporate matters will now go to Sidley & Austin. (The two Reuben partners in charge of tax work for the Tribune, Alfred Spada and William Schmidt, are both gone, leaving that area thinly covered.) Employee benefits and tax work will go to McDermott, Will & Emery.

"I think people were disappointed [about losing the work]," says Reuben partner Thomas Ging. "Of course the more senior people realized that when we left Kirkland with the Tribune Company we had the mission of building a corporate area. . . . One of the purposes of the merger was to fulfill that."

Reuben & Proctor previously did about two thirds of the Tribune Company's legal work, Gunnels says, Billings for corporate and tax work were more than $1 million in years when there were a lot of acquisitions, according to several sources. Gunnels declines to estimate what percentage of the Reuben & Proctor work he has redistributed. "It's not earthshaking or radical or anything," he says. "It's not a big divorce. I think they'll still be doing a lot of work for us."

Most departing partners have not received their capital contributions, and some say they may sue. But, says Reuben dryly, "I cannot say that I have high on my personal agenda concerning myself with my former partners' capital until all our obligations are discharged." The defectors left the firm responsible for the leases on the Isham offices in Chicago – $10 million commitment – and in Washington. The Washington space has been sublet at no cost to the firm, but turning over the Chicago lease cost $2.2 million. The capital left behind by Isham partners amounts to about $80,000.

Lawyers are still speculating about what sort of deal Ferguson may have struck before he retired last year. Neither Reuben nor the co-managing partners would comment on the terms of Ferguson's retirement.

Chicago headhunter Bert Early was the original matchmaker in the merger deal and attended the fateful initial meeting between Reuben and Ferguson. "There were no major conflicts between them, their earnings were in the ballpark," says Early in his own defense. "One of them needed more corporate securities work, and the other one needed more litigation support. That was a natural complement." Now, he concedes, "It's gone sour, and everybody's unhappy that it has. I certainly am."

Reuben is not happy, but he admits to no regrets. After all, as much as he believed in the merger, he always knew there was a big risk involved; what he didn't know was just how big. As he wrote a year and a half ago: "We all believe we are on our way to a very successful, professional end result; however, candor and prudence compel me to say to all those who ask: Come back in 18 months. It's not over until the fat lady sings."

Reuben stoically continues to repeat this credo, but others have already heard the aria. "I think she sang," says one former Isham lawyer.

Amy Singer

Appendix 10

Inland Revenue Press Release 18/6/79

Accounts on a cash basis

A company, whether limited or unlimited is normally required to prepare accounts for tax purposes on an earnings basis, as defined in TA 1970 S.151(2) [now TA 988 S.110(3)]. An individual or a partnership carrying on a trade is similarly required to prepare accounts on an earnings basis, but in the circumstances set out below, accounts prepared on a cash basis, or on a conventional basis such as bills issued or work completed which is neither full 'earnings' nor pure 'cash' may be accepted from an individual or partnership carrying on a profession or vocation.

Where a profession or vocation is newly set up, or is treated as new for tax purposes (under TA 1970 S.154(1) [now TA 1988 S.113(1)] the profits of the first three years from the date of setting up or of the change to which S.154(1) applies, are required to be computed on the earnings basis (as defined in S.151(2)) [now TA 1988 S.110(2)] in determining all tax liabilities affected by the profits of these years.

The computation of subsequent profits will continue on the earnings basis until the taxpayer asks to change to a cash or other conventional basis. Such a basis will be accepted if the new basis seems likely to provide a reasonable measure of the taxpayer's profit. This is interpreted as meaning that the profits computed on the new basis will not, taking one year with another, differ materially from the profits computed on the earnings basis.

The change must also be a complete one. For example receipts after the change for work done before the change must be brought into the computation of profits on the cash basis notwithstanding that they have already been brought into account in the computation on the earnings basis; similarly expenses accrued due but unpaid which were debited in the accounts on the earnings basis may again be debited in the subsequent accounts on the cash basis when they are paid.

A further condition is that the taxpayer wishing to make such a change is required to give a written undertaking that he will issue bills for services rendered or work done (that is in the normal way, completed work but also including work in progress where interim payments or payments on account are contemplated by the terms of the contract or are customary) at regular and frequent intervals. The intervals may be chosen by the taxpayer but they should be quarterly or more often, and they should be specified in the undertaking.

Attention is drawn to the possibility of liability under TA 1970 S.144, [now TA 1988 S.104] wherever accounts are prepared on a basis other than earnings: in computing such liability there is no provision for any relief in respect of any profits which may have been brought into the computation twice when the change from the earnings basis was made.

Where accounts are prepared on a cash or other conventional basis and it is desired to change to an earnings basis, no objection will be raised but attention is again drawn to the liability that will arise under TA 1970 S.144. A subsequent claim to revert to a conventional basis would not be accepted.

This statement is not applicable to barristers (a separate statement applicable to barristers was published in November 1969).

Appendix 11

Inland Revenue Statement of Practice SP 9/86

Income tax – partnership mergers and demergers

1 This statement explains the basis on which the Inland Revenue apply the provisions of TA 1970 S.154 [now TA 1988 S.113] (change in ownership of trade, profession or vocation) to mergers and demergers of partnership businesses. In the following paragraphs, the word "business" means trades, professions or vocations carried on in partnership.

Mergers

2 When two businesses which are carried on in partnership and which are different in nature merge, it may be that the result of the merger is a new business, different in nature from either of the previous businesses. Whether this is so is a question of fact to be determind according to the circumstances of each case. Where it is the case, the old businesses will have been permanently discontinued, and a new business commenced; TA 1970 S.154 will therefore not apply and the normal commencement and cessation provisions will apply to each business respectively.

3 However, where two partnership businesses in different ownership carrying on the same sort of activities are merged and then carried on by the joint owners in partnership, the total activities of both businesses may continue, even though in a merged form, ie the new partnership may succeed to the businesses of the old partnerships. In that event the partners have the following options –

(a) TA 1970 S.154(1) applies to both businesses so that the cessation and commencement provisions are deemed to apply to both;
(b) an election under TA 1970 S.154(2) is made in respect of one business, and the cessation and commencement provisions are deemed to apply to the other;
(c) elections are made in repsect of both businesses.

4 Where (b) applies, it will be necessary to apportion the profits of the combined business to apply the commencement provisions to the business in respect of which no election is made. It will of course be a question of fact whether succession has occurred and in this connection disparity in size between the old partnerships will not of itself be a significant matter.

De-mergers

5   When a business carried on in partnership is divided up, and several separate partnerships are formed, it will again be a question of fact, to be determined according to the circumstances of each case, whether any of the separate partnerships carries on the same business as was carried on previously by the original partnership. It might be that one of the businesses carried on after the division was so large in relation to the rest as to be recognisably 'the business' as previously carried on; but that will frequently not be the case, and if it is not the case an election under S.154(2) will not be possible.

6   The Inland Revenue would want to look carefully at any case where it was claimed that a demerger of a partnership had occurred but it appeared that the demerger was more apparent than real, and that the demerger seemed to have taken place for fiscal reasons. The Revenue might wish to argue that in such a case the same trade was being carried on after the demerger as before, that a S.154(2) election could be made, and that FA 1985 S.47 [now TA 1988 S.62] therefore applied.

Appendix 12

Schedule of selected mergers since 1.1.87

	Merged with	Now styled
Coward Chance	Clifford Turner	Clifford Chance
Withers	Crossman Block & Keith	Withers Crossman Block
Kinneir & Co	Bevan Hancock *and* Ashford Sparkes & Harward	Bevan Ashford
Shoosmith and Harrison (amal)	Seabroke Harris	(no change)
Knapp-Fisher	Winckworth and Pemberton	W&P incorp K-F
Mills and Reeve	Francis	Mills and Reeve Francis
Mackrell & Co	Turner Garrett & Co	Mackrell Turner Garrett
Sharman Jackson & Archer	Vincent Sykes and Son	Sharman Jackson & Vincent Sykes
Ryland Martineau	Johnson & Co	Martineau Johnson
Frederick Hall & Co	Colin Hayward & Co	(no change)
Greenways	Whitford & Sons	–
Charles Russell & Co	Williams & James	Charles Russell Williams & James
Cobbetts	Leak Almond and Parkinson	Cobbetts Leak Almond
Hawkins	Russell Jones & Co	Hawkins and RJ&Co
Daynes Hill & Perks	Moreton Phillips & Son	–
Argles & Court	Winch, Greensted & Winch	Argles & Court
Bradfield Howson & Chalkey	Thomson Snell & Passmore	Thomson Snell & Passmore
Morgan Bruce & Hardwickes	Geo L Thomas, Nettleship & Co	–
Beachcrofts	Stanleys & Simpson, North	–

243

Successful Mergers

	Merged with	Now styled
A V Hammond & Co	last Suddards	Hammond Suddar
Stanley Wasbrough	Veale Benson	–
Lees Moore and Price	Edward Lloyd & Co *and* Whitley & Co	Lees Lloyd Whitley
Alsop Stevens	Wilkinson Kimbers	Alsop Wilkinson
Weightmans	Rutherfords	Weightmans Rutherfords
Steele Raymond	Luff, Raymond & Williams	Steele Raymond
Druces & Atlee	Hickmans	Druces & Atlee
Burroughs Day	Robert Smith & Co	Borroughs Day Robert Smith
Neill Clerk & Plant Hill	Smith Crawford *and* Galts	–
Jaques & Lewis	(purchased IOM practice)	Shakespeare Duggan Lea
Batten & Co	Burridge Kent & Arkell	Batten & Co
Payne Hicks Beach	Francis & Crookenden *and* Roper Piese	PHB
Evershed & Tomkinson	Daynes Hill & Perks *and* Alexander Tatham & Co *and* Broomheads (in stages to mid '89)	Eversheds
Woolf Seddon	Rosko Phillips	Woolf Seddon Rosko Phillips
Moss Toone & Deane	Lathan New & Smythe	Moss Lathan & Toone

Appendix 13
Bibliography

How to effect a successful merger. (Of law firms). John Harrison.
S.J. 1988, 132(5), 142-144

Keeping expansion under control. (Merger of Crossman Block & Keith and Withers). Julian Harris.
S.J. 1988, 132(7), 218-219

Mechanics of merger: the birth of Clifford Chance. Lorna Montgomerie and Paul Brown.
N.L.J. 1987, 137(6302), 377-379

Merger, a commitment to principle. (Merger as a route to increased success for law firms). Tom Marshall and David Salway.
L.S.G. 1987, 84(37), 2914, 2917

Merger mania: disease or cure? (Mergers between law firms). Michael Simmons.
L.S.G. 1987, 84(7), 471-473

Merger mania: the way forward. (Law Society conference session).
L.S.G. 1987, 84(42), 3308-3309

Mergers – legal supply responds to new client demand. (Rationale behind mergers between law firms). Richard Clayton.
Lawyer 1987, 21 May, 12-14

Merger and take-overs – what to look for. (In proposed mergers between law firms). T.G.F. Harris.
L.S.G. 1987, 84(7), 474, 477

Mergers and tax considerations. (For law firms). Jerry Burley.
S.J. 1988, 132(6), 174-176

To merge or not to merge? (Factors to be considered in possible law firm mergers). John Harrison.
S.J. 1988, 132(4), 102-104

The transatlantic merger: is it already here? (Mergers and increased contacts between UK and US law firms). Graham Whybrow
I.F.L. Rev. 1987, 6(6), 8-9

Mixing the practices: a solution or recipe for disaster? (Allowing the mergers of law firms and accountancy practices).
I.F.L. Rev. 1988, 7(3), 5-6

Considering a merger? looking behind accounts. Robert Ivison.
L.S.G. 1988, 85(21), 20-21

When is a merger not a merger? (Linking of five top law firms in the Australian Legal Group). Peter Curtain.
I.F.L. Rev. 1987, 6(7), 8-10

Amalgamation, conflict of interest and "Chinese walls". (Comment from Law Society's Ethics and Guidance Committee).
L.S.G. 1987, 84(20), 1546

Amalgamations. (Of law firms).
S.J. 1987, 131(10), 271

Anatomy of a merger. (Mills & Reeve and Francis & Co). Charles Christian.
S.J. 1987, 131(20), 642-643

Bringing the city to Cardiff. (Merger of Morgan Bruce and Nicholas and Hardwickes in Cardiff). Richard Clayton.
Lawyer 1987, 7 May, 11-12

Cultures must mesh to achieve success. (Professional help available to law firms contemplating merger). Nick Gillies.
Lawyer 1988, 2(13), 16-17

First national chain becomes a reality. (Amalgamation of four substantial provincial practices). Nick Gillies
Lawyer 1988, 2(14), 6-7

'Law Firm Mergers'
Editor in Chief: Nancy Gurwitz Sambul. New York State Bar Association.

'Mergers and Acquisitions of Professional Firms.'
By Hugh T Nicholson F.C.A. Institute of Chartered Accountants in England and Wales. 1978.

Multidiscipline and the Megabuck. Accountancy (UK), VOL: v103n1135, p: 67-71, (5), Mar 1988

How Beautiful Is Big?
International Mgmt (UK), VOL: v43n1, P: 52-54, (3), Jan 1988.

When Is a Merger Not a Merger?
International Financial Law Review (UK), VOL: v6n7, P: 8-10, (3), Jul 1987.

Small Firm Mergers.
Legal Economics, VOL: v13n4, P: 50-57, (5), May/Jun 1987.

Clifford Chance – The City Cats Which Stole the Cream.
International Financial Law Review (UK), VOL: v6n3, P: 5 – 8, (4), Mar 1987.

London's Medium-Sized Law Firms.
International Financial Law Review (UK); VOL: v6n8, P: 8-11, (4), Aug 1987.

Dial M for Merger.
Canadian Business (Canada), VOL: v60n3, P: 48-54, 105-106, (7), Mar 1987.

Bid Fever Grips Lawyers.
International Financial Law Review (UK), VOL: v4 n11, P: 5-8, (4), Nov 1985.

Mergers of Solicitors' Firms
Law Society's Young Solicitors' Group 1988

INDEX

Index

Accountability 5
Accountancy
  computers 89, 105
  management 145
Accountants 13, 16
Accounting bases 49-51, 103
  bills issued 49
  cash 49
  dates 57
  differences 61
  earnings 49, 53
  incompatible 49-51
  work in progress 60
Acquisitions 1, 36
Administration 70-73
  computers 71
  director 123
  estimates 70
  filing 72
  furniture 72
  inventories 71
  removal day 72
  schedule 71
  stationery 71
  staff 87
  telephones 71, 89
Advertisements 13, 151
Agencies 14
  fees 14
Announcements 25, 150, 159
Annuity arrangements 56
Arbitration 158
Audits 147

Back-up staff 115
Bills
  book 67
  issued 49
Break off 7
Brochures 66

Brokers 33
Buy-out
  management 12

Candidates 17
Capital
  gain 63-64
  requirements 143-148
Cash
  accounting bases 49
Chinese wall 100
Clients 38-39
  development 2
  informing 24, 35
  retention of 150-151
  strategy 2, 34
Committees 68, 98
Communication 5, 42-45, 77-79
  equipment 89
Computers 88-91
  accounts 89, 105
  consultants 91
Confidentiality 23, 95
Conflicts 35
  of interest 99
Constitution 69
Consultants
  administration 70
  brokers 33
  computer 91
  functions of 46
  management 33
  public relations 46, 159
Costs 47, 54, 116
Cultures
  differing 19, 36, 95
  changing 19

Databases 91, 118

Debts 141
   discontinuance 142-143
   doubtful 142
   debtors 49-60
   forward reserving 142
   statutory liability 142
Decisions 5, 23, 26, 33
Depreciation
   of fixed assets 62
Discussions 32, 112
Distraction
   partners 6, 25
   staff 25
Documentation 41, 44, 66-69
Draftsmen 26, 67
Drawings 145

Earnings
   accounting bases 49, 53
Efficiency 74, 80
Employment
   registers 13
Entrepreneurs 20
Equalisation 134-136
Equipment 89
Exhibits 35, 41

Fax 89
Fees
   agencies 14
Financial advisers 26
   secrecy 48
Firm name 36, 45, 104
Firm management 109
Fixed assets 61-63, 141-143
   depreciation 62
   non-property assets 61
   write off 62
Forward reserving
   debts 142
Freehold property 63-64
Furniture 72

Hiving off 11
Human relations 75-81
   staff needs 79

Identity
   loss of 7
Implementation 44
Information 95, 133
Initial approach 23
Inland Revenue 50
Institutionalists 20
Investment 4

Law Society
   registers 13
   rules 99
Liabilities
   taxation 52
Lifestyle 21, 150
Leasehold property 64-65
Local associations 13
Logistics 40-44

Machines
   systems 89
Management
   accounts 145
   buy out 11
   consultants 33
   functions 5
   merger 31-47
   people 74
Media 150-151
Meetings 43
Morale 74, 111
Motivation 79, 106

Organisation 35, 40

Partners 40, 99
   distraction 6
Partnership
   Act 157

253

Questions 35, 41

Rainmakers 19
Rationalisation 11, 134, 153
Recruitment 108, 118, 120
Registers
 employment 13
 Law Society 13
Merger 13
Reorganisation 11
Reserving policy
 taxation 142–145
Retirement
 obligations 56
Restrictive covenants 158
Reverse takeover 18
Risk 4
to acquired firm 6

Public relations
 consultant 46, 159
Provincial offices 108
Property
 freehold 63–64
 leasehold 64–65
 shares 48–49
Profit
 differing absolute 48–59
 plan 39
Premises 98, 106
Preliminaries 34
Personnel officer 86
parallel 55
deed 157
agreement 26, 67

Search 13–16, 34
Service 2
Size
 of firm 96, 107
Specialisation 134
Spin off 4
Staff
 administration 87
 distraction 25
 Stationery 71, 104
 Statutory liability
 debts 142
 Strategy 2, 34
 clients 2, 34
 planning 11, 80
 Supervision 134
Systems
 machines 89
Synergy 7

Takeover
 reverse 18
Taxation
 basis of merged firm 57
 liabilities 52
 relief 62–64
 reserving policy 142–145
 Taxes Act 1988 58
 Telephones 71, 89
 Timetable 26
 Training 118

Valuation
 of work in progress 60
Work in progress 7, 60